PAT BROWN

Financial Literacy For The Culture

"Teaching What Wasn't Taught—Credit, Budgeting, Investing, and Legacy for the Culture"

ABRAM · 47 · BROWN

First published by AbramBrown47 2025

First edition

ISBN: 978-1-967737-14-7

This book was professionally typeset on Reedsy.
Find out more at reedsy.com

Contents

Preface

Why This Book Had to Be Written

Both of my parents were college-educated.

We had the structure, the expectations, the ambition. But one thing we didn't have in my household growing up was regular conversations about money. Not because it wasn't important—but because we just didn't talk about it.

We talked about grades. We talked about doing the right thing.

We talked about responsibility, respect, and how to carry yourself in this world.

But we didn't talk about credit scores.

We didn't talk about compound interest.

We didn't talk about building wealth—because like many families, we were focused on staying afloat.

Now that I'm older, a father, and a financial educator, I realize how much that silence shaped me. And I made a promise: the cycle would stop with me. My kids would grow up with the conversations I never had.

And let me tell you—it's already happening.

My oldest daughter, **Peyton Brown**, doesn't just listen when I talk about money—she *applies* it. She's locked in. The other day, I was trying to pay for something for her over the phone—just being a dad, wanting to take care of my baby girl—and she stopped me mid-sentence.

"Wait, Dad," she said, "I want to put it on my card so I can get the points."

I couldn't help but laugh. I was ready to handle it—glad to, even. But here she was, calm and calculated, choosing the smarter route. Not because she had to—but because she's been paying attention. She's internalized the lessons. She's thinking about how to make every dollar do more. That moment told me everything I needed to know: her path has shifted.

And my youngest, **Ryan Brown**, is right there behind her.

Ryan is watching, soaking it up. She's starting to ask questions about money and how it works. She's learning the vocabulary. She's seeing her big sister move differently—and I can already feel her mindset changing too. She may not be arguing with me about credit card points yet, but trust me... it's coming.

As a father, this is what legacy looks like in real time.

Not just buying them things. Not just showing up.

But *equipping* them.

Giving them a lens to see money not as something to fear or fumble, but as something to manage, grow, and use with purpose.

That's why I wrote this book.

Because too many of us are still walking around with brilliance and hustle—but no blueprint.

Because too many of us are still trying to figure out what nobody ever explained.

Because financial literacy has always felt like it belonged to "them"—but now, it's *ours.*

Financial Literacy For The Culture is written in our voice. For our experience.

It's not a textbook—it's a conversation.

It's not about shame—it's about power.

It's not about doing it perfectly—it's about finally doing it *intentionally.*

So if you've ever felt behind... you're not.

If you've ever wished someone had taught you this... now they will.

If you've ever wanted to change the money narrative in your family... this is the moment.

Because I believe when we talk about money, we talk about freedom.

And I believe the more we talk, the more we teach, the more we pass down—the more we reclaim what's always been possible for us.

This book is for Peyton. For Ryan.

For every young person who deserves a head start.

For every parent doing the best they can with what they know.
And for every household ready to stop surviving and start building.
Let's shift the conversation.
Let's shift the culture.
Let's build something that lasts.
— *Patrick Brown*
Author, *Financial Literacy For The Culture*

Meet the Author – Who I Am and Why This Matters to Me

Before we dive into all things money, let me introduce myself.

My name is **Pat Brown**. I'm a financial advisor, educator, speaker, former Division I athlete, proud husband, and most importantly—**a father** to two incredible daughters: **Peyton** and **Ryan**.

I grew up in a household with two college-educated parents. We had discipline, we had love, and we had expectations. But like many families, we didn't talk about money—not in a real way. Not about credit scores. Not about building wealth. Not about investing or budgeting or legacy. We just... didn't go there. And it wasn't because my parents didn't care—it just wasn't part of our normal family conversation.

I didn't realize how much that mattered until I got older—until I started seeing how much that silence around money had cost us.

That's when everything changed.

After my football career at the University of Kansas—where I served as team captain—I went on to play briefly in the CFL. But life after sports hit me with some real questions: What does retirement actually look like? How do taxes work? Why was nobody talking about building wealth in a way that spoke to *us*?

That curiosity turned into a calling. I earned my MBA. I became a financial advisor. And for over two decades now, I've been helping individuals, families, and professionals make smarter financial decisions—not with fancy jargon, but with real talk and real strategy.

But I didn't stop there.

I wanted to create spaces where our people could see themselves in the conversation. Where money wasn't this intimidating, shame-filled topic—but something we could talk about at the barbershop, around the dinner table, or while riding in the car with your kids.

Speaking of kids—this book is deeply personal to me because of **Peyton and Ryan**.

My oldest, Peyton, doesn't just hear me when I talk about money—she absorbs it. She applies it. The other day, I tried to pay for something over the phone for her (being a dad, doing what dads do), and she straight-up stopped me. "No, Dad—I want to put it on my card. I want the points."

I laughed, shook my head, and realized... she *gets it*. She's not just learning—she's owning her financial future.

And my youngest, Ryan? She's catching on, too. Watching. Asking questions. Leaning in. I can already feel her path shifting just by being in the room with these conversations.

That's what this book is about.

It's about helping our kids, our communities, and ourselves do better—because we *know* better.

I wrote this book for the culture.

For every family that avoided the money talk. For every young person who never learned about credit or compound interest in school. For every grown man or woman who feels behind but doesn't know where to start. For everyone who's tired of just surviving—and ready to start building.

You don't need to be rich to get started.

You just need to be **ready**.

Let's change the narrative—together.

How to Use This Book

Let's Talk Strategy

This book wasn't written to sit on your coffee table collecting dust like that unopened game of Monopoly your cousin swore he was gonna teach you. This is not just a "good read"—this is a playbook, a conversation starter, a mirror, and a blueprint. It's something you come back to again and again as your money mindset, income, and life evolve.

Here's how to make the most of it:

Start Where You Are—Not Where You Think You Should Be

You don't have to read this book cover to cover in one sitting like it's the latest season of *Snowfall.* This ain't a binge-watch—it's a journey. If you're already budgeting but don't know how credit works, jump straight to the credit chapter. If you're good with saving but struggle with talking to family about money, skip to that section. Flip around, fold corners, highlight quotes, and write in the margins. Make it yours.

Treat It Like a Playlist, Not a Lecture

This ain't school. There's no test at the end. This book is a playlist of money topics, each with its own beat and vibe. Pick what hits you in the moment. Some chapters will feel like a wake-up call. Others will feel like confirmation that you've been on the right track. Let the content meet you where you are.

Use the Examples—Then Replace Them with Your Own

Every story, every analogy, every "remember when" moment is designed to help connect the dots. But eventually, this stops being *my* voice and starts becoming *your* strategy. Swap out the names, tweak the scenarios, and apply it to your actual life: your rent, your card, your job, your mama asking for a little help. Turn these lessons into real moves.

Share It—Out Loud

Read a chapter and talk about it at dinner. Screenshot a quote and send it to your cousin. Use it to start a conversation with your kids. You'll be surprised how quickly the silence around money begins to crack when someone's finally brave enough to start talking.

Revisit It Every Season

Your money life is going to change. Maybe you're graduating. Maybe you're switching jobs. Maybe you just had your first baby or lost someone close. Whatever season you're in, this book can meet you there. Reread it once a year—just like you check your insurance policies, your goals, or your sneaker rotation. Let it evolve with you.

Write in the Margins

Seriously. Get messy. Underline what hits. Circle what confuses you. Write down questions. Mark the stuff you want to come back to when you've got more time—or more courage.

Use It as a Family Manual

Pass it to your kids. Read it with your partner. Let your auntie borrow it. Give it to that one friend who's always "figuring stuff out." This book is meant to multiply—not sit lonely on your shelf.

You Don't Have to Agree with Everything

You might read something and think, "Nah, that ain't me." Good. That means you're thinking. You're reflecting. This book isn't about perfection—it's about starting the conversation and customizing the path that works for *you*.

If It Feels Heavy—That's Okay

Talking about money can bring up some stuff. Shame. Regret. Guilt. Confusion. You might feel like you should already know this. Breathe. Nobody handed you a playbook before. But you've got one now. This book is here to meet you with grace, not judgment.

Final Thought

This book isn't just about money—it's about power.

About freedom.

About healing what we weren't taught.

About passing down more than just struggle.

So take your time.

Take notes.

Take action.

And take pride in the fact that *you showed up*—because most people never even do that part.

Let's build.

Let's learn.

Let's grow.

And most importantly—let's make sure this book doesn't stop with you.

Part I: The Foundation – Understanding Where We Came From

You can't fix what you don't understand. That's why Part I of *Financial Literacy for The Culture* doesn't start with budgets, credit scores, or investment strategies—it starts with truth. It starts with our story.

Understanding Where We Came From lays the groundwork for everything that follows in this book. It's the emotional and historical core of our journey toward financial empowerment. Before we talk numbers, we talk **narratives**—how money has been used *against us*, how we've made a way *in spite of it*, and how we can now use it *for us*.

This section connects the dots between slavery, redlining, media messaging, systemic exclusion, and today's financial mindsets in the Black community. It explores not just what happened, but how it *felt*—what we inherited emotionally, mentally, and behaviorally about money from our grandparents, parents, and society itself.

Chapter 1: Generational Financial Trauma

Let's get one thing straight—this ain't just about dollars and cents. When we talk about generational financial trauma, we're not just talking about what's in your wallet—we're talking about what's in your wiring. It's the tension in your shoulders when bills come in. It's the fear of opening a bank account because your auntie swore banks were crooked. It's how you never saw a will in your household, but you knew to wear black and bring a covered dish when somebody passed.

It's deeper than broke. It's cultural. It's emotional. It's systemic. And it didn't start with us—it was passed down, like Grandma's cornbread recipe or Uncle Earl's record collection. Except this inheritance comes with interest—emotional, financial, and generational.

See, when a community survives 400 years of economic exclusion, exploitation, and erasure, it doesn't just walk away untouched. That kind of damage settles into habits. Into fears. Into silence. You've got folks with good jobs and solid credit still afraid to talk to a financial advisor because "they don't mess with our kind." You've got folks who grew up hearing "never trust a bank," and now they're adults cashing paychecks at corner stores and hiding their savings in sock drawers. That's not just personal preference—that's legacy.

In this chapter, we're unpacking the trauma we didn't sign up for but still carry. From the plantations to the projects, from Wall Street to the welfare line, from sharecropping to subprime loans—our relationship with money has always been complicated. It's been shaped by policies that locked us out, burned down what we built, and handed out loans and land and access to everybody but us.

You ever watched *The Fresh Prince of Bel-Air* and seen how Will clashed with Carlton? Will came from a place of struggle and survival. Carlton was born into comfort. But even Carlton, with all his prep school and privilege, still had to deal with being a Black man in America. That's the tension. That's the trauma. Even when you "make it," you're still carrying the weight of history.

Our financial behavior didn't fall from the sky. It came from somewhere. It came from watching Big Mama stretch meals, from watching Daddy work two jobs and still be behind, from watching uncles hustle not because they wanted to—but because they had to. It came from watching GoFundMes pay for funerals because nobody had life insurance. From watching the one person in the family with a steady income carry everybody else.

And let's not pretend like trauma doesn't shape how we see the world. If you've ever seen eviction notices on the front door, you don't just "budget better"—you hustle different. If your lights ever got cut off, you remember that feeling every time you see a utility bill, even when you can afford it now. That's what trauma does—it sticks. It lives in the background of your financial life, whispering worst-case scenarios even when things are okay.

So why don't we talk about it? Because shame is loud. Because survival doesn't leave much room for reflection. Because if we're honest, many of us grew up thinking being broke was just part of the deal. Like it was normal. Expected. Like it was our lane.

But complicated doesn't mean unfixable. You just need context, clarity, and a little game. You need to understand that what you're feeling isn't failure—it's history. And once you name it, you can start to heal it.

This chapter is the mirror and the flashlight. It's the cousin who tells you the truth at the cookout—not to shame you, but to lift you. Because if we can trace the trauma, we can interrupt the cycle. If we can name the patterns, we can break them. If we can see where we came from, we can decide where we're going.

So pull up a chair. This is the conversation your school never had and your family never felt safe enough to start.

Let's begin at the root.

What follows in the next 5,000+ words is a deeper dive into the ways this trauma was planted, watered, and passed down—from slavery to segregation, from redlining to predatory lending, from inherited poverty to invisible wealth. Each section is layered with historical facts, personal reflections, cultural references, and action steps—not just to educate, but to *empower*.

Because the point isn't just to survive anymore.

The point is to build. To heal. To reclaim.

1.1 The Legacy of Slavery and Wealth Suppression

The Starting Line Was Never Even

Let's just say it plain: we didn't start on equal footing. When we talk about financial literacy, budgeting, and building generational wealth, it's easy to make it sound like a level playing field where everybody just needs to "work hard" and "make better choices." But if we keep it 100, Black folks in America were never even given a chance to get to the starting line—let alone run the same race.

We weren't immigrants chasing a dream—we were capital fueling somebody else's. Our ancestors weren't allowed to own land, learn to read, build businesses, or pass anything down. We were owned. We were bought and sold. We were the investment that built the American economy—and when that economy started to boom, we were locked out of the profits.

Now fast forward to 2024. You see folks saying "Black people need to invest more" or "y'all need to own property." And yes, we do—but let's not act like we're starting from the same financial inheritance as everybody else. Our story is one of survival first, strategy second. It's not because we're lazy. It's because we've been locked out and locked down in every era of this country's history.

From Enslavement to Economic Exploitation

Slavery wasn't just a human rights violation—it was a business model. Cotton, sugar, rice, and tobacco were all billion-dollar industries that made white folks rich. The labor was free, the risk was low, and the profit was high. Think about that. While enslaved Black people were working sunup to sundown, generating generational wealth for white slaveowners, we weren't even considered human—just property on a balance sheet.

When slavery "ended," we didn't get paid back wages. We didn't get equity in the businesses we built. We didn't even get an apology. What we got was a new version of oppression—sharecropping, convict leasing, Jim Crow laws—that continued to rob us of wealth, dignity, and opportunity.

Imagine working a job for 200+ years and not getting paid. And then, after being "freed," your employer tells you that you can rent a shack on the same land, buy seeds from the same store, and if your crop doesn't hit, you still owe money. That's sharecropping. That's financial slavery with a new name.

The Inheritance We Never Got

White families who owned land, businesses, and even slaves were able to pass down wealth. They passed down farms, houses, insurance policies, railroad stock—real generational assets. Meanwhile, Black families passed down hustle, prayer, survival skills, and resilience. All valuable, but they don't earn compound interest.

In *Good Times*, the Evans family was always trying to get out the projects—but no matter how hard they worked, something always knocked them back. That wasn't just for laughs. That was a reflection of real-life financial systems that made it nearly impossible for Black families to build lasting wealth.

Let's break it down:

- No access to loans
- No protection from labor exploitation
- No property rights
- No education funding

It's not that we didn't want to build wealth. We just weren't allowed to.

Systemic Sabotage: The Long Reach of Oppression

Even when we tried to play the game by the rules, the rules changed. We started our own towns—places like Greenwood in Tulsa, Oklahoma (Black Wall Street)—only to watch them be bombed and burned. We opened banks, built schools, and created self-sufficient communities, but white mobs and complicit governments destroyed them.

That's not just loss. That's trauma. And that trauma still lives in our bodies, in our choices, in our bank accounts. It's why we might be hesitant to trust financial institutions. It's why we overextend to help family. It's why we say "I'm broke" even when we have money—because we remember what broke feels like.

Pros and Cons of Financial Survival Modes

Pros:

- Resourcefulness: We know how to stretch a dollar.
- Community: We've always supported each other.
- Resilience: We keep pushing, no matter the obstacle.

Cons:

- Fear-Based Spending: Making decisions out of panic.

- Lack of Investment: Holding onto cash instead of letting it grow.
- Generational Strain: One person supporting the whole family.

Action Steps: Turning Awareness into Power

1. **Acknowledge the History** Don't let anybody gaslight you into thinking your financial position is just about choices. Context matters. Study your family's financial journey. Ask your elders what they went through.
2. **Educate Yourself** Once you know the history, get the tools. Learn about credit, investing, insurance, estate planning, and entrepreneurship. Don't be afraid to ask questions. Don't let pride block your progress.
3. **Break the Silence** Have those money talks at the dinner table, in the group chat, at church. Normalize financial transparency. Share resources. Celebrate wins.
4. **Invest in Community** Support Black-owned businesses. Bank Black. Build networks of professionals who understand your story.
5. **Build Strategically** Budget with intention. Save with purpose. Plan for the next generation, even if it starts with $25/month.

Healing From the Root

Healing generational financial trauma is not just about making more money—it's about changing our relationship with money. It's about transforming fear into confidence, silence into knowledge, and pain into power.

It's about unlearning the idea that wealth isn't for us. That comfort is a betrayal. That success means you "left the hood." Nah—success means you turned pain into a platform.

Just like *The Cosby Show* gave us a picture of what a thriving Black family could look like, we need to give ourselves permission to dream—and to do the work to get there.

This legacy of slavery and wealth suppression doesn't have to be our ending. It's the beginning of a new chapter. One where we write the rules, protect our wealth, and build something real.

One dollar at a time. One decision at a time. One generation at a time.

Let's build.

1.2 "40 Acres and a Mule" – Reparations Promised, Then Denied

Setting the Stage: A Promise That Could've Changed Everything

Let's take it back to 1865. The Civil War just ended. The chains are off. Black folks are no longer enslaved—at least not legally. For the first time in generations, our people had a glimpse of something they'd never been allowed to hold: possibility.

But freedom with no foundation is a setup. Imagine being kicked out of prison after decades, with no clothes, no ID, no money, and no family. "You're free" sounds good, but what does it *mean* when you've got nothing to stand on?

That's where "40 acres and a mule" comes in. General William Tecumseh Sherman issued Special Field Order No. 15 in January 1865. The order promised formerly enslaved Black families up to 40 acres of land on the coasts of Georgia, South Carolina, and Florida. The idea was to give newly freed people a shot at independence, self-sufficiency, and real freedom—the kind that comes with economic control.

And just so we're clear: this wasn't a rumor, a myth, or a wish list. This was policy—signed, sealed, and delivered by the Union Army. Thousands of Black families started to settle that land. They were farming, building homes, creating communities. For a brief, beautiful moment, the promise of reparations was real.

Then President Andrew Johnson came through and snatched it all back.

Let's talk about what that meant—and what it means today.

The Power of Land: Why 40 Acres Mattered

Land isn't just dirt. It's power. It's leverage. It's legacy.

In 1865, owning land meant you could feed your family, build a home, start a business, grow crops, and—most importantly—pass something down. It meant you didn't have to ask for work. You *made* work. It meant you weren't just free on paper; you were free in practice.

To put it in today's terms, 40 acres and a mule back then would be like giving every formerly enslaved family a house, a truck, and startup capital to launch their lives. That land would've been the platform for generational wealth—just like white families got through the Homestead Act, the GI Bill, and countless other policies that deliberately excluded us.

And let's not play like this wouldn't have made a difference. Imagine how many Black children would've grown up on inherited land instead of rented tenements. How many Black businesses could've launched with land as collateral. How many Black elders would've aged on property that stayed in the family, instead of dying in public housing.

We're not just talking about a few acres. We're talking about a generational ripple that could've transformed everything.

The Reversal: Reparations Revoked

When President Lincoln was assassinated, Andrew Johnson took over—and he had no love for the formerly enslaved. Within months, he overturned Sherman's order and returned the land to Confederate plantation owners. Let that sink in.

The very people who had rebelled against the country got their land back. The very people who had built that land, who had dreamed of ownership, were forced off it.

Black families who had begun building lives were evicted, sometimes violently. Homes were burned. Crops were destroyed. And just like that, what could've been a financial revolution for Black America became one of its greatest betrayals.

Imagine working overtime, finally saving enough for a down payment, buying your first house—and then the government shows up and hands the deed to your ex-landlord. That's what happened. That pain echoes through generations.

Cultural Echoes: How It Shows Up Today

You ever notice how some folks treat land like gold, while others see it as stress? That's generational. That's legacy talking.

In *The Fresh Prince of Bel-Air*, Uncle Phil talked about legacy and land. That family had built something, and they protected it. They knew what it meant to have something to pass down. Now imagine Will's side of the family never even getting that shot.

For so many Black families, land is a touchy subject. Either we lost it, couldn't afford it, got scammed out of it, or never believed we'd get it in the first place. That disbelief? That doubt? That didn't come from nowhere. It came from 1865, when our shot got stolen.

Even now, Black Americans own less than 2% of all rural land in the U.S. That's not an accident—it's a consequence.

Pros and Cons: What Reparations Could've Meant

Pros of Delivering on the Promise:

- Laid the foundation for intergenerational wealth
- Reduced long-term government dependency
- Built political power through property ownership
- Dignity, autonomy, and economic security

Cons of Breaking the Promise:

- Generational poverty and housing insecurity
- Deep distrust of government institutions

- A wealth gap that compounds over time
- Reinforced white supremacy by prioritizing Confederates over freed people

Action Steps: What Do We Do With This Now?

We can't undo the past, but we can reclaim the narrative—and start building now.

1. **Study Your Family History** Ask about land. Who owned it? Who lost it? What stories were buried? Look through county records. If your family once owned property and lost it unjustly, document everything.
2. **Reconnect with the Land** You don't have to buy a 40-acre farm tomorrow. But look into land co-ops, community gardens, or shared ownership models. Reframe land as a tool, not a burden.
3. **Advocate for Reparative Policies** Whether it's local tax relief, land grants, or national reparations—speak up. Vote with intention. Write to your reps. Policy didn't get us here alone, but it can help us out.
4. **Build Wealth With Purpose** Invest in property if you can. But also invest in knowledge, business, insurance, and estate planning. It's not just about ownership—it's about strategy.
5. **Teach the Next Generation** Talk to your kids and nieces and nephews about legacy. Show them what equity means. Make financial literacy part of family dinner.

Final Word: The Dream Deferred Ain't Dead

Langston Hughes asked what happens to a dream deferred. We've lived that answer. But here's the thing—we're still dreaming.

"40 acres and a mule" wasn't just about land. It was about being seen. Being valued. Being included in the American promise. That promise was broken—but we're still here, still building, still thriving.

They took the land, but not the vision. They broke the promise, but not our power.

So now we make our own promises—to ourselves, to our families, to our community. We promise to get educated. To protect our assets. To build even when the blueprint was burned.

Because even without the mule, we still got muscle. Even without the acres, we still got access to knowledge, strategy, and each other.

Let's build the inheritance they tried to steal.

Let's honor our ancestors not just with memory—but with movement.

Let's get what's ours, by building it from the ground up.

One brick. One dollar. One generation at a time.

We are the reparations we've been waiting for.

1.3 The Freedman's Savings Bank Collapse (1874)

The Setup: Hope After Emancipation

Alright, family—picture this. It's the end of the Civil War. Slavery is officially over. You and your people are finally free. You've got dreams bigger than the plantation that tried to bury you. You want land, you want work, and—most of all—you want to save. Not just survive. Thrive.

Now here comes the government, saying: "We got you." They help open a new bank—just for us. A place where formerly enslaved Black people could deposit their money, build credit, and finally begin the journey toward wealth.

Sounds like a blessing, right? Like finally being invited to the table after being locked outside for centuries.

That bank? It was called the Freedman's Savings Bank. And what happened next? Straight-up betrayal. Think *Good Times* when James dies—just when you think things are turning around, the rug gets pulled out.

Let's walk through what this bank was, how it played our people, and why that pain still lingers in our financial DNA.

A Bank Built on Broken Promises

The Freedman's Savings Bank was established by Congress in 1865, the same year slavery officially ended. Its mission was clear: help newly freed Black Americans save money, invest, and learn financial literacy. It was like the financial version of a fresh start.

And let's be honest—we needed it. Black soldiers, teachers, barbers, preachers, laundresses—we were ready to bank. To build. To believe in the American promise.

By 1870, the bank had grown to more than 37 branches in 17 states and over 60,000 depositors. That's over 60,000 Black folks trusting a system that had only recently enslaved them. Think about that level of faith.

They deposited a total of more than $3 million. That's over $70 million in today's money. This was not play money. This was *real.*

But here's the problem: the people running the bank didn't look like us, didn't know us, and didn't respect us.

Where It All Went Left

The Freedman's Bank wasn't managed by the people it was supposed to serve. Most of its trustees were white men—politicians, clergymen, businessmen. People with no connection to the community. Many didn't even visit the branches.

At first, the bank was only supposed to take deposits and hold them. No risky loans. No investments. Just safekeeping.

But over time, that rule went out the window. The bank started making bad investments—mainly in railroads. Money was lent out recklessly. And when things got shaky, they kept playing with people's deposits like it was Monopoly money.

To make it worse, they tried to boost public trust by putting Frederick Douglass in charge at the very end. Yes, *that* Frederick Douglass. But by the time he stepped in, the damage was already done. Even he couldn't save it.

In 1874, the Freedman's Savings Bank failed. It collapsed, and tens of thousands of Black depositors lost everything.

The Aftershock: More Than Just Money

This wasn't just a financial loss—it was a spiritual gut-punch.

Imagine putting every dime you earned into a system that told you, "You're safe here," only to wake up broke. That's not just trauma—that's betrayal. And that kind of betrayal doesn't disappear. It gets passed down.

Ask your grandma why she never trusted banks. Ask your uncle why he cashes checks at the corner store instead of direct deposit. That fear? That suspicion? That's legacy trauma. That's Freedman's Bank energy still floating through our financial habits.

It's why so many of us prefer cash. Why we keep our money "where we can see it." Why we're skeptical of "too good to be true" investments—even when they're legit.

We've been burned before. And we never fully healed.

Cultural Echoes: Why It Still Matters

In *The Cosby Show,* we saw a Black family with financial stability, savings, and legacy planning. But that's not everyone's story. For many of us, wealth is new—and scary. Because deep down, we remember how fast it can vanish.

The Freedman's Bank collapse isn't just a footnote in history. It's a foundational story. It's part of why the racial wealth gap exists. Why Black families have five to ten times less wealth than white families. Why trust in financial systems is still so low.

This wasn't about mismanagement—it was about exploitation. And it laid the groundwork for everything that came after: redlining, predatory lending, payday loans, subprime mortgages.

The game has always been rigged. The Freedman's Bank was the first round.

Pros and Cons: The Legacy in Perspective

Pros of the Freedman's Bank (on paper):

- Created access to banking for newly freed Black people
- Offered an early model of financial empowerment
- Showed the desire and ability of Black communities to save and invest

Cons (the reality):

- Mismanagement and corruption by white trustees
- No protection or regulation for depositors
- Crushed trust in financial institutions
- Contributed to long-term financial exclusion

Action Steps: Turning Pain into Power

1. **Reclaim the History** Learn the full story of the Freedman's Bank. Don't let this be forgotten. Teach your kids. Talk about it at your church. Share it in your group chats. Knowledge is the first step to ownership.
2. **Build Financial Trust Again—But on Our Terms** Start with safe, transparent options. Credit unions. Black-owned banks. Community-based financial programs. Use budgeting apps that speak your language.
3. **Get Educated—Not Just Informed** There's a difference. Information is everywhere, but education is empowerment. Learn how banks work, how credit operates, how to spot shady deals.
4. **Heal Financial Trauma** Acknowledge the fear. Talk about it in therapy. Pray on it. Journal about it. But don't let it control you. Just like you heal from heartbreak, you can heal from financial betrayal.
5. **Build Legacy—Even if You Start Small** Open that savings account. Start that Roth IRA. Get that life insurance. Make that will. Legacy

doesn't start with wealth—it starts with intention.

Final Word: We Still Rise

Yes, we were robbed. But we're still rising.

The Freedman's Bank took our savings, but it couldn't take our spirit. We kept going. We started churches, schools, businesses. We sent our kids to college. We bought homes. We fought for civil rights—and economic rights, too.

This chapter of history doesn't end in defeat. It ends in awareness. And from awareness comes action.

You are your ancestor's wildest financial dream. They saved so you could succeed—even if the system failed them.

Now it's your turn.

Save smarter. Move wiser. Build louder.

Because this time?

The bank's in our name.

1.4 Wall Street Slave Auctions and the Birth of American Finance

Let's Start With the Truth: The Game Was Rigged From the Jump

We gotta be honest. Real talk. When most people hear "Wall Street," they think of stocks, suits, CNBC, and the hustle of money changing hands in fancy buildings. They think of power. They think of wealth. They think of institutions that define global economies. But you know what they don't think of? Enslaved Africans.

And yet, that's exactly where it all started.

Wall Street, as in *the* Wall Street in New York City—the one they teach you about in economics class—was literally built on the labor, bodies, and suffering of Black people. Not metaphorically. Not symbolically. *Literally.*

There was a time when the "street" in Wall Street hosted open-air slave auctions. Where human beings—our ancestors—were bought, sold, and traded like cattle. Right there. Downtown Manhattan.

So before we get into savings accounts and investment portfolios, we need to take a step back. We need to know the history. Because you can't heal from something if you don't understand what happened. And you sure can't talk about building Black wealth until you understand the original blueprint was drawn in chains.

Let's get into it.

The Wall That Became Wall Street

Wall Street gets its name from an actual wall. Back in the 1600s, the Dutch built a wooden wall across lower Manhattan to protect their settlement. Guess who built that wall? Enslaved Africans.

The wall was gone by the early 1700s, but the name stuck. And so did the business that took place there. That area—Broad Street and Wall—became the go-to spot for commercial activity, including slave trading.

From the late 1600s through the early 1800s, enslaved people were bought and sold right on Wall Street. It wasn't hidden. It wasn't some back-alley, underground deal. It was in the open. It was a normal part of daily business. Like grabbing a coffee and checking the stock ticker.

Our ancestors were treated as commodities. They had a market value, just like gold or tobacco. Families were split. Children were auctioned. Trauma was turned into profit. And the very institutions that built the U.S. economy—including insurance companies, banks, and brokerage houses—profited directly from it.

Let that settle in.

Receipts: Who Benefited From the Trade

Let's name names. Companies like Aetna, JPMorgan Chase, Bank of America, and New York Life have all been tied to slavery. These weren't small side hustles. These were foundational business practices.

Insurance companies offered policies on enslaved people's lives—paying the *slave owners,* of course, not the enslaved families. Banks accepted slaves as collateral on loans. Plantation owners got the capital to build and expand based on how many Black bodies they owned.

And who was managing those deals? Brokers, traders, investment houses. The same kind of institutions we now associate with Wall Street prestige.

So when folks say "slavery ended in 1865, why are you still talking about it?"—this is why. Because wealth isn't about what happens in one generation. It's about accumulation. And while white families were stacking money from the slave trade and reinvesting it for generations, Black families were being robbed of that same opportunity before it ever started.

That's the root of the wealth gap.

From Chains to Capital: How Slavery Built Finance

The slave economy didn't just impact agriculture. It touched *everything.*

Textiles? Cotton. Shipping? Transporting enslaved people. Railroads? Funded by profits from plantations. Insurance? Policies on human lives.

Wall Street didn't grow in spite of slavery. It grew *because* of it.

Even when the transatlantic slave trade was banned, domestic trade within the U.S. continued. Financial markets adjusted. Investment flowed. Banks grew.

The foundation of the American financial system is soaked in our ancestors' sweat and blood. But somehow, we're expected to just pick up the pieces, catch up, and "build wealth" without even being given the manual.

That's not a lack of effort. That's a lack of *justice.*

Cultural Echoes: What We Inherited

This kind of history leaves a mark. It doesn't disappear after a few generations. It shows up in our culture, our conversations, and our choices.

Think about how some families won't talk about money at all. Or how others treat wealth like it's suspicious—as if too much comfort means something bad is coming.

That's trauma. That's inherited fear. That's the legacy of being stolen, sold, and suppressed by the very system that now asks us to "trust the process."

You know that scene in *The Fresh Prince* when Will's dad leaves him, and he breaks down saying, "How come he don't want me, man?" That pain? That's the kind of generational abandonment we feel when we realize our ancestors were abandoned by the very government and institutions meant to protect them.

It's hard to trust banks when you know they once sold your people. It's hard to talk legacy when no one handed you a foundation.

But here's the truth: we can't change what happened. But we can understand it. Name it. Learn from it. And move differently.

Pros and Cons of Knowing This Truth

Pros:

- Builds financial self-awareness
- Provides context for generational habits and struggles
- Empowers us to advocate for systemic change
- Helps heal generational trauma by telling the truth

Cons:

- Emotionally heavy to process
- May trigger anger, frustration, or hopelessness

- Can lead to distrust without a plan for action

Action Steps: Reclaiming the Narrative

1. **Learn Your Personal Money Story** Ask your elders how they were taught about money. What did they learn? What didn't they know? Start connecting your family's choices to the systems that shaped them.
2. **Teach the Truth** Don't let this history stay buried. Teach your kids. Share in classrooms. Use your platforms. Post about it. Tweet about it. The more we know, the stronger we grow.
3. **Demand Transparency and Accountability** Call out institutions that profited from slavery. Push for investment in Black communities. Ask questions when you bank or invest. Put your money in places that honor your people.
4. **Start Where You Are** Yes, we were behind. But now we know the game. So play it smart. Budget. Save. Invest. Build community. Buy land if you can. Protect your assets. Create a will.
5. **Connect With Black Financial Professionals** Find folks who get it. Financial advisors who understand the culture. Accountants who speak your language. Lawyers who know the legacy. Build your team.

Final Word: From Auction Blocks to Ownership

Wall Street was once a place where we were sold. Now it's a place where we're buying stocks, launching businesses, and flipping property. That's evolution. That's resilience.

But we can't pretend the past didn't happen. We have to face it. Talk about it. Learn from it. And make moves that honor our ancestors.

Because every time you invest, every time you save, every time you say "I want more for my kids," you are rewriting a story that started in chains.

You are your ancestors' wildest *financial* dream.

Now let's build like they knew we could.

One dollar. One share. One community at a time.

Chapter 2: Black Wealth Destroyed – The Crises No One Taught Us

Let's not sugarcoat it—Black wealth in America didn't just struggle to grow; it was actively destroyed. Over and over again. And most of us didn't even learn about it in school. They gave us Harriet Tubman and MLK, maybe Rosa Parks, and then skipped straight to Barack Obama. But in between were decades of systemic destruction of Black financial progress—entire communities burned, homes lost, land stolen, businesses erased from history.

They don't tell us about the fires. They don't teach us about the deals made in backrooms that robbed generations. And so we grow up thinking we're starting from scratch, when really—we're starting from *what's left*.

This chapter is about the wealth we built that got bulldozed. The businesses, neighborhoods, and institutions we created in spite of the odds—only to have them targeted. It's about the erasure, the policies, the violence, and the manipulation that set us back every time we stepped forward.

We're going to talk about Black Wall Street, the urban renewal hustle, redlining, the war on drugs, and even subprime mortgages—all wrapped in everyday terms. No academic lecture, just a real convo. Like you're talking to your big cousin on the porch, sipping something cold and spitting facts.

Because once you know what was stolen, you'll stop blaming yourself for what you didn't inherit.

And once you understand the patterns, you'll start seeing the power in building differently.

Let's go back and uncover what they buried.

Black Wall Street and the Blueprint They Feared

Everybody's heard of Tulsa now—but let's really talk about it.

Greenwood, a neighborhood in Tulsa, Oklahoma, was one of the most affluent Black communities in America in the early 1900s. Doctors, lawyers, real estate agents, grocery store owners. They had their own schools, newspapers, movie theaters, banks, and a strong network of support. It was dubbed "Black Wall Street" not because it mimicked whiteness, but because it embodied *Black excellence.*

But in 1921, white mobs burned it to the ground. Over 1,000 homes destroyed. Hundreds of businesses wiped out. Hundreds of people killed. No insurance payouts. No rebuilding funds. No justice.

Imagine your whole life's work being destroyed in 48 hours—and the government doing nothing. Now multiply that across families and generations.

That wasn't an isolated incident. Similar attacks happened in Rosewood, Florida; Wilmington, North Carolina; and many more cities. Black wealth was seen as a threat, and so it was attacked—by mobs, by laws, and by silence.

The Redlining Playbook

Fast-forward to the 1930s. The government launches programs to help Americans buy homes. Sounds good, right?

Here's the catch: the Home Owners' Loan Corporation (HOLC) created maps grading neighborhoods for investment risk. Black neighborhoods? Automatically marked in red—"hazardous." That's where the term "redlining" comes from.

That red ink was a death sentence. It meant no loans, no mortgages, no investment. Black families couldn't buy, build, or borrow—even when they had the income. Meanwhile, white families got loans, homes, and the beginning of generational wealth.

By the 1960s, the average white family had equity and property. The average Black family had rent receipts and shut doors. Even today, you can trace poverty patterns directly back to those redlined maps.

This wasn't personal finance—it was policy.

Urban Renewal = Black Removal

Now let's talk about the 1950s and '60s. Post-war America. Cities are expanding. Highways are being built. "Urban renewal" becomes the buzzword.

Translation? Bulldozing Black neighborhoods to make way for freeways, stadiums, and suburbs.

Thousands of families displaced. Entire communities erased. If you were living in a thriving Black district near downtown, chances are it got labeled "blight" and bulldozed. And when they offered compensation? It wasn't enough to rebuild.

This happened in cities like Detroit, Atlanta, Los Angeles, Kansas City, and more. Our communities weren't just pushed aside—they were paved over.

The Subprime Setup

Let's slide into the 2000s. Black folks are finally getting mortgages. Owning homes. Making moves.

But here's the twist: we were targeted with subprime loans. Higher interest rates. Complex terms. Predatory practices. Even when our credit was good, we were steered into bad deals.

Then the 2008 crash hit—and who lost the most? Black families. We lost homes, equity, and wealth at rates double or triple our white peers.

We didn't fail the system. The system scammed us.

Cultural Echoes: What All This Did to Us

You ever notice how your family talks about money? The fear? The silence? The hustle mentality? That's not just cultural—it's survival mode.

If your grandma lost her home to redlining, she's not gonna teach you about refinancing. If your uncle's barbershop got pushed out by urban renewal, he's not gonna trust city officials. If your parents got burned by a bad mortgage, they might warn you away from ownership altogether.

That's trauma talking. It's also grief. And we carry that in our decisions.

We're taught to "never owe nobody," but never taught how to leverage credit. We're told to "hold onto cash," but not taught how to grow wealth. We're praised for being independent, but punished for not having assets.

Pros and Cons of Knowing the Truth

Pros:

- You stop internalizing shame.
- You understand the root causes of inequality.
- You get motivated to build with strategy.
- You learn to protect what you build.

Cons:

- The truth can make you angry.
- It may feel overwhelming.
- It might trigger grief over what was lost.

Action Steps: Rebuilding with Wisdom

1. **Learn the Real History** Go beyond textbooks. Read about Tulsa, Rosewood, and redlining. Watch documentaries. Share stories. Bring your people into the light.

2. **Talk About Wealth** At the dinner table. In the group chat. After church. Don't let silence steal another generation's power.
3. **Get Financial Education** Follow Black financial educators. Take free classes. Learn about credit, insurance, investing, homeownership. It's never too late.
4. **Buy Strategically** If you're in a position to buy land or property—research, network, protect it. Use estate planning tools. Get a will. Set up a trust if you can.
5. **Join or Create Wealth-Building Circles** Start a savings club. Invest with friends. Learn together. Build together. We've always been strongest as a unit.
6. **Support Policy That Protects Us** Vote for housing reform. Support reparations. Push for financial equity. Local policy matters just as much as national.

Final Word: It Was Taken—Now We Take It Back

This chapter isn't about guilt or despair. It's about clarity. Because clarity is the beginning of healing.

Yes, Black wealth has been destroyed. But not completely. Because you're still here. We're still here. Breathing. Learning. Building.

We may not have inherited stocks, but we inherited *vision.* We may not have been handed land, but we've got hustle. We've got genius. We've got community.

We are the architects now. And we're building a new blueprint.

One that can't be bulldozed. One that can't be burned down. One that's too strong to be erased.

2.1: The Tulsa Race Massacre (Black Wall Street, 1921)

The Introduction They Never Gave Us

You ever hear somebody talk about "Black excellence" and wonder where that started? Not just in terms of vibes or hashtags, but real, tangible, legacy-building, community-powered Black success. For a lot of us, we think of folks like Madam C.J. Walker, or maybe the Cosbys showing what an upper-middle-class Black family could look like. But way before TV gave us the Huxtables, and long before social media let us hashtag our wins, there was Greenwood. There was Tulsa. There was Black Wall Street.

And it wasn't a metaphor. It was a *movement.*

This chapter right here? It's about what we built—and what they burned. It's about the pride and the pain, the resilience and the rage. It's about Black wealth, Black entrepreneurship, and Black self-determination—torn down not because it failed, but because it thrived.

So grab your seat. We're going back to 1921. And this time, we're telling the full story.

What Was Black Wall Street?

Greenwood, a neighborhood in Tulsa, Oklahoma, was one of the wealthiest Black communities in the United States during the early 20th century. We're talking over 600 businesses: movie theaters, hotels, barbershops, newspapers, grocery stores, banks, doctors' offices—you name it.

This wasn't a side hustle economy. This was a full-blown, self-sufficient Black economic ecosystem. People owned homes. Sent their kids to college. Wore suits on Tuesdays. There was dignity, structure, and strategy.

And it wasn't by accident—it was by design. Black folks weren't allowed to shop or do business in white neighborhoods due to segregation laws. So what did we do? We built our own. And not just "good for Black folks"—we're talking generational wealth, circulation of dollars, cooperative economics.

Imagine the energy of *Coming to America*'s Zamunda, mixed with the self-reliance of *Good Times,* and the ambition of every Nipsey Hussle lyric.

That was Greenwood. That was Black Wall Street.

The Day the Dream Burned

But on May 31, 1921, everything changed.

The spark? A 19-year-old Black boy named Dick Rowland was accused of assaulting a 17-year-old white girl, Sarah Page, in an elevator. No proof. No investigation. Just a rumor.

White mobs gathered outside the courthouse demanding Rowland's lynching. Black men, many of them WWI veterans, showed up armed to protect him. A scuffle broke out. Shots were fired. And just like that, the match was lit.

For the next 18 hours, white mobs—backed by law enforcement—looted, burned, and destroyed Greenwood. They set buildings on fire, shot people in the streets, dropped bombs from private planes (yes, bombs), and reduced one of the most successful Black neighborhoods in America to ashes.

Over 300 Black people were killed. 1,200 homes were destroyed. 35 city blocks obliterated. And you know how many people were prosecuted for the violence?

Zero.

Why They Burned It

Let's not get it twisted. This wasn't just about an elevator ride.

This was about Black success. About economic independence. About a community that didn't need white approval or assistance. Greenwood was proof that we could win without them. And that was a threat.

It's the same reason why so many Black neighborhoods were "urban renewed" out of existence in the '50s and '60s. It's the same reason our schools are underfunded and our businesses are undercapitalized.

They didn't hate us because we were poor. They feared us because we weren't.

Cultural Echoes: How It Still Lives in Us

Think about how we treat success sometimes.

We're afraid to shine too bright. We joke about "crabs in a barrel." We don't trust the system because the system has *never* shown up for us. And that's not paranoia—it's historical memory.

In *The Fresh Prince,* Uncle Phil always wanted Will to understand the value of legacy. Not just money—but *dignity.* The idea that you belong in the boardroom as much as the barber chair. That you can have both culture and capital.

But imagine if Uncle Phil had grown up hearing stories about his father's law office being torched by a mob. Imagine if Aunt Viv's beauty salon was burned down in front of her. That trauma doesn't disappear—it passes down.

That's why this story matters.

Pros and Cons of Knowing This History

Pros:

- You realize that we've *already* built wealth before.
- You stop believing the lie that we never tried.
- You feel empowered to rebuild with wisdom and intention.
- You understand why certain fears, hesitations, and habits exist.

Cons:

- It can be heartbreaking to learn what was lost.
- It may trigger anger or hopelessness.
- It reminds us how fragile our progress can feel without protection.

Action Steps: Turning Grief into Groundwork

1. **Learn and Teach the History** Don't let Greenwood be a hashtag. Read books, watch documentaries, tell your kids. Make it part of the family legacy.
2. **Support Black-Owned Businesses** Every dollar is a vote. Circulate your money where your people are. From the corner store to the tech startup.
3. **Build Cooperative Economics** Start investment clubs. Buy property together. Use group economics like our ancestors did. The dollar circulates longer in unity.
4. **Protect What You Build** Get life insurance. Write a will. Set up a trust. Trademark your business. Don't let what you build be easy to take.
5. **Create Spaces That Uplift** Whether it's a school, a co-working space, or a pop-up shop—create environments where Black excellence isn't just possible, it's expected.
6. **Push for Policy Change** Demand investment in Black neighborhoods. Fight for reparations. Hold local officials accountable. Policy burned Greenwood down—policy can help build it back.

Final Word: The Fire Didn't Win

They burned our homes, but not our hope. They dropped bombs, but couldn't destroy our brilliance. We've always rebuilt—out of scraps, out of dreams, out of sheer determination.

Black Wall Street wasn't just a place—it was a blueprint. And that blueprint still lives in us. In every Black entrepreneur. In every family saving for their child's future. In every church, barbershop, and book club talking about legacy.

We are not just survivors. We are architects. Engineers. Visionaries.

So the next time someone says Black people need to "learn how to build wealth," tell them we already did. And we're doing it again.

This time, with fireproof floors.

2.2: The Rosewood Massacre (1923)

Setting the Scene: Florida Sun and Southern Tension

Let's set the scene. Early 1920s. Rosewood, Florida—a small, predominantly Black town tucked away on the Gulf Coast. It wasn't massive like Tulsa's Greenwood district, but it was stable. Solid. Quiet.

The folks in Rosewood had built something out of nothing. They owned land. They worked hard. They had schools, churches, businesses, and dignity. Families looked out for each other. Kids played in the dirt. Neighbors shared meals. You could call it a rural version of Black Wall Street—tight-knit and self-sufficient.

And then, like too many times in our history, the lie of a white woman and the fury of white mobs turned everything to ash.

This chapter is about what happened in Rosewood—and what it means for us today. It's about the loss, the silence, and the legacy. But it's also about the power of memory, the necessity of truth, and the responsibility of building again.

Because Rosewood wasn't just a tragedy. It was a warning. And if we don't remember, we risk repeating.

What Happened in Rosewood?

On January 1, 1923, a white woman in a nearby town named Fannie Taylor claimed she had been assaulted by a Black man. The story spread fast—and just like in Tulsa, it didn't take long for a white mob to mobilize.

No investigation. No questions. Just fury.

They were looking for a man named Jesse Hunter, an escaped convict who may not have even existed. But truth wasn't the goal—terror was.

The mobs moved in. They burned Black homes. They lynched a local

Black man named Sam Carter. They stormed churches and businesses. Over several days, they completely destroyed the town of Rosewood.

Black families fled into the swamps to survive. Many never returned.

Estimates vary, but it's believed that up to 150 people may have been killed. And the town? Erased. Vanished from maps. Forgotten by history books.

For decades, survivors didn't speak of it. The trauma was too deep. The risk too high.

Why It Hit So Hard

Rosewood wasn't a place where people were "just getting by." These were landowners. Businesspeople. Teachers. Families who had *worked* to build something lasting.

They weren't on welfare. They weren't dependent. They were self-made—and that's what made them dangerous in the eyes of white supremacy.

The destruction of Rosewood wasn't just violence—it was an economic attack. Homes were destroyed. Property was seized. Generations of wealth were wiped out.

Sound familiar?

We saw it in Tulsa. We saw it in Wilmington. We saw it in Detroit, Harlem, Atlanta. Black success is too often seen as a threat—and punished accordingly.

Cultural Echoes: Trauma in the Silence

Here's the thing about Rosewood—it almost disappeared from public memory.

For over 70 years, there were no reparations. No formal recognition. No public teaching. Survivors kept quiet. Some out of fear. Some out of shame. Some just trying to survive.

You ever have an elder who refuses to talk about the past? Who gets quiet when certain names come up? That's Rosewood trauma. That silence? That's inherited grief.

Think about it: you lose your home, your business, your family—and no one comes to help. No one's held accountable. No one even says your name.

That's erasure. And we've lived with it for generations.

The Cost of the Cover-Up

Because Rosewood was kept out of the history books, many of us didn't learn about it until a 1997 movie or a quick social media post decades later. And that's by design.

If you don't know what was stolen, you don't ask for it back. If you don't know you've been wronged, you internalize the struggle. If you don't see the pattern, you think the failure is personal.

The loss of Rosewood isn't just about land—it's about narrative. About how history is written, remembered, and erased.

But we're flipping the script.

Pros and Cons of Revisiting This Pain

Pros:

- We restore dignity to the lives lost.
- We break the silence for future generations.
- We empower ourselves to build with protection.
- We fuel the movement for justice and reparations.

Cons:

- It's painful. No way around that.
- It can feel like reopening a wound.
- It may shake your belief in systems you once trusted.

Action Steps: Learning, Building, Protecting

1. **Learn the Names and Stories** Don't let Rosewood be just another headline. Read survivor accounts. Watch the documentary. Study the details. Know the names.
2. **Teach It Forward** Bring it up in your circles. Share the knowledge. Add it to family conversations, community workshops, classrooms. Our kids deserve the full story.
3. **Protect What You Build** Insure your assets. Keep records. Set up wills and trusts. Document your property and your plans. Be ready.
4. **Advocate for Reparations and Historical Justice** Support local and national efforts that push for compensation, historical recognition, and investment in Black communities. Justice delayed isn't always justice denied—but we have to demand it.
5. **Build Stronger Together** Use cooperative economics. Build networks of trust. Don't try to do it all solo. Rosewood was strong because it was united. Let's honor that.

Final Word: We Carry the Fire

They tried to burn Rosewood off the map.

But what they didn't know is—you can burn a house, but not a legacy. You can destroy buildings, but not spirit. You can silence voices, but not truth.

Rosewood lives in us.

Every time we invest in our communities, every time we teach our children their real history, every time we rise despite the odds—we resurrect what they tried to kill.

We are the dream and the defense.

And this time, we're not asking for permission.

We're building again.

2.3: Redlining and the HOLC Maps

Setting the Record Straight: It Was Never Just About Credit Scores

You ever wonder why the hood stays the hood even when the people in it are grinding hard? Why some neighborhoods have great schools, clean streets, and rising home values—and others, despite the hustle and heart, are stuck in struggle mode?

The answer isn't just economics or effort. It's policy. It's red ink. It's a series of maps that quietly told banks, "Don't invest in Black folks."

This chapter is about redlining—the original neighborhood discrimination tool—and how it still affects us today. We're gonna talk about HOLC maps, the housing hustle, and the invisible fences drawn around our futures.

We'll break it down like you're sitting on your front porch, chopping it up with your favorite uncle who's seen some things and is finally ready to put you up on game.

Because the first step to breaking the cycle is knowing where the trap was set.

What Is Redlining?

Redlining is when banks, lenders, and the government literally drew red lines around certain neighborhoods on maps and said, "Don't lend here."

These neighborhoods? Always Black. Sometimes Latinx. Almost always working-class.

It wasn't subtle. It wasn't accidental. It was strategic exclusion. And it didn't just block loans—it blocked opportunity.

The term comes from the color-coded maps created in the 1930s by the Home Owners' Loan Corporation (HOLC). These maps graded neighborhoods from green (best) to red (worst). Red areas were marked as risky for investment, regardless of the actual creditworthiness or income of residents.

Green zones? White folks. New suburbs. Good schools.

Red zones? Black folks. Inner cities. "Undesirable elements."

You could be a Black war veteran with a steady job and still be denied a loan just because you lived in a redlined zone. Your zip code told the bank all it needed to know.

And the worst part? These maps were used for decades.

The HOLC Maps: America's Financial Color Code

Let's break this down a little more.

The HOLC (Home Owners' Loan Corporation) was created during the Great Depression to help people avoid foreclosure and make home ownership more accessible.

Sounds good, right?

But when they started evaluating where to invest, they didn't just look at home prices or property conditions. They looked at race.

Neighborhoods were graded based on "inhabitants," which was code for whether or not Black people lived there. If Black folks were present—or even nearby—that area was marked as a no-go.

Banks, insurance companies, and mortgage lenders used these maps to make decisions. And once your neighborhood was redlined, it meant:

- No home loans
- No business loans
- No insurance
- No investment

Just stagnation. Disrepair. Devaluation.

It was financial segregation—with a spreadsheet.

Real-World Impact: The Wealth Gap on Paper

You know that stat about the average white family having 6 to 10 times more wealth than the average Black family?

This is one of the biggest reasons why.

White families in green and blue zones got loans, bought homes, built equity, and passed that wealth down.

Black families in red zones were stuck renting, couldn't fix their homes, couldn't get loans, and watched their neighborhoods deteriorate—not because they didn't care, but because they were systematically locked out.

Even today, you can overlay a redlining map from the 1930s on a current poverty map, and it matches. The wealth (or lack of it) in Black communities wasn't random. It was engineered.

And we're still living with the results.

Cultural Echoes: The Long Shadow of Red Ink

You ever heard a relative say, "Don't buy in that neighborhood"? Or seen how your people have to jump through extra hoops just to get a mortgage? Or maybe you've wondered why the Black side of town always has fewer banks and more payday lenders?

That's redlining residue. The ghosts of policies past.

It's why gentrification hits so hard—because the same banks that refused to lend to us in the '50s are now handing out loans to developers flipping our grandma's block.

It's why Black homeowners often see slower appreciation rates, even when they buy in "hot" markets.

It's why we hustle so hard to buy, only to find out our zip code is still being judged.

Like *Martin* said: "Damn, Gina." Sometimes all we can do is shake our heads.

Pros and Cons: Unpacking the Knowledge

Pros of Knowing This History:

- You realize your struggle isn't just personal—it's systemic.
- You stop blaming yourself for what was strategically denied.
- You learn to ask better questions and demand accountability.
- You build with eyes wide open.

Cons:

- It can feel overwhelming to realize how deep the roots are.
- It might trigger anger or frustration.
- It can make you wary of traditional financial systems (which is fair, but limiting).

Action Steps: Reclaiming Our Blocks, Rebuilding Our Futures

1. **Learn the Redlining Map in Your City** You can find most HOLC maps online. See if your neighborhood was redlined. Share that history. Connect the dots.
2. **Invest With Intention** If you're able to buy property, buy smart. Buy where you can add value, protect legacy, and push for reinvestment.
3. **Demand Local Investment** Push your city to reinvest in historically redlined areas. Advocate for affordable housing, business grants, and community development.
4. **Build Together** Start cooperatives. Pool funds. Invest with family or friends. We've always had the talent—we just need systems that work *for* us.
5. **Document Everything** If you're building, protect it. Get it in writing. Use contracts. Set up estate plans. Make your moves permanent.
6. **Teach the Babies** Don't let this be forgotten. Tell your kids about redlining, equity, credit, and how to build with wisdom. Their

foundation is your legacy.

Final Word: Red Ink, Black Power

They drew red lines around us to box us in. But we don't do boxes.

We create. We flip. We reclaim.

Redlining was real—but so is our resilience. We've survived the maps. Now we're making our own.

And this time?

Our blocks will be protected. Our homes will be insured. Our stories will be told.

Because the same system that once excluded us is now being questioned by us, challenged by us, and rebuilt by us.

Let's draw new lines—ones filled with hope, equity, and ownership.

2.4: GI Bill Discrimination After WWII

The Promise That Skipped Us

Alright, let's talk real. Imagine you fight for a country, risk your life overseas, wear the uniform with pride, and come home ready to build a better life. That's the setup. That's what was promised to the millions of men and women who served in World War II.

Now imagine coming home, ready to start fresh, but instead of a handshake and a home loan, you're handed a roadblock. That's what happened to thousands—actually, *millions*—of Black veterans after WWII. The G.I. Bill, which was supposed to be the launchpad to middle-class life, turned out to be just another door slammed in our faces.

This chapter is about the discrimination baked into one of America's most celebrated policies. We're diving into how the G.I. Bill worked, how it didn't work for us, and how it created a racial wealth divide that still shows up on your cousin's paycheck, your grandma's mortgage, and your student loans.

Let's get into it.

What Was the G.I. Bill?

Formally known as the Servicemen's Readjustment Act of 1944, the G.I. Bill was created to help returning WWII veterans transition back into civilian life. It offered a wide range of benefits:

- Free or low-cost college tuition
- Low-interest home loans
- Unemployment compensation
- Business loans

On paper? It was a generational game-changer.

And for millions of white veterans, it absolutely was. It helped them go to school, buy homes in the suburbs, start businesses, and move from working-class to middle-class in one generation.

But for Black veterans? It was a different story.

The Loopholes That Locked Us Out

The G.I. Bill didn't explicitly say "no Black people allowed." It didn't have to.

The federal government left the implementation of the G.I. Bill up to *local* officials. And you already know what that meant in the Jim Crow South—and even in many so-called progressive northern cities.

Let's break it down:

1. Education Discrimination Many colleges and universities didn't accept Black students. So even though the G.I. Bill would've paid tuition, there were few places for Black veterans to actually use it.

Historically Black Colleges and Universities (HBCUs) were already underfunded and overcrowded. They didn't have enough space for the flood of returning vets.

2. Housing Discrimination VA home loans required cooperation from banks and real estate agents. But many banks refused to lend to Black applicants. And redlining maps (remember those?) meant even Black folks who *could* get a loan couldn't buy in "good" neighborhoods.

That means no access to rising property values. No equity. No generational wealth.

3. Employment Discrimination The G.I. Bill included job placement support, but many industries openly discriminated against Black applicants. So Black vets often ended up in low-wage, low-opportunity jobs—if they could get hired at all.

So yeah, technically we "had access" to the benefits. But practically? The system was stacked.

The Impact: White Wealth Grows, Black Progress Stalls

Let's talk numbers. By 1950, nearly 8 million veterans had used the G.I. Bill to attend school or job training. But only a tiny fraction of them were Black.

In Mississippi, for example, out of over 3,000 VA home loans issued in 1947, only *two* went to Black veterans.

Let that sink in.

Two.

Meanwhile, white families bought homes, built equity, passed it down, and moved to the suburbs. They built the American Dream off a federal program. And we paid taxes into that same system—but couldn't touch the benefits.

Sound familiar?

It's like paying into a family BBQ and being told you can't have a plate.

Cultural Echoes: Generational Residue

You know that cousin who's working three jobs but still can't get ahead? Or that uncle who never went to college because he didn't think it was "for us"? Or that grandma who rented for 50 years and never owned a home?

That's G.I. Bill residue. That's what happens when opportunity skips a generation.

When we say Black folks are "behind" in wealth, this is what we're talking about. It's not laziness. It's legacy.

It's also why we often say, "We gotta work twice as hard to get half as far." Because structurally, we started *way* back.

Pros and Cons of Understanding the G.I. Bill Discrimination

Pros:

- You see how wealth gaps were created by policy, not just personal choices
- You stop carrying shame for systemic outcomes
- You get inspired to demand and design better systems for the next generation

Cons:

- It can make you angry
- It can make you feel hopeless
- It reveals just how deep the rabbit hole goes

Action Steps: From Betrayal to Blueprint

1. **Learn the History in Your Family** Was your grandfather or great-uncle a WWII vet? What happened when he came home? Did he try to get a loan or go to school? These stories matter.

2. **Document the Disparity** Use your platform to tell the truth. Social media. Family events. Schools. Let folks know how this played out in real life.
3. **Build and Protect Wealth** Start with what you can do now:

- Buy property, if possible
- Open a Roth IRA or 529 college fund
- Set up a will and estate plan
- Insure your life, your business, and your assets

4. Advocate for Reparative Policy Push for student loan forgiveness, Black homeownership programs, and real reinvestment in Black communities.

5. Educate the Next Generation Teach your kids about credit, ownership, and financial planning. They don't have to start at zero.

Final Word: We Remember, We Rebuild

The G.I. Bill could've been a bridge. For us, it was a barricade. But now that we know what was taken, we can begin to reclaim.

Not just for ourselves, but for every vet who came home to closed doors.

We're still building. Still rising. Still passing down the blueprint.

And this time?

We're not waiting for permission.

We're creating policy, platforms, and power that includes *all* of us.

2.5: Urban Renewal or "Negro Removal"

Let's Call It What It Was

Let's not play polite with the language. "Urban Renewal" might sound like progress, like new buildings and fresh streets. But if you talk to the people who lived through it—your grandma, your great-uncle, that elder at church—they'll tell you the real name: "Negro Removal."

This chapter is about the bulldozers that came through our blocks in the name of "development." It's about the highways that cut through our homes, the stadiums that replaced our churches, and the policies that tore apart communities like they were playing SimCity with real lives.

We're not just talking demolition—we're talking displacement. Erasure. And financial devastation. We're unpacking what urban renewal really did to Black wealth, Black families, and Black futures.

And most importantly, we're talking about how we fight back—with knowledge, with strategy, and with receipts.

What Was Urban Renewal?

After World War II, the federal government launched a wave of infrastructure and housing projects to modernize cities and accommodate a growing population.

It sounded good on paper. The goal was to clear out "blighted" areas and replace them with new housing, business districts, and transportation systems.

But guess what? Blight became code for Black.

Whole neighborhoods were labeled as rundown—not because of the people in them, but because the government had already redlined them, underfunded them, and disinvested in them.

Then, once they were labeled "problematic," the bulldozers came.

The Process: How It Went Down

1. **Label the Area Blighted** City officials would designate a Black neighborhood as a slum or unfit for living—even if people owned their homes, took care of them, and had vibrant community life.
2. **Use Eminent Domain** The government would take over the property "for public good." Translation? They forced people out, often with lowball payments.
3. **Clear the Land** Bulldozers would destroy homes, churches, schools, and businesses. Sometimes people weren't even given time to pack.
4. **Build Something Else** Usually a highway, a stadium, a government building, or a private development. And nine times out of ten? The folks who were pushed out couldn't afford to come back.

You ever see *Good Times* when they talked about moving out of the projects but never quite made it? That's what urban renewal did. Every time we were ready to rise, here came the system with another setback dressed like a favor.

The Numbers Don't Lie

Between 1950 and 1980, over 1,600 Black communities were displaced by urban renewal projects.

In cities like New York, Atlanta, Chicago, Detroit, Los Angeles, and Kansas City, Black families were pushed out to make room for highways and new developments.

In St. Paul, Minnesota, nearly 700 Black families were displaced from the Rondo neighborhood to make way for I-94.

In Atlanta, the Sweet Auburn district—once dubbed the richest Black street in the world—was cut in half by an expressway.

In New York, Lincoln Center sits on what used to be a thriving Black neighborhood.

Urban renewal destroyed more Black homes than any other single program in U.S. history.

Let that sink in.

Cultural Echoes: What It Did to Us

Displacement doesn't just move your address. It shatters your foundation.

You lose your neighbors. Your corner store. Your Sunday church routine. Your community watch. Your sense of safety. Your memories.

And when you lose those, you also lose:

- Stability for your kids
- Opportunities to build wealth
- Cultural preservation
- A support network

It's like somebody coming into your house, telling you it's too old, and then kicking you out and selling it to someone else for three times the price.

Urban renewal created cycles of generational instability. Renters instead of owners. Transit deserts. Food deserts. Trauma.

And we're still feeling that loss today.

Pros and Cons of Learning This Truth

Pros:

- You finally see the full picture of Black wealth loss
- You understand why certain areas are underdeveloped
- You gain fuel to protect and rebuild your own

Cons:

- It's painful to realize how planned it all was
- It may trigger feelings of powerlessness

- It highlights how slow justice can be

Action Steps: Protect, Plan, Push Back

1. **Learn the History of Your Neighborhood** Ask elders. Research maps. Check city archives. Know what was there before the highways and stadiums.
2. **Document What You Own** If you own property, get the deed. If you don't, make a plan to start. Protect your assets. Set up a trust. Put it in writing.
3. **Get Involved in Local Planning** Go to city council meetings. Pay attention to zoning laws. Speak up when development is proposed.
4. **Create a Neighborhood Network** Know your neighbors. Form a tenants' union. Share knowledge. Strengthen your block before outsiders do.
5. **Build Our Own Developments** Support Black developers. Invest in co-ops. Start a community land trust. Let's be the ones building, not just reacting.
6. **Teach the Next Generation** Make sure your kids know how we got here. Teach them about gentrification, home ownership, and legacy planning.

Final Word: Renewal Starts With Us

They called it progress. We call it robbery. They called it modernization. We call it memory loss.

But here's the thing: we're still here.

We may have been moved, but we weren't removed. We may have been scattered, but we ain't silent.

Now it's our turn.

To rebuild communities that center us. To protect homes that hold our stories. To fight for policies that don't erase us—but elevate us.

Urban renewal wasn't our ending.

It's just another chapter we're rewriting.

2.6: FHA Lending Discrimination (1930s–1970s)

Let's Talk About the "American Dream" They Sold—But Didn't Deliver

We've all seen the image: white picket fence, two-story house, maybe a swing on the front porch and a grill out back. That's what they told us the American Dream looked like, especially post-WWII. They told us that if you worked hard, played by the rules, and kept your nose clean, you could get a mortgage, buy a home, and start building generational wealth.

But like a lot of things in American history, that dream came with a disclaimer—especially if you were Black.

Between the 1930s and 1970s, one of the most powerful tools for building middle-class wealth was homeownership. And the engine behind that explosion of suburban growth was the Federal Housing Administration (FHA).

The FHA wasn't just a player in the housing game—it *was* the game. It made homeownership affordable. It backed mortgages. It set the rules.

But here's the twist: the FHA built the suburbs while burying Black communities under decades of denial, disinvestment, and deliberate exclusion.

Let's get into it.

What Was the FHA and Why Did It Matter?

Created in 1934 during the Great Depression, the FHA was designed to stimulate the housing market by making it easier for Americans to buy homes. It offered insurance on loans, so banks would take less risk. That meant lower down payments, longer loan terms, and lower interest rates.

In other words? It made homeownership accessible for the everyday

American.

But not for everyone.

From the jump, the FHA refused to insure loans in Black neighborhoods or even in white neighborhoods that were "at risk" of becoming racially mixed. They called it "maintaining property values."

We call it what it is: discrimination.

The Playbook: How FHA Discrimination Worked

1. **Redlining Maps** FHA adopted the HOLC's redlining maps. If you lived in a red zone—which was almost always Black—you were automatically disqualified from receiving an FHA-backed loan.
2. **Restrictive Covenants** Many FHA-insured developments included deed restrictions that banned the sale of homes to non-white families. These were legally enforced until 1948 and socially enforced long after.
3. **Suburban Flight** The FHA poured money into white suburban developments. Entire towns were built on government-backed loans that excluded Black buyers.
4. **Urban Disinvestment** Because Black families couldn't access FHA loans, they were stuck renting or buying homes with shady contracts (contract selling) that offered no equity, no protection, and high risk.

So while white families were buying into neighborhoods with rising property values, Black families were boxed out—again.

The Legacy: Wealth Built on Our Exclusion

Let's keep it real: the average American family's wealth is tied to homeownership. That equity turns into college tuition, emergency funds, retirement savings, and something to leave behind.

So when Black folks were denied access to FHA-backed home loans for decades, we weren't just denied homes—we were denied wealth.

And that wealth gap didn't just happen—it was *engineered.*

From 1934 to 1962, the government underwrote $120 billion in new housing. More than 98% went to white families.

Black families? We got crumbs—if that.

Cultural Echoes: How It Still Hits

You ever wonder why your grandparents rented their whole lives?

Or why your neighborhood never got upgraded—while one zip code over they got new sidewalks, schools, and Starbucks?

Or why your family didn't inherit a house, but your white college roommate got one as a graduation gift?

That's FHA fallout. That's how a 30-year mortgage denial turns into 3 generations of delay.

Even today, Black families are still less likely to own homes, more likely to be denied for mortgages, and more likely to live in areas with low property value growth.

And it's not just about money—it's about *mobility.* Economic, geographic, and generational.

Pros and Cons of Understanding the FHA's Role

Pros:

- You see how housing discrimination wasn't just social—it was federal policy
- You stop believing the myth of meritocracy
- You're motivated to fight for equity and reparative housing programs

Cons:

- The truth can be heavy
- You might question whether homeownership is still the path

- It reveals how fragile progress can be

Action Steps: Reclaiming the Blueprint

1. **Learn the History of Your Block** Find out if your neighborhood was affected by FHA redlining. Talk to your elders. Check the records. Tell the story.
2. **Buy Smart, Build Strong** If you're buying a home, study the market. Use reputable lenders. Avoid predatory contracts. Protect your investment.
3. **Advocate for Equity** Support Black homeownership initiatives. Push for fair lending. Vote for housing policy that includes us, not excludes us.
4. **Teach the Next Generation** Teach your kids about credit, loans, equity, and how the system *was* built so they can learn to build better.
5. **Support Community Investment** Shop local. Invest in Black-led real estate projects. Strengthen your block. Reclaim the land we were locked out of.

Final Word: They Built a Fence—Now We Build a Foundation

The FHA handed the keys to white America and left us standing on the porch.

But we're still here.

We're still buying. Still building. Still planting roots.

And now that we know what was done, we know what to undo—and how to move.

Because home isn't just where the heart is.

It's where the *wealth* is.

2.7: The Highway Act and Mass Displacement

When Progress Paved Over Our Communities

You ever hear someone say, "We used to have a whole block here"? Or maybe your elders mention how their childhood home got bulldozed, how the old church is under an overpass now, or how the vibrant strip of Black-owned businesses disappeared without a trace.

That's the Highway Act at work.

It didn't come through with sirens and warnings—it came in the name of "progress," "modernization," and "national defense." But when the bulldozers came, they didn't roll through the white suburbs. They rolled through us.

In this chapter, we're breaking down how the Federal-Aid Highway Act of 1956 became one of the largest, most destructive tools of Black displacement in American history. We're going to talk about how it changed the geography of our cities, the economics of our neighborhoods, and the structure of our communities—while making it look like it was all for the greater good.

Let's get into the real story.

What Was the Highway Act?

Signed into law by President Dwight D. Eisenhower in 1956, the Federal-Aid Highway Act authorized the construction of 41,000 miles of interstate highway across the country.

The public narrative? National security, economic growth, and traffic efficiency. You know, apple pie and all that.

But underneath the surface, something else was happening. The highway system didn't just go around cities—it went straight through them.

And guess which communities were labeled as the most "cost-effective" to demolish?

You guessed it: Black ones.

The Blueprint for Displacement

The government called it "urban planning." But for many Black communities, it was an eviction notice.

1. **Target "Low-Value" Land** Planners identified land that had been redlined or labeled as "blighted." These areas were "cheaper" to acquire because property values had been deliberately suppressed for decades.
2. **Use Eminent Domain** Local governments used eminent domain to seize homes, churches, schools, and businesses. Owners were underpaid, renters were often given nothing, and families were left scrambling.
3. **Construct Highways Right Through the Heart** Rather than route highways around established Black neighborhoods, they routed them directly through. Destroying community centers, displacing thousands, and leaving behind noise, pollution, and concrete.

Real Places, Real People

Let's talk specifics.

- **Detroit:** The Black Bottom and Paradise Valley neighborhoods—once the heart of Black culture and commerce—were gutted by the construction of I-375.
- **New Orleans:** Claiborne Avenue was a tree-lined boulevard filled with Black-owned businesses. Today? It's a concrete highway overpass.
- **Miami:** The Overtown community, home to countless Black residents and historic landmarks, was torn apart by I-95.
- **Nashville:** Jefferson Street, a vibrant Black cultural corridor, was decimated.

The pattern? Consistent.

Black progress was seen as an acceptable casualty of white convenience.

Cultural Echoes: The Trauma of Disruption

You don't just bulldoze a street—you bulldoze trust, safety, history.

When the highway came through, it didn't just take homes. It took identity.

Churches gone. Businesses shut down. Elders separated from neighbors they'd known for decades. Kids taken out of their schools. And no infrastructure to catch them after the fall.

It's why so many of our elders talk about "back in the day" like it was a paradise. Because before the highways came, there *was* a sense of place, of community, of possibility.

That's not nostalgia. That's truth.

Pros and Cons: Understanding the Big Picture

Pros:

- You see how "neutral" policies can have targeted impacts
- You understand the role of infrastructure in systemic racism
- You get motivated to protect what we build

Cons:

- It's painful to realize how much was lost
- It can feel overwhelming to fight against city planning machines
- It highlights the fragility of our progress

Action Steps: Reclaim the Map

1. **Learn Your City's History** Research which communities were displaced by highway construction. Ask elders. Check archives. Tell the story.
2. **Advocate for Community Reinvestment** Push your city to reinvest

in displaced communities. Support reparative infrastructure projects and economic redevelopment grants.

3. **Protect What's Left** If your community is still intact, organize. Watch zoning proposals. Attend planning meetings. Stay vocal.
4. **Support Smart Growth** Development doesn't have to mean displacement. Support projects that build with—not over—Black communities.
5. **Reconnect the Roots** Map out where your family's home used to be. Talk about it. Walk those streets. Let your kids know the legacy. Bring memory back to life.

Final Word: They Drew the Roads—We're Redrawing the Routes

They cut through our homes to create shortcuts for others.

But what they didn't expect? That we'd still be here.

Still building. Still loving. Still remembering. Still rising.

Now it's our turn to pave the way—on our terms.

Not just highways, but *byways* back to legacy, connection, and empowerment.

Because our neighborhoods were never "in the way."

They were *the way.*

2.8: The Destruction of Seneca Village and Mill Creek Valley

Black Roots, Bulldozed Dreams

Before Harlem, before the South Bronx, before all the big stories of urban struggle and survival, there was Seneca Village—a peaceful, thriving Black community in the heart of Manhattan. And before interstate highways gutted Black neighborhoods in the Midwest, there was Mill Creek Valley in St. Louis, a cultural and economic anchor for thousands of African Americans.

These stories aren't just history lessons—they're cautionary tales. They're the roots of why we distrust developers, question "progress," and still feel the sting of displacement generations later.

This chapter dives into the deliberate erasure of Black neighborhoods long before redlining and highways became common practice. Seneca Village and Mill Creek Valley weren't just torn down—they were covered up. Hidden. Forgotten. Until now.

Let's bring their names back into the light.

Seneca Village: New York City's Forgotten Black Eden

Let's rewind to the early 1800s—New York City, just before the skyscrapers, before Wall Street took over everything. On the western edge of Manhattan, between 82nd and 89th Streets, a small but mighty Black community called Seneca Village began to grow.

Founded in 1825 by free Black Americans, Seneca Village was a safe haven. Families bought land. Built homes. Started churches. Raised kids. It was one of the few places in the city where Black people could own property, which meant they could *vote*. Let that sink in.

By the 1850s, about 225 residents lived in Seneca Village, including Irish and German immigrants, but the backbone of the community was Black.

And then came Central Park.

Progress with a Price Tag

In 1853, the state of New York authorized the creation of Central Park. The land they wanted? Smack dab in the middle of Seneca Village.

They didn't negotiate. They didn't listen. They used eminent domain, paid folks pennies on the dollar for their land, and demolished everything.

Gone. Just like that.

No monuments. No markers. No apology. For over a century, most people didn't even know Seneca Village existed. It was buried—physically and historically.

And that's the blueprint. Label it progress, bulldoze the people, erase the memory.

Mill Creek Valley: The Heart of Black St. Louis

Now fast forward to the mid-1900s—St. Louis, Missouri. Mill Creek Valley was a vibrant Black neighborhood between Union Station and Saint Louis University. Over 20,000 residents called it home. There were more than 800 Black-owned businesses, dozens of churches, and a deep-rooted culture of self-determination.

But like so many Black communities, Mill Creek was labeled "blighted." The city decided it was time for "renewal."

By the 1950s, urban renewal plans claimed over 450 acres of land. Bulldozers rolled in, families were forced out, and nearly 5,000 buildings were destroyed. Public housing projects and highways replaced what used to be one of the most vibrant Black areas in the Midwest.

Once again, Black wealth, Black culture, Black identity—bulldozed for the comfort of white America.

The Pattern Repeats

Whether it was Seneca Village in the 1800s or Mill Creek Valley in the 1950s, the formula was always the same:

- Identify a thriving Black community.
- Label it undesirable.
- Use eminent domain or urban renewal.
- Displace the people.
- Erase the memory.
- Profit from the land.

You see it in stories like the Cosby Show's brownstone—a symbol of Black success in a historically Black neighborhood. But too often, real-life versions of those homes were taken before they could become legacies.

Cultural Echoes: What We Lost

Displacement didn't just remove buildings—it severed relationships.

- Grandmas lost their front porches.
- Children lost their classmates.
- Entrepreneurs lost their storefronts.
- Communities lost their anchors.

You ever wonder why Black folks are so deeply connected to where they came from—even if that place is gone? It's because we know how fast it can be taken.

You ever hear an elder talk about "how things used to be" with tears in their eyes? That's not nostalgia—it's grief.

And we carry that grief in our decisions today. In our hesitation to trust institutions. In our deep skepticism of "development." In our passion for preserving the block.

Pros and Cons of This Truth

Pros:

- Restores erased history
- Validates community memory and cultural trauma
- Strengthens the call for reparations and justice
- Inspires future building with intention

Cons:

- Reopens old wounds
- Can feel emotionally overwhelming
- Reminds us how vulnerable our progress has been

Action Steps: Reclaim, Restore, Remember

1. **Teach the Names** Put Seneca Village and Mill Creek Valley in the same breath as Tulsa and Rosewood. Tell your kids. Talk about it in barbershops, salons, classrooms, and pulpits.
2. **Support Local Preservation Efforts** Many cities are working to restore and honor displaced communities. Get involved. Speak up. Fund it. Name it.
3. **Document Your Family's Story** If your family lived in a neighborhood that no longer exists—write it down. Record the stories. Create your own archive.
4. **Protect Your Block** Learn the zoning laws. Know the development plans. If your neighborhood is next on the "revitalization" list, organize. Build coalitions. Make noise.
5. **Build Where You Can** Invest in Black-led projects. Develop land in our names. Leave something for the next generation. Let them inherit ownership, not eviction.

Final Word: Their Names Weren't Lost—They Were Stolen

Seneca Village and Mill Creek Valley weren't accidents. They were *intentional* communities, full of hope and hustle. They were dreams made real—until someone decided they didn't belong.

But now, we decide.

We decide to remember. To honor. To rebuild.

Their stories don't end in the rubble. They rise in every Black homeowner who says, "This is mine." They breathe in every kid who learns about what was taken. They echo in every neighborhood meeting where we say, "Not this time."

We've seen what they'll do to take.

Now let's show them what we'll do to protect.

2.9: The MOVE Bombing (1985)

The Day the Government Bombed Black Folks in Philly

This ain't ancient history. This didn't happen back when folks were wearing top hats and monocles. This happened in the 1980s—when *The Cosby Show* was topping the ratings, when Run-DMC was rocking Adidas with no laces, and when your auntie probably had a salt-and-pepper asymmetrical haircut.

May 13, 1985. Philadelphia.

A city government dropped a bomb—*a bomb*—on a residential neighborhood. On American citizens. On Black families.

Let that marinate.

This chapter is about the MOVE bombing, one of the most shameful, tragic, and under-taught acts of state violence in U.S. history. It's about a Black liberation group, a city's fear of Black resistance, and the destruction of an entire city block by its own police department.

Let's unpack what happened, why it matters, and what it means for how we move forward today.

Who Was MOVE?

MOVE was a Black radical organization founded in Philadelphia in the early 1970s by John Africa (born Vincent Leaphart). The group preached a back-to-nature lifestyle, a deep mistrust of government, and a commitment to liberation for Black people and all life.

They were vegetarians. They believed in natural living. They had long hair, raised children communally, and gave all members the surname "Africa" to symbolize unity and ancestry.

But they also clashed hard with the city. Constantly.

MOVE protested police brutality, animal cruelty, and systemic racism. They were loud, unapologetic, and deeply committed. But their methods were controversial—they used bullhorns, resisted government intrusion, and carried firearms (legally, mind you).

To some, they were radicals. To others, freedom fighters. But to the Philadelphia Police Department and city officials? They were a "problem" that needed to be handled.

What Led Up to the Bombing?

MOVE had already been in conflict with the city. In 1978, there was a violent police confrontation at another MOVE house that led to the death of a police officer and life sentences for nine MOVE members.

By 1981, remaining MOVE members relocated to a row house on Osage Avenue in West Philadelphia. Neighbors complained about the noise, the confrontations, and the presence of armed adults and children living in a fortified house.

But rather than de-escalate or find peaceful solutions, the city planned a full-on siege.

May 13, 1985: The Attack

At 5:30 AM, nearly 500 police officers surrounded the MOVE home. They used tear gas, floodlights, water cannons, and eventually, gunfire—over 10,000 rounds were fired in 90 minutes.

But the climax? Around 5:30 PM, the police dropped a satchel bomb from a helicopter onto the house.

Let's run that back.

They dropped a bomb.

It ignited a massive fire.

But instead of putting the fire out, officials let it burn.

Why? Because they wanted it to burn the house down. But that fire spread—to the whole block.

The Toll

- **11 people killed**: 5 children, 6 adults
- **61 homes destroyed**
- **250 residents left homeless**

The city let an entire Black neighborhood burn.

And the people responsible? None of them went to jail. Not the mayor. Not the police commissioner. Not the fire chief. Not the bomb squad.

Not. One. Person.

Cultural Echoes: Fire in the Neighborhood, Fire in the Soul

If you ever hear your elders talk about how the system doesn't care about Black lives, this is what they mean.

This wasn't some distant war zone. This was Philadelphia—home of the Liberty Bell, birthplace of the Constitution. And they bombed babies.

It's the same fear that makes Black families skeptical of government intervention. That side-eye when a city says, "We're here to help." That reflex to protect your own first—because history shows we've been burned before. Literally.

And it's why we teach our kids to ask questions. To film the police. To organize. Because silence won't save you—and loud truth might be the only thing that keeps you safe.

Pros and Cons of Remembering This History

Pros:

- Names the violence that systems try to hide
- Honors the lives lost with truth
- Pushes back against propaganda and whitewashing
- Empowers community control and self-defense

Cons:

- Emotionally overwhelming
- Can fuel mistrust and fear
- A reminder that justice is often delayed—or denied

Action Steps: Learning From the Fire

1. **Tell the Story** Don't let the MOVE bombing be forgotten. Share documentaries. Talk about it in schools, churches, and family circles. Say their names.
2. **Demand Accountability** Push your city to revisit past state violence. Demand transparency, reparations, and reform.
3. **Protect Your Communities** Know your rights. Teach your neighbors. Organize safety plans and networks. Don't wait for a crisis to get involved.
4. **Build Independent Media** Tell our stories from our perspective. Write. Film. Record. Document. MOVE was misrepresented for decades—until we started speaking up.
5. **Invest in Community Healing** Trauma lingers. Support counseling. Fund youth programs. Create safe spaces. Generational pain needs generational repair.

Final Word: Bombs, Babies, and the Blueprint for Resistance

The MOVE bombing was state-sponsored violence, plain and simple.

But the lesson isn't just in the tragedy—it's in the resilience. The community rose. The truth came out. And the memory lives on.

We don't tell this story to dwell in pain—we tell it to honor the past, protect the present, and build a future they can't erase.

Because the fire may have burned the houses.

But it didn't burn the truth.

2.10: Predatory Lending and the Subprime Mortgage Crisis

When the American Dream Became a Nightmare—for Us, Again

You remember when everybody and their mama was buying a house in the early 2000s? When folks you knew were getting approved with "no money down," low intro payments, and promises of flipping that property for a bag in a year or two?

Yeah... it felt like Black folks were finally getting a seat at the table. We had our church members closing on homes. Your cousin who just fixed his credit was talking about getting investment property. Even your auntie who used to rent for 30 years was finally holding keys in her hand.

But fast forward a few years—and it all fell apart.

Foreclosures. Evictions. Dreams deferred *again.*

This chapter is about the trap that was laid for us, called subprime lending. It's about how they dangled homeownership in front of us—after decades of redlining, FHA denial, and housing discrimination—and then set us up to lose it.

We're going to talk about what happened, how it hit us harder than anyone else, and what we can do to never let history play us twice.

What Is Predatory Lending?

Predatory lending is when lenders give loans with unfair, deceptive, or even abusive terms. That includes high-interest rates, hidden fees, balloon payments, and shady contract language.

But it's not just about bad numbers. It's about *targeting.*

Predatory lenders don't just show up in wealthy white suburbs. They pull up where they know folks are tired, underinformed, underserved—and desperate to believe in something.

They especially target:

- Low-income communities

- Elderly people
- First-time homebuyers
- Black and Brown communities

They don't just offer loans. They sell *dreams.*

Subprime Lending: The Setup

Subprime loans are mortgages given to people with lower credit scores or limited financial history. Because the borrowers are seen as "high-risk," the loans come with higher interest rates, less favorable terms, and more traps.

Between 2000 and 2008, subprime loans exploded. Lenders were giving out money like Oprah gave out cars. "You get a loan! You get a loan! Everybody gets a loan!"

But here's what they didn't say:

- Many of the loans were adjustable rate mortgages (ARMs), meaning your interest rate (and payment) could jump up after a few years.
- Some had balloon payments—giant amounts due after a short period.
- Some included prepayment penalties, trapping borrowers in bad terms.

Banks and lenders knew they were bad loans. But they kept pushing them because they were profitable—especially when bundled and sold to investors as mortgage-backed securities.

You were a number in someone else's bonus plan.

How It Hit Black America

Here's the messed-up part: many Black borrowers who *qualified* for better loans were *steered* toward subprime loans anyway.

Why? Because loan officers made more money that way.

Even Black folks with good credit, stable income, and down payments were offered bad loans. Entire Black neighborhoods were targeted. Lenders set up shop in our churches, our community centers, even our beauty salons.

It felt like opportunity. But it was a setup.

When the market crashed in 2008, we were hit the hardest:

- **53% of Black wealth was wiped out.**
- Millions of homes were lost to foreclosure.
- Property values in Black communities plummeted.
- Renters in Black neighborhoods were evicted at record rates.

It wasn't a housing crisis. It was a *targeted financial assault.*

Cultural Echoes: The Pain We Don't Talk About

You know how you don't see as many "Welcome Home" BBQs like we used to? Or how some families went from homeowners back to renting? Or how some elders talk about the housing market with this look of betrayal?

That's subprime trauma.

It's why folks are scared to buy again.

It's why some of us would rather rent and save than take on another mortgage.

It's why we side-eye every real estate agent like they're trying to run game.

And who could blame us?

We were told, "This time, it's for you."

But when the market collapsed, the same banks that gave us the loans got bailed out. We got put out.

Pros and Cons: Facing the Realities

Pros:

- Builds awareness of predatory financial systems
- Encourages smart, informed borrowing decisions
- Shows the importance of financial literacy and community accountability

Cons:

- May trigger anger or regret
- Can reinforce distrust in banking and finance
- Might make homeownership feel too risky

Action Steps: How We Push Back

1. **Learn the Language** Know the terms: interest rate, APR, fixed vs. adjustable rate, balloon payment, prepayment penalty. Don't sign what you don't understand.
2. **Use Trusted Lenders** Shop around. Compare offers. Use credit unions, reputable banks, or Black-owned mortgage companies with a track record.
3. **Educate the Fam** Make sure your kids, cousins, and church members know what happened—and what to look out for. We don't gatekeep knowledge.
4. **Demand Accountability** Push for financial reform, regulation, and reparations. Call out companies that profited from the crisis.
5. **Build Back with Strategy** If you're buying again:

- Get pre-approved
- Review your credit
- Choose a fixed-rate mortgage

- Work with ethical real estate professionals
- Get everything in writing

6. Invest in Financial Literacy Create money circles. Host workshops. Watch YouTube channels. Learn together. Heal together.

Final Word: The Next Time, We Move Different

They offered us the keys, but locked us out the back door.

But now we know.

Now we ask questions. Now we read the fine print. Now we pull up to the closing table with wisdom, not just hope.

Homeownership is still possible. Wealth is still within reach. But it has to be on *our* terms.

Because the dream is still alive—but we're not falling for the hustle.

2.11: Black Farmers and USDA Discrimination

The Land We Tilled but Never Fully Got to Own

We all got that one uncle, cousin, or grandparent who told us about the land they used to have. Maybe it was a few acres down South. Maybe it was a farm. Maybe it was just a patch of land they hoped to build on one day.

But here's the hard truth: Black folks in America didn't just lose land because we couldn't manage it. We lost it because the system was *designed* to take it.

This chapter is about Black farmers. About how we once owned millions of acres of land and how, piece by piece, it was stripped away—often with the help of the very agency that was supposed to support farmers: the USDA.

It's about discrimination that spanned generations, lawsuits that took decades, and the dream of land ownership that still lives in our DNA.

Let's get into it.

A Legacy in the Soil

In 1920, Black farmers owned over 15 million acres of land in the United States.

We weren't just farming—we were building communities. Feeding our people. Creating independence. Having land meant you didn't have to beg nobody. It meant freedom, security, and a way to pass something down.

But by 1997, that number dropped to less than 2 million acres.

What happened?

The story is long, but it's rooted in racism, exploitation, and one powerful gatekeeping institution: the U.S. Department of Agriculture (USDA).

The USDA: Jim Crow in a Suit

On paper, the USDA was supposed to help farmers with loans, crop insurance, technical support, and grants.

But for Black farmers?

The USDA was often a wall instead of a bridge.

Local county agents—usually white—had the power to approve or deny loans. They could delay processing. They could "lose" paperwork. They could prioritize white farmers for aid, disaster relief, and assistance programs.

And they did. Over and over again.

Black farmers were denied the tools to keep their farms afloat. They couldn't buy seed. They couldn't buy equipment. They couldn't upgrade their land. And when hard times hit, they couldn't get help.

So what happened?

They lost the land.

Some were forced to sell. Others lost it to foreclosure. Some had it stolen outright through shady legal loopholes and deceitful practices.

And nobody was held accountable.

The Pigford Case: Too Little, Too Late

In 1997, Black farmers came together and filed a class-action lawsuit against the USDA—*Pigford v. Glickman*.

The lawsuit revealed decades of discrimination, unfair practices, and intentional exclusion. In 1999, a settlement was reached: the USDA agreed to pay $1 billion in damages.

But guess what?

- Thousands of claims were denied or delayed.
- Many farmers died before they saw a dime.
- Others didn't qualify because of technicalities.
- And still, the USDA never fully admitted wrongdoing.

Pigford II was opened later for those left out—but by then, most of the land was long gone.

A check can't replace a legacy.

Cultural Echoes: Land Lost, Trust Broken

You ever wonder why so few Black folks talk about farming anymore? Why we're suspicious of land deals? Why we hesitate to move back South?

That's USDA trauma.

It's in the stories we don't tell. It's in the silence around inheritance. It's in the mistrust of institutions. It's in the heartbreak of watching something grow, only to have it ripped away.

We were farmers. Landowners. Caretakers of the earth.

Now we rent apartments, live in food deserts, and wonder what happened.

That loss didn't just happen—it was made to happen.

Pros and Cons: Naming the Truth

Pros:

- Restores a sense of pride in Black agricultural history
- Validates generational pain and economic loss
- Encourages land reclamation and rural development

Cons:

- Painful to relive what was taken
- Highlights how little restitution has been made
- Can trigger feelings of helplessness

Action Steps: Planting New Roots

1. **Learn Your Family's Land Story** Ask your elders: Did we own land? What happened? Write it down. Record it. Archive it. Truth is power.
2. **Support Black Farmers Today** Buy from Black-owned farms. Join a Black-led CSA. Support Black agricultural cooperatives. Keep the money and food in the community.
3. **Reclaim Land, If Possible** Look into rural land auctions. Invest as a family. Buy together. Even a small plot can be the start of something generational.
4. **Push for USDA Accountability** Support legislation that holds the USDA responsible. Demand funding for Black agricultural programs. Attend public meetings. Stay in the loop.
5. **Build Food Sovereignty Locally** Start community gardens. Partner with urban farms. Teach kids how to grow something—anything. Reconnect with the soil.

Final Word: They Tried to Uproot Us—But We Still Bloom

They didn't just take land. They took legacy. They stole futures. They tried to erase our connection to the earth.

But here's what they forgot:

We come from people who knew how to grow, build, nurture, and feed entire communities.

That knowledge is still in us. That power is still in our hands.

We may have been pushed off the land—but we were never disconnected from it.

Now it's our time to return. To reclaim. To rebuild.

Let's plant something new.

Part II: The Psychology of Money

How the Past Lives in Our Pockets

Money ain't just math. It's memory. It's mindset. It's muscle memory passed down like recipes, rituals, and warnings.

You ever stop to ask yourself *why* you treat money the way you do? Why you freeze up when it's time to talk numbers? Why that direct deposit hits different—but never seems to stay? Why some of us can hustle like legends but still feel broke inside?

That's the psychology of money.

This part of the book ain't about budgets or bank accounts. It's about beliefs. Stories. Emotional wiring. Trauma. Culture. It's about that moment when you realize that your wallet ain't just carrying cash—it's carrying your childhood, your culture, and your community's pain and pride all at once.

We're going to unpack the mental side of money—the fear, the guilt, the shame, the pressure to provide, the pressure *not* to outgrow your people, the silence at the dinner table, the missed opportunities, and the generational echoes that whisper: "Don't trust them," or "That's not for us," or "Just survive."

But we're also going to talk about healing.

About how to rewire what's been hardwired. How to move from surviving to thriving. From reacting to planning. From scarcity to strategy.

This is where therapy meets financial literacy. Where hip-hop meets

Harvard Business Review. Where grandma's cash-under-the-mattress wisdom meets asset protection strategies.

Because until we heal the relationship we have with money, we'll keep repeating the same cycles—no matter how many commas are in the account.

This is for the folks who grew up on "we can't afford that."

This is for the ones who felt guilty for having more than their parents.

This is for every Black person who's ever been told "money changes people"—and deep down feared it might.

Let's break the cycle.

Let's get free—inside and out.

Chapter 3: The Mental Side of Not Having Money

Let's Get Real: Being Broke Ain't Just About Money

Let's just call it what it is—being broke messes with your mind. It ain't just a line in your bank account or a minus sign next to your balance. It's in your body, your breath, your sleep, your relationships, and your self-worth.

You ever had a moment where your card declined and your whole chest tightened like you just got called out in front of the whole class? You ever walked into a store and started calculating tax in your head before you even looked at the price tag? You ever had to smile through dinner even though you were praying they wouldn't ask to split the bill evenly?

Yeah. That part.

This chapter is about the psychology of lack. The toll it takes on your mind, your heart, your spirit—and how, even when your income goes up, that trauma can still live with you like an unwanted roommate.

This ain't theory. This is lived experience.

What Scarcity Does to the Brain

Science has a name for it: *scarcity mindset.*

When you're constantly trying to stretch a dollar, your brain is stuck in survival mode. It starts focusing on the urgent instead of the important. You start making short-term decisions—like payday loans, late fees, skipping the dentist—because you're too busy trying to make it to *next week*.

Scarcity eats your focus. It lowers your ability to plan. It makes you reactive. It keeps you in the hustle, not the strategy.

And you're not lazy or irresponsible—you're tired.

You're not broken—you're broke. There's a difference.

But this mental load? It's heavy. And we carry it everywhere.

Growing Up Without—What It Teaches You

Let's talk childhood.

If you grew up in a house where the lights got cut off, where food stamps were a lifeline, where every "no" came with a side of guilt—then you've already been trained to see money a certain way.

You might have learned:

- Money is always stressful.
- Asking for help is weakness.
- We don't talk about money in this house.
- Having money means you're showing off.
- We're not like "them"—we survive.

And even when you're doing better, those lessons linger.

You get the promotion, but still feel like an imposter. You save up, but can't stop feeling like it's gonna disappear. You don't spend on yourself, even when you can, because guilt's got you on a leash.

It's not just money—it's muscle memory.

Cultural Messaging: Black, Broke, and Blamed

In America, being Black and being broke often get lumped together in the media and the culture. We're called lazy, entitled, financially illiterate—while ignoring centuries of systemic blocks.

You ever notice how when a Black celebrity goes broke, it's headline news, but when a white CEO bankrupts a company, it's called a business risk?

We are shamed, scrutinized, and stereotyped—even when we're grinding.

And that pressure creates a mental loop:

- We feel like we have to "prove" our success.
- We avoid asking for help because we don't want to confirm the stereotype.
- We carry guilt when we do better than our families.

Being broke feels personal, but it's deeply cultural.

Mental Health Effects: It's Deeper Than Stress

Let's talk about what financial scarcity can actually *do* to your mind and body:

- **Anxiety:** Constant worry about bills, debt, rent.
- **Depression:** Feeling stuck, hopeless, embarrassed.
- **Sleeplessness:** Your mind can't shut off because the hustle never stops.
- **Low self-esteem:** You start to think your value is tied to your income.
- **Relationship strain:** Money fights, resentment, feeling like a burden.

And it don't matter if you grew up in the 'hood or had a two-parent household—money stress doesn't discriminate.

The "Money PTSD" Nobody Talks About

Ever been so broke that even when you start doing better, you still feel poor?

That's financial trauma. And it sticks.

You might:

- Hoard money and never feel safe spending it.
- Overspend to "feel" rich for a moment.
- Avoid checking your bank account entirely.
- Feel triggered by financial conversations.

This is real. And you're not alone.

But here's the good news: what was learned can be unlearned.

Pros and Cons of Facing the Mental Side

Pros:

- You stop blaming yourself for survival choices.
- You gain self-awareness and emotional clarity.
- You begin to heal, not just hustle.

Cons:

- It might bring up shame or buried memories.
- It can be emotionally exhausting to confront.
- You may need outside help (therapy, coaching, etc.)

Action Steps: Healing While Hustling

1. **Name the Wounds** Write down the money messages you learned growing up. Whose voice is that? What were you taught? What do you want to keep—and what do you want to leave behind?
2. **Practice Financial Self-Compassion** When you make a mistake with money, don't spiral. Pause. Reflect. Learn. Nobody gets it perfect—especially not in survival mode.
3. **Set Emotional Boundaries** You don't owe everyone access to your finances or guilt about your success. Set limits. It's okay to say no with love.
4. **Get a Money Therapist or Coach** There are therapists who specialize in financial trauma. There are coaches who can walk you through mindset blocks. You don't have to figure this out alone.
5. **Celebrate Small Wins** Paid off a credit card? Saved $100? Didn't impulse-buy out of sadness? That's a win. Honor it.
6. **Redefine What Wealth Looks Like** Wealth isn't just money. It's peace of mind. It's having options. It's being able to rest without guilt. Chase that.

Final Word: Broke Wasn't Your Fault—But Healing Is Your Power

Listen—being broke is hard.

But what it does to your mind and spirit? That's the part nobody prepares you for.

The shame. The fear. The survival habits that become default.

But you are not your bank account. You are not your overdraft. You are not your financial past.

You're learning. You're unlearning. You're evolving.

And once you see how deeply this runs, you'll stop beating yourself up and start building yourself up.

Because your money mindset isn't just about wealth—it's about wellness.

And when we heal that?

We don't just rise—we *reclaim.*

3.1: Scarcity Thinking

What Is Scarcity Thinking, Really?

Scarcity thinking isn't just being broke—it's being *stuck*. It's that feeling like you're always running out: of time, money, energy, peace. It's when your first thought isn't "How can I grow this?" but "How long until it's gone?"

If you grew up hearing "we don't have it" more than "let's figure it out," you already know what scarcity sounds like.

Scarcity thinking is when you:

- Grab what you can, when you can, even if it's not the best move.
- Don't invest because you're scared to lose anything.
- Don't plan long-term because you've never had long-term security.
- Struggle to believe there's enough—for you, your family, or your community.

It shows up in everyday life. When you don't apply for that new job because you think you're not qualified. When you don't start that side hustle because "too many people already doing it." When you get nervous just checking your bank account.

Scarcity isn't just a financial problem. It's a mindset problem. And it's deeper than you think.

Where It Comes From: Generational Survival Mode

You ever notice how our grandparents saved foil and rinsed out plastic containers like it was gold? That wasn't just being frugal—it was being trained by scarcity.

From slavery to sharecropping, from Jim Crow to redlining, Black folks have lived through generations of systemic *not enough.* Not enough jobs. Not enough credit. Not enough freedom to just live without looking over your shoulder.

So we learned to:

- Stretch what we had.
- Protect what little we got.
- Expect it all to fall apart tomorrow.

And even when the money finally comes, the mindset stays. That's how you can make six figures and still feel broke. That's how you can save $10,000 and still not feel safe.

Scarcity taught us to survive—but it never taught us to *thrive.*

How Scarcity Shows Up in Black Culture

Let's keep it 100. We all have seen scarcity thinking in action:

- **At the cookout**: That one cousin who grabs five plates to-go before anyone even sits down? Scarcity.
- **In relationships**: Settling for less because "Black love is rare"? Scarcity.
- **In business**: Thinking someone else's success means less for you? Scarcity.
- **In career**: Staying in a toxic job because "at least it's a check." Scarcity.

Even the way some of us react to wealth—judging, questioning, side-eying—is rooted in scarcity. Because when you've only seen struggle, success can feel like betrayal.

But let's flip it.

What if success isn't betrayal? What if it's a breakthrough?

The Psychology Behind It

Scarcity isn't just about how much money you have—it's about how much *mental space* you have.

Studies show that when you're in scarcity mode, your brain literally changes. Your focus narrows. Your decision-making declines. You make quick fixes instead of long-term moves.

That's why people in poverty aren't "bad with money"—they're just overwhelmed. They're managing survival, not strategy.

It's like driving on E—you're not thinking about a road trip; you're just praying to make it to the next gas station.

Scarcity vs. Abundance: The Real Difference

Scarcity says:

- "I'll never get ahead."
- "If they win, I lose."
- "It's too late."

Abundance says:

- "There's enough for me too."
- "Their success shows what's possible."
- "Every day is a new chance."

Abundance thinking doesn't mean ignoring your reality—it means believing your reality can *expand*.

You don't have to be rich to think abundantly. You just have to believe in possibility.

Pros and Cons of Scarcity Thinking

Pros (yep, there are a few):

- Teaches resilience and resourcefulness
- Builds community through shared struggle
- Helps people learn how to stretch a dollar

Cons:

- Limits imagination and risk-taking
- Traps you in survival cycles
- Undermines trust and collaboration

Action Steps: Shifting From Scarcity to Strategy

1. **Name It When You See It** Pay attention to your inner voice. When you catch yourself saying, "That's not for me," or "That'll never happen," pause and ask: Is this fact or fear?
2. **Create an Abundance Habit** Every week, list three things you *do* have—skills, resources, relationships. Build gratitude like muscle.
3. **Stop Competing, Start Collaborating** If you see someone doing what you want to do, don't hate—connect. Ask questions. Build together.
4. **Learn Something New About Money** Abundance is powered by knowledge. Take a course, read a book, follow a money coach online. Make learning your flex.
5. **Invest in Yourself** Even if it's small. A class, a side hustle, a tool that saves you time. Show your mind it's safe to grow.
6. **Say "Yes" to Bigger Things** Apply for the job. Pitch the idea. Take the leap. Abundance doesn't mean you won't feel fear—it means you move anyway.

Final Word: Scarcity Was a Season, Not Your Story

Let's be real—scarcity helped us survive.

But survival ain't the finish line.

It's time to break up with lack. To unfollow fear. To stop living like everything's about to collapse.

You are not cursed. You are not behind. You are not the struggle story they try to sell us.

You are capable. You are worthy. You are enough.

And there *is* enough.

It's time to live like it.

3.2: Anxiety, Guilt, and Financial Shame

The Emotions Money Brings That Nobody Prepares Us For

We talk about money like it's just math. Add this, subtract that, boom—you good.

But that's a lie. A bold-faced, teeth-showing, Sunday-dinner kind of lie.

Because if money was just about numbers, most of us wouldn't feel so much every time we look at a bill, hear someone say "credit score," or get that text that says, "Hey, can I borrow $100 until next Friday?"

This chapter is for the feelings we've learned to hide. The ones that don't come with dollar signs but hit our pockets all the same. We're talking anxiety, guilt, and financial shame—those emotional side effects of money trauma that linger long after the check clears.

Let's name them. Let's face them. And let's heal from them, together.

Let's Start With Financial Anxiety

You ever had your heart race just looking at your bank app? You ever avoided opening the mail because you knew a bill was waiting? You ever delayed logging into your student loan portal even though you *know* you're out of the grace period?

That's financial anxiety. And it's real.

It's not just stress—it's chronic. It follows you. It eats at you. And it's deeper than "being bad with money."

It's:

- Growing up watching your parents argue about bills.
- Remembering how the lights got cut off right before your birthday.
- Feeling like one bad break could erase everything you've built.

Financial anxiety is when your nervous system doesn't feel safe—because your bank account hasn't felt safe. Ever.

The "Good Times" Guilt Complex

Let's talk guilt. That low-key, creeping feeling that makes you second-guess every little thing you do with your money.

You saved $500—and now you feel guilty you didn't help your cousin with rent. You booked a vacation—and now you feel bad because your mama still doesn't have central air. You got a raise—and you're low-key hiding it from your family so they don't come asking.

Guilt comes from this belief that having more means you're *doing people wrong*—even when you earned it.

It's a trauma response, rooted in generations of "We all we got." So when you step out and start getting yours, it can feel like betrayal. But it's not. It's growth.

Still, that guilt? It don't care about logic. It whispers:

- "Why you and not them?"
- "You think you better now?"
- "Don't forget where you came from."

And before you know it, you're backpedaling your blessings.

Shame: The Heavyweight Champ of Financial Emotions

Now let's talk about shame. Not the quick kind that hits you when you bounce a check. I'm talking deep shame—the kind that sticks to your skin.

Financial shame sounds like:

- "I should've known better."
- "I'm grown, I shouldn't be struggling."
- "I make good money, why can't I figure this out?"

It looks like:

- Dodging friends because you can't afford the dinner.
- Lying about your situation to keep up appearances.
- Feeling like a fraud, no matter how hard you work.

And because shame thrives in silence, most of us never talk about it. We just carry it like a weighted blanket—heavy, private, and always present.

Where It Comes From: Culture, Family, and Capitalism

Let's break it down:

Culture says we're supposed to grind and never complain. To get the bag and stay humble. But what happens when getting the bag breaks you down?

Family says we stick together. But that often means you're the safety net for everybody. And if you say no? Now you're "acting funny."

Capitalism says if you're broke, it's your fault. If you're rich, you better keep it quiet or you'll get judged. Either way, it's set up for you to feel like you're never doing enough.

And when you put all that on one person—plus race, plus gender, plus class? Whew. No wonder we're anxious.

Pros and Cons: The Truth About These Emotions

Pros:

- Signals that something's out of alignment
- Pushes us to examine our relationship with money
- Can motivate us to seek support and community

Cons:

- Can lead to secrecy, poor decision-making, or avoidance
- Makes us feel alone or unworthy
- Stops us from celebrating progress

Action Steps: Healing Your Money Emotions

1. **Talk It Out Loud** Shame dies in sunlight. Say it to a friend, a therapist, a journal. Tell the truth. You're not the only one.
2. **Make Room for Both/And** You can feel anxious *and* still make progress. You can feel guilty *and* still grow. You can feel shame *and* still deserve abundance.
3. **Build Boundaries Without Apology** You're not a bad person for saying no. For not being the family ATM. For choosing your peace over pressure.
4. **Replace Guilt With Generosity** If you feel led to give, give with joy. But not from guilt. Let your giving be a choice, not a chain.
5. **Celebrate the Small Wins** Paid a bill early? Opened your mail

without flinching? Didn't cry in the Target checkout line? Celebrate that.

6. **Invest in Financial Therapy or Coaching** Sometimes the numbers aren't the problem—it's the story behind them. Get help if you need it. No shame in the healing game.

Final Word: You Are Not Your Balance

Money is emotional.

And when you grow up in lack, or around pressure, or carrying your whole family's hope—it *will* show up in how you move.

But hear this: you are not your account. You are not your credit score. You are not the loan you took or the mistake you made.

You are not the debt. You are not the guilt. You are not the shame.

You are human. You are healing. You are learning.

And there is room for grace.

Let's rise.

Chapter 4: Breaking the Cycle

When You've Had Enough of Just Getting By

Let's keep it a buck: there comes a point when surviving just ain't enough anymore. When you're tired of living check to check, tired of watching your family repeat the same mistakes, tired of feeling like money owns *you* instead of the other way around.

This chapter is for that moment. The moment you say, "Nah, we not doing this anymore."

Breaking the cycle isn't just about getting out of debt or finally opening a savings account. It's about shifting the mindset, the habits, the trauma, and the silence around money that's been passed down like hand-me-down clothes.

It's about deciding that the story ends *with you*. And a new one starts *because of you*.

Let's get into it.

What Does "The Cycle" Even Mean?

When we say "the cycle," we're talking about that repeating loop of:

- Lack of financial literacy
- Overspending out of emotional need
- Under-earning from self-doubt or systemic barriers

- Avoidance of budgeting or planning
- Guilt around having or not having money
- Silence around financial struggles and wins

That cycle isn't just in your checking account—it's in your childhood, your choices, your culture. It's why you might panic when money comes in—or feel shame when it goes out. It's why your family never talked about wills, but always passed around the GoFundMe link.

But cycles are meant to be *broken*.

Where It Starts: The Mirror

Before you can break the cycle, you gotta face it.

You can't heal what you don't acknowledge. So ask yourself:

- What did I learn about money growing up?
- Who did I watch handle money, and how did they do it?
- What money habits do I have that don't serve me?
- What am I afraid of when it comes to wealth?

This ain't about blame—it's about clarity. Because once you see it, you can change it.

The First Break: Financial Literacy

You can't win a game you don't know the rules to.

Start with the basics:

- What's a budget? It's just a plan for your money—not a punishment.
- What's a credit score? It's your financial GPA.
- What's debt? A tool when used right, a trap when used wrong.
- What's investing? Planting seeds now so you can eat later.

You don't need a finance degree—you need the right info and the will to *use* it.

And if school didn't teach you? Cool. We got books, YouTube, apps, mentors. Tap in.

The Second Break: Boundaries With Your People

This one's tough, but necessary.

You can't break a cycle in your house if everyone else is dragging you back into theirs. That means:

- Saying no to that $500 "emergency" request that keeps popping up every month.
- Telling your family you're saving to build, not to ball.
- Teaching your kids early instead of sheltering them into struggle.

You're not abandoning your people—you're showing them a new way.

And when you stop rescuing everyone, you'll have the energy to actually *lead* them.

The Third Break: Emotional Spending

Retail therapy feels good—until it doesn't. Until the Amazon boxes come and the rent check bounces. Until the closet's full but your peace is empty.

Emotional spending is often how we cope when we feel:

- Powerless
- Unseen
- Tired
- Unworthy

But no purchase can fix what healing needs to handle.

Start checking in with yourself:

- Am I buying this because I need it—or because I feel low?
- What could I do instead that supports my peace without draining my wallet?

Healing is free. But it saves *everything*.

The Fourth Break: Accountability and Consistency

You don't have to do it perfect. But you *do* have to do it on purpose.
Accountability means:

- Checking your budget weekly.
- Reviewing your bank statement monthly.
- Setting goals and tracking them.
- Finding a money buddy, mentor, or coach.

Consistency builds trust with yourself. Every time you keep your financial promise—even if it's small—you remind yourself: "We don't do chaos anymore. We do clarity."

Pros and Cons of Breaking the Cycle

Pros:

- You build a foundation for generational wealth.
- You heal the emotional wounds tied to money.
- You create peace and confidence in your decisions.

Cons:

- It might feel lonely or uncomfortable at first.
- Some people around you won't understand the new you.
- You'll have to face hard truths and forgive old versions of yourself.

Action Steps: How to Break Free, For Real

1. **Start a Money Ritual** Pick one day a week to check in with your money. Light a candle, grab your favorite playlist, and make it a vibe. Normalize treating your finances like self-care.
2. **Automate What You Can** Set up auto-transfers to savings. Schedule bill payments. Take the stress out of remembering.
3. **Say "No" Without Explaining** Practice it. "No, I'm not able to do that." Period. Not "let me see" or "maybe next time." Say it and mean it.
4. **Teach One Person** What you learn—share. That's how we multiply the healing. That's how we shift the culture.
5. **Celebrate Milestones** Paid off a debt? Saved $1,000? Made a budget and actually stuck to it? Celebrate. That's big.
6. **Visualize Your New Normal** What does a financially free life look like for you? Visualize it. Speak it. Write it. Live like it's already yours.

Final Word: You Are the Chainbreaker

You're not selfish for wanting more. You're not disloyal for doing better. You're not a fraud because you started from behind.

You are the one. The one who said, "It stops here."

You are the one who looked poverty in the face and said, "You won't raise my kids."

You are the one who took the shame, the struggle, and the silence—and turned it into strategy.

You are the new chapter. You are the new legacy.

You are the breakthrough your bloodline has been waiting on.

4.1: Talking About Money at Home

The Conversation We Didn't Grow Up Having

Let's be honest—growing up, money was one of those topics that stayed behind closed doors. If it came up, it was either in hushed tones or during a blowout fight in the next room. You might've heard "money doesn't grow on trees" more times than you heard "I love you."

We didn't have money talks—we had money silences. And that silence? It left us unprepared.

This chapter is all about flipping the script. It's about breaking the generational hush-hush and making money conversations normal—healthy, honest, and consistent.

Whether you're raising kids, living with your partner, supporting your parents, or healing your own financial past, talking about money at home is where the cycle breaks for good.

Let's talk about how to talk about it.

Why We Don't Talk About It

We come from a culture where:

- Privacy is survival.
- Struggle is normal.
- And vulnerability around money feels like weakness.

Add in some shame, fear, generational trauma, and a history of systemic economic exclusion—and you've got a recipe for silence.

You ever hear your mama say, "That's grown folks' business"? You ever ask your daddy about the rent and he just told you to stay in a child's place?

That's not their fault. That was protection. But in the long run, it left us without a playbook.

So now that *we're* grown, it's time to change the play.

Where It Starts: Your Money Story

Before you can talk about money with other people, you've got to understand how *you* feel about it.

Ask yourself:

- What's the first memory I have about money?
- Was money a source of stress or security growing up?
- What did I learn (or not learn) from my parents?
- Do I feel confident or anxious talking about finances?

Knowing your money story helps you name your patterns—and break the ones that don't serve you.

How to Talk to Your Kids

Kids don't need a full lecture on compound interest at age 5. But they *do* need exposure, honesty, and empowerment.

Here's how:

- Use everyday moments. Grocery shopping? Talk about budgets. Giving? Talk about generosity.
- Be honest. If money is tight, don't lie. Say, "We're being smart with our money right now."
- Normalize the vocabulary. Use words like budget, savings, debt, credit.
- Let them see you make decisions. "We're not eating out because we're saving for something important."

And most importantly: Let them *ask*. And don't shut them down.

We don't raise financially confident kids by keeping them in the dark. We raise them by showing them the light.

How to Talk to Your Partner

Money and love are inextricably tied. If you don't talk about money with your partner, you're building your relationship on vibes instead of values.

Here's how to get on the same page:

- Start with your goals. "Where do we want to be in five years?"
- Don't lead with blame. Lead with curiosity.
- Share your money stories. Understand each other's financial upbringing.
- Build a plan *together*. Joint account? Separate accounts? Do what works—but do it *on purpose*.

And check in regularly. Weekly money dates. Monthly budget meetings. Make it a ritual, not a reaction.

How to Talk to Your Parents

This one's tough. Especially in Black families, where roles are sacred and pride runs deep.

But we can't wait until somebody passes away to find out where the life insurance policy is—or if it even exists.

Here's a script to get started:

- "Hey, I've been learning more about money lately and I want to make sure our family is straight. Can we talk about your plans for the future?"
- "If something ever happened, do you have a will or anything written down?"
- "Are you comfortable with your finances? I'm not trying to be nosy—I just want us to be prepared."

Lead with love, not interrogation.

And if they shut down? Don't force it. Leave the door open. Come back with more grace.

How to Talk to Yourself

This one might be the most important.

You can't shift the conversation until you shift the voice in your head. If your inner monologue around money sounds like:

- "I'm so stupid with money."
- "I'll never get ahead."
- "I don't deserve to be wealthy."

Then baby, we gotta change that tape.

Speak life over your finances:

- "I'm learning."
- "I make better decisions every day."
- "I deserve peace and prosperity."

The way you talk about money *to yourself* sets the tone for everyone else.

Pros and Cons of Talking About Money at Home

Pros:

- Builds trust and transparency
- Reduces shame and secrecy
- Creates alignment around shared goals
- Prepares the next generation

Cons:

- Can be uncomfortable at first

- May reveal painful truths
- Might expose tensions or disagreements

But silence? Silence is the most expensive thing we never paid for.

Action Steps: Making Money a Normal Topic at Home

1. **Schedule a Money Talk** Pick a date. Set a vibe. No tension. No stress. Just transparency. Whether it's with your kids, your partner, or your parents—make the space.
2. **Create a Family Budget Board** Even if it's just you. Make it visual. Set goals. Track progress. Let everyone see where the money's going and why.
3. **Use Media as a Springboard** Watch a documentary, read a book, or play a podcast at home. Use it to spark conversation.
4. **Set Financial Goals Together** Big or small. "Let's save for a family trip." "Let's pay off this credit card." Goals create unity.
5. **Normalize Mistakes** When someone messes up financially (including you), don't shame—teach. We all fall. The goal is to fall forward.
6. **Keep the Conversation Going** Don't wait for tax season or emergencies. Make money talks a monthly thing. Keep it regular. Keep it real.

Final Word: From Hush to Healing

The silence stops with us.

We're done with pretending. Done with hiding. Done with letting shame and fear keep us stuck.

Money is a part of life—and so is talking about it.

You don't have to have it all figured out. You just have to *start the conversation.*

Because every time you talk about money with love, honesty, and clarity—you're planting seeds of wealth.

And one day, your kids, your partner, your family—they'll thank you for the table you built.

4.2: Financial Healing and Emotional Wealth

Let's Talk About Healing, Not Just Hustling

For the longest time, we've been told to chase the bag. Secure the bag. Protect the bag.

But what if you get the bag and still feel empty? What if the bank account is up, but the anxiety is still high? What if you finally buy the house, but can't sleep in peace?

That's where financial healing comes in.

This chapter isn't about budgeting or investing—it's about *recovery*. About reconnecting with yourself after years of money stress, trauma, and survival mode. It's about building emotional wealth—peace, clarity, confidence—that money can't buy but money sure can disturb when it's out of alignment.

Let's dig in.

What Is Financial Healing?

Financial healing is the process of unlearning the pain, guilt, shame, and fear that's attached to your money story—and replacing it with intention, self-trust, and joy.

It's when you:

- Forgive yourself for past mistakes.
- Stop beating yourself up about what you didn't know.
- Create safety and peace in your financial life.
- Reclaim your power from systems and beliefs that made you feel small.

It's like emotional physical therapy. You might limp at first, but you get stronger over time. You learn new ways to move.

What Is Emotional Wealth?

Emotional wealth is what holds you steady when life shakes your coins. It's that inner knowing that you're good—not because of your income, but because of your *insight*.

It's:

- Peace of mind.
- Financial confidence.
- Self-trust in how you make decisions.
- Gratitude, not guilt.
- Boundaries, not burnout.

When you're emotionally wealthy, money works *for* you—not *on* you.

Why We Need Financial Healing in Our Community

We didn't just wake up anxious about money.

We inherited trauma from slavery, segregation, redlining, stolen land, denied loans, burned-down businesses. From being the last hired and the first fired. From being told we don't belong in boardrooms or investment meetings.

We also inherited silence.

We weren't allowed to ask about the bills. We didn't know if the house was paid off or not. We found out about debt collectors from the voicemails we weren't supposed to hear.

We learned survival. But healing? That's new territory.

And now it's on us to chart it.

Signs You Might Need Financial Healing

- You feel anxious even when your bills are paid.
- You feel guilty for earning more than your family.
- You avoid looking at your bank account.
- You sabotage yourself when money starts flowing.
- You overgive out of obligation, not love.
- You judge yourself harshly for past money mistakes.

These aren't just habits—they're wounds.

And they deserve care.

The Connection Between Money and Mental Health

You know how when you're stressed about money, everything else gets worse? Your sleep. Your mood. Your patience. Your self-esteem.

Financial stress is one of the leading causes of depression, anxiety, divorce, and even physical illness. It weighs on your chest. It messes with your head.

So when we talk about healing—we're not just talking about feeling better. We're talking about *being better,* inside and out.

Steps Toward Financial Healing

This ain't about fixing everything overnight. This is about building muscle.

1. Tell Yourself the Truth Start by writing your money story. The real one.

- What did you grow up believing about money?
- Who taught you?
- What patterns do you repeat?
- What do you want to let go of?

No judgment. Just truth.

2. Make Peace With Your Past You messed up? Cool. Join the club. The question is—what did you learn?

- If you blew your refund check—what were you trying to heal?
- If you stayed in debt—what need was being met?

You weren't stupid. You were coping.

Now you can choose different.

3. Create a Safe Money Space Design a ritual around your money. Light a candle. Put on some Sade or Kendrick. Open your statements. Review your goals. Breathe.

Create a vibe of care—not chaos.

4. Forgive Who Needs Forgiving That parent who never taught you. That ex who drained your account. That friend who borrowed and never paid back.

You don't have to forget—but you *do* need to free yourself.

5. Define Your Version of Wealth Maybe it's not six figures. Maybe it's not a big house. Maybe it's:

- Sleeping peacefully.
- Taking care of your people.
- Doing work that doesn't drain you.

You get to decide. Your wealth, your rules.

6. Set Boundaries and Honor Them If it costs you your peace, it's too expensive. If it drains your energy, it's not profitable.

Say no when needed. Say yes with clarity.

7. Seek Support Therapists. Coaches. Podcasts. Books. Friends.

Healing doesn't happen in a vacuum.

Pros and Cons of Financial Healing

Pros:

- Builds confidence and clarity
- Reduces anxiety and emotional spending
- Helps create peace and purpose

Cons:

- Takes time and patience
- May reveal pain or patterns you tried to ignore
- Requires consistency and self-reflection

But the long-term reward? Priceless.

Emotional Wealth Habits to Practice Daily

- Speak affirmations: "I am safe. I am worthy. I am capable."
- Celebrate small wins: "I paid that bill. I honored my budget."
- Check in weekly: "What's working? What needs adjusting?"
- Stay in community: "Who's holding me accountable?"

Emotional wealth is built like a savings account—slow, steady, and sacred.

Final Word: You Deserve Peace With Your Paper

Healing is wealth.

Healing is sitting down with your bank statement and not feeling shame. Healing is paying your bills without flinching. Healing is saying no without guilt. Healing is knowing you are not what you lacked—you are what you've learned.

We don't just want money. We want meaning. We want freedom. We want joy. We want legacy.

And we're building it—one healed step at a time.

4.3: Building a New Financial Identity

You Are Not Your Past—You're the Blueprint

Let's get this out of the way early: who you've been with money does *not* have to be who you become.

You might've messed up. You might've grown up broke. You might've been bad with credit, took out loans you shouldn't have, gave when you didn't have it, spent when you should've saved.

Cool.

We all been there.

But the beautiful thing about identity? You can *build* a new one. Not just wish for it. Not just talk about it on New Year's Eve. But actually, intentionally, brick by brick, build the version of you that's aligned with where you're going—not stuck in where you've been.

That's what this chapter is about. We're gonna build something different.

Let's go.

What Is a Financial Identity?

Your financial identity is how you see yourself when it comes to money. It's not just what's in your account—it's what's in your *mind*.

Do you see yourself as broke? As bad with money? As "not a math person"? As the family bank? The spender? The hustler? The avoider?

Or do you see yourself as a builder? A steward? A wealth creator? A peaceful planner?

The identity comes *before* the outcome.

You don't wait until your credit score hits 750 to act like someone with good credit. You act like it now. That's how you get there.

You embody the person you're becoming—starting today.

Why Identity Shifts Matter More Than Budgets

Budgeting is a tool.

But if you still see yourself as someone who "ain't good with money," no budget in the world is gonna work for long.

This is deeper than spreadsheets. This is about:

- Your habits
- Your environment
- Your beliefs
- Your language
- Your posture

Do you walk like someone with a plan? Do you speak like someone who knows what they're building? Do you invest time, energy, and attention like someone who values their future?

Or do you keep shrinking yourself?

Identity work rewires your financial life from the *inside out.*

Let's Talk Cultural Identity and Money

For many of us—especially in the Black community—our financial identity was handed to us:

- "We always gotta hustle."
- "Money don't stay long in Black hands."
- "We don't invest, that's for white folks."
- "We don't talk about money in this house."
- "You better get a good job and keep your head down."

That's not identity—that's survival programming.

And we thank it for getting us through.

But now? We're rewriting it.

Because your financial identity can be:

- Wealth-minded
- Legacy-focused
- Generous *and* smart
- Disciplined *and* joyful
- Free from guilt, fear, and shame

Let's build it.

Step 1: Define the Old Identity

Start with the truth.

Ask yourself:

- What did I used to believe about money?
- What were my go-to behaviors when I felt stress around money?
- How did I talk about money—out loud and in my head?
- Who did I model my financial behavior after?

Write it down.

That's not who you *are*. That's who you *were programmed* to be.

Big difference.

Step 2: Design the New You

Now create the new version.

Ask yourself:

- How do I want to feel about money?
- How do I want to act when it comes to spending, saving, investing, and

giving?
- What kind of financial future do I see myself creating?
- What would my financially free self *never* do again?

Give your new financial identity a name if you want. "Investor Me." "Peaceful Planner." "Debt-Free Auntie." "Next-Gen Millionaire."

Own it.

Step 3: Speak the New Language

Watch your mouth. Seriously.

The old identity says:

- "I'm just bad with money."
- "I'll never get ahead."
- "Money makes people greedy."

The new identity says:

- "I'm learning how to handle money wisely."
- "Every day, I'm getting better at this."
- "I attract abundance with clarity and discipline."

Talk to yourself like you *believe* in your growth.

Because you're listening.

Step 4: Set Identity-Based Goals

Don't just set goals like "Save $5,000."

Ask: "What would someone with my new identity do?"

If your new identity is "Peaceful Provider," you might:

- Create a cushion fund to eliminate anxiety.

- Automate savings for therapy and wellness.
- Get insurance to protect your people.

If your identity is "Next-Gen Investor," you might:

- Open a Roth IRA.
- Learn about index funds.
- Buy a book on real estate.

Let your identity *inform* your goals—not the other way around.

Step 5: Walk It Daily

Do the small things that reinforce your new identity:

- Check your accounts weekly.
- Read one finance article per day.
- Make spending decisions based on alignment, not emotion.
- Teach someone else what you're learning.

Don't wait for perfection.

Practice is proof.

Pros and Cons of Building a New Financial Identity

Pros:

- Shifts your whole relationship with money
- Creates lasting change, not just quick fixes
- Aligns your goals with your values

Cons:

- Takes time and intentionality
- May cause you to outgrow some relationships
- Requires constant self-reflection and honesty

But trust—who you become is *worth* it.

Identity Affirmations to Practice

Say these daily:

- "I am the first wealth builder in my family—and not the last."
- "I make wise, intentional decisions with my money."
- "I am allowed to grow, evolve, and outgrow."
- "I lead with vision, not fear."
- "I define success for myself."

Affirmations are like mental reps. Keep lifting.

Final Word: You're the Architect Now

This is your time.

You don't have to wait for someone else to give you permission. You don't have to hold onto old beliefs that kept you small.

You are the designer, the builder, the keeper of the vision.

Build a financial identity that reflects your *real* values. Build a legacy that feels like freedom—not just flexing. Build a version of you that your future self will thank you for.

You're not the one who's just trying to make it.

You're the one who's changing everything.

Part III: Building the Blueprint

From Vibes to Vision—This Is the Game Plan

Now that we've unlearned the lies and started healing the emotional wounds, it's time to get into *strategy*.

Because healing is the foundation—but planning is the structure. And if we're gonna build something that lasts, we need more than just good intentions—we need a blueprint.

Part III is about action. It's about creating a real game plan for your life and your money. We're talking budgets that make sense, credit that works for you, investments that grow with you, and plans that reflect your *actual* life—not just what looks good on Instagram.

This is where we get tactical without being boring. Intentional without being stiff. We still keeping it real, still keeping it rooted in culture, still keeping it practical—but now, we're building.

Brick by brick. Choice by choice. Dollar by dollar.

This part of the book is your playbook for what comes *next*. It's how you go from surviving to thriving. From reacting to directing. From making do to making moves.

You've done the internal work. Now let's stack that work into wealth—mental, emotional, and financial.

Welcome to the blueprint.

Chapter 5: Budgeting – Telling Your Money Where to Go

Real Talk: If You Don't Tell Your Money Where to Go, It Will Ghost You

Let's be honest—most of us didn't grow up with a budget. We grew up with vibes. With survival. With the "pay what you can, when you can" system. With maybe enough for groceries or gas, but never both at the same time.

We watched our mamas make magic with half a check. Watched our uncles flip side hustles just to cover the light bill. We learned how to juggle—but we never learned how to *plan*.

And planning? That's where budgeting comes in.

Budgeting isn't about restriction. It's about direction. It's not about saying "no" to everything—it's about saying "yes" *on purpose*.

This chapter is about flipping the script and turning your budget from a punishment into a power move. Let's tell your money what to do—before it disappears on payday.

What Is a Budget, Really?

A budget is just a plan for your money.

That's it. No shame. No stress. Just you being the boss of your dollars.

It's saying:

- "Rent is due—let me make sure that's handled."
- "I want to take that trip—I'm going to plan for it."
- "Groceries cost *what* now? Okay, let's adjust."

A budget is your money's GPS. Without it, you'll stay lost.

Why Most People Avoid Budgeting

Let's call it out:

- We think it's too complicated.
- We're scared to face the numbers.
- We associate budgeting with lack, not abundance.
- We tried before and "failed."

But here's the thing: budgeting isn't just about numbers. It's about *values.*

What matters to you? What are your priorities? Your budget should reflect that.

This isn't about living off rice and beans and never going out. It's about aligning your money with your mission.

Step 1: Know What's Coming In

Before you can tell your money where to go, you need to know how much is walking through the door.

That means:

- Your salary (after taxes)
- Side hustles
- Child support
- Freelance work
- Any consistent income

Add it up. Be real. Be thorough. Be honest with yourself.

Don't plan your month on your *best case* paycheck. Plan it on your *guaranteed* one.

Step 2: Know What's Going Out

List every bill. Every obligation. Every automatic draft you forgot about.

Include:

- Rent/mortgage
- Utilities
- Car note
- Insurance
- Groceries
- Gas or transit
- Cell phone
- Internet
- Subscriptions (Netflix, Hulu, Spotify—don't act brand new)

Then add:

- Eating out
- Haircuts and nails
- Clothes
- Tithes or giving
- Entertainment

Track where every dollar is going. Use an app, a spreadsheet, a notebook—whatever works. Just be *accurate*.

Step 3: Give Every Dollar a Job

Now that you know what's coming in and going out—it's time to assign roles.

Every dollar needs a job:

- Pay bills
- Save for emergencies
- Pay off debt
- Invest
- Enjoy life

You don't leave money sitting around with no direction. That's how it ends up buying things you forgot about.

Make categories. Make limits. Make it *make sense*.

Step 4: Build in Flexibility

Your budget shouldn't choke you.

Give yourself grace:

- Create a "miscellaneous" line for unexpected stuff.
- Leave room for joy—fun money is not a sin.
- Adjust month to month. Groceries up? Tweak elsewhere.

You're not failing because life shifts. You're learning to pivot.

Step 5: Review Weekly

Set a weekly money date with yourself.

- Pull up your budget.
- Check what's been spent.
- Adjust what's left.
- Celebrate your wins.

This isn't just about control—it's about *connection*.

The 50/30/20 Budget Rule (And How to Remix It)

This classic framework suggests:

- 50% of income = needs (rent, food, utilities)
- 30% = wants (fun, leisure, treats)
- 20% = savings and debt payoff

But you can flip it based on your life. Maybe you:

- Spend less on wants to pay off debt faster.
- Save more because you're tired of living on edge.
- Budget by week instead of month.

Customize it. Make it yours.

Budgeting on an Irregular Income

If your paycheck isn't steady—welcome to the club. Bartenders, barbers, freelancers, entrepreneurs—this part's for you.

- Budget based on your *lowest* average month.

- Prioritize the essentials first.
- Build a buffer when money's good.
- Use a "rolling budget" that adjusts weekly.

Irregular income just means you need regular *discipline*.

Budgeting as a Family

If you're sharing life with someone (partner, roommate, kids, etc.), your budget has to reflect the team.

- Have monthly money meetings.
- Agree on shared goals.
- Divide responsibilities clearly.
- Keep transparency.

A house divided will bust the budget every time.

Emotional Spending & Budget Sabotage

Sometimes you overspend not because you're careless—but because you're *coping*.

Ask yourself:

- What do I feel before I click "add to cart"?
- What am I trying to soothe?
- Is this purchase aligned with my goals?

Budgeting isn't just financial—it's *emotional.* Heal your triggers, and your spending will start to heal too.

Pros and Cons of Budgeting

Pros:

- Gives you control over your money
- Reduces financial anxiety
- Helps achieve goals faster
- Creates peace and clarity

Cons:

- Requires discipline
- Takes time and consistency
- May feel restrictive at first

But once you see results? Game-changer.

Action Steps to Start Budgeting Today

1. Download a budgeting app (YNAB, EveryDollar, Goodbudget, Mint)
2. Track your last 30 days of spending
3. Create categories based on *your* real life
4. Assign every dollar a job
5. Commit to weekly check-ins for the next 30 days

And give yourself grace. It's progress, not perfection.

Final Word: You're the CEO of Your Coins

Budgeting isn't boring—it's *boss behavior*.

This is how you stop wondering where your money went and start telling it where to go. This is how you build wealth—not just in numbers, but in confidence. In peace. In purpose.

You're not broke—you're building.
You're not behind—you're becoming.
And every dollar you direct is a brick in your freedom.

Chapter 6: Credit – Your Financial Reputation

Let's Talk Credit—Because the Streets Are Watching

Credit ain't just a score. It's your financial reputation. It's what the money world says about you when you're not in the room. Just like your name carries weight in the streets, your credit carries weight in the financial world.

And just like a bad rumor can follow you, so can bad credit.

But here's the twist: you can clean it up, build it up, and walk in any financial room with your head held high. Just like your mama told you to fix your posture before going into church—you gotta fix your credit before you go for that loan.

Let's break it all the way down.

What Is Credit, Really?

Credit is borrowed money with a receipt.

It's a system that says, "We'll lend you this now if we believe you'll pay it back."

And the better your track record, the more doors it opens:

- Lower interest rates

- Easier approval for loans
- Bigger buying power
- Leverage for business deals

Credit is a tool. It's not your identity. But it sure can influence your access.

What Makes Up Your Credit Score?

Your credit score is like your GPA in the world of money. It ranges from 300 to 850. Here's the breakdown:

35% – Payment History Did you pay your bills on time? Creditors want to know if you keep your word.

30% – Credit Utilization How much of your available credit are you using? If you've got a $1,000 limit and you're always maxed out, that's a red flag.

15% – Length of Credit History How long have you had credit? The longer, the better—like seasoning on cast iron.

10% – New Credit Have you applied for a bunch of new cards lately? Too many "hard inquiries" make you look thirsty.

10% – Credit Mix Do you have different types of credit? Like a student loan, a car loan, and a credit card? That variety shows range.

Why Credit Matters in Our Community

Historically, Black folks have been locked out of traditional banking and credit systems. From redlining to discriminatory lending, we've had to build from the outside.

That's why it's crucial to master credit. Not just for approval—but for *autonomy*.

You want to:

- Start a business? You'll need credit.
- Buy a home? You'll need credit.

- Rent a decent apartment? Yup—credit check.

It's the modern-day gatekeeper. We don't have to love it. But we do need to learn how to *leverage* it.

Common Credit Myths (And the Real Deal)

Myth: I need to be in debt to build credit. Truth: You just need to use credit wisely and pay it off responsibly.

Myth: Closing old accounts helps your score. Truth: That shortens your credit history. Keep them open if there's no annual fee.

Myth: Checking my score hurts it. Truth: Only *hard inquiries* (like when you apply for credit) hurt. *Soft checks* (like using Credit Karma) don't.

Myth: Cash is king, so I don't need credit. Truth: That's cool until you want a mortgage or car loan. Cash doesn't build a history—credit does.

Building or Rebuilding Credit

Here's your starter pack:

1. **Get a Secured Credit Card** You put down a deposit, and they give you a card with that same limit. Use it like a regular card. Pay it off each month. That deposit is your training wheels.
2. **Become an Authorized User** Got a family member with great credit? Ask them to add you to their card. You get their history on your file—without using their money.
3. **Pay Bills On Time, Every Time** Set reminders. Automate it. Write it on the bathroom mirror. Late payments are credit killers.
4. **Keep Your Utilization Low** Use less than 30% of your credit limit. Bonus points if you can keep it under 10%.
5. **Don't Open a Bunch of New Accounts** Slow and steady. Credit is a long game.
6. **Check Your Reports** Go to annualcreditreport.com. Pull your free

reports from Equifax, TransUnion, and Experian. Look for errors. Dispute anything shady.

Credit and Relationships

You know what's less romantic than red roses? Red flags on a credit report.

Talk about credit early with your partner. Don't wait until y'all are applying for a home together to find out one of you is carrying $80K in debt.

Share your credit goals. Build together.

Money arguments break up homes. Transparency builds them.

Credit and Generational Legacy

We talk about generational wealth—but let's talk generational *access*.

- Add your kids to your cards (when they're ready) as authorized users.
- Teach them how to manage credit before the world does.
- Show them how to pull a report before they co-sign for somebody.

Normalize credit education in your house like you do sports stats or TikTok dances.

Pros and Cons of Using Credit

Pros:

- Builds your financial reputation
- Gives access to opportunities
- Can be used strategically for travel, cash back, or rewards

Cons:

- Easy to misuse
- Interest rates can be predatory
- Missed payments can follow you for years

Credit is a tool. Use it like a hammer—not like a grenade.

Action Steps to Level Up Your Credit

1. Pull your credit reports today
2. Pay off any collections or negotiate pay-for-delete agreements
3. Start using a card for one bill and paying it off every month
4. Set payment reminders
5. Track your score with free tools (Credit Karma, NerdWallet, etc.)

Stay consistent. Your score will start rising like a gospel choir at revival.

Final Word: Protect Your Name—And Your Number

Credit is power.

It's not a flex. It's a foundation.

You don't need to be perfect—you need to be *intentional.*

Build your credit with care. Build your reputation with wisdom. Build your legacy with clarity.

Because when your name is good, your options grow.

Chapter 7: Banking – More Than Just a Checking Account

Let's Get Real About the Bank

For a lot of us, the bank has felt more like a barrier than a bridge. Some of us still remember being dragged to the branch to cash a paper check, standing in long lines, or hearing our parents talk about how the bank denied their loan application for the third time.

Truth is, many Black families have a complicated relationship with banks—thanks to years of being overlooked, underserved, and straight-up discriminated against.

But here's the deal: we can't build wealth if we're keeping our money in a shoebox, a mattress, or riding around with it in the glove compartment.

Banking right—and I do mean *right*—can level us up.

This chapter is about reclaiming the banking system and making it work *for* us, not *against* us. Because your bank account shouldn't just hold your money—it should help you grow it.

Let's talk about it.

Banking Isn't Just a Place to Hold Money

Banking is access. It's infrastructure. It's your money's home base. But more importantly—it's strategy.

When used wisely, a good banking system helps you:

- Protect your money
- Track your financial flow
- Automate your savings
- Build credit history
- Qualify for loans
- Earn interest
- Create documentation for taxes, business, and investing

It's not just about checking your balance before payday—it's about building a system that works while you sleep.

Understanding Bank Types: Choose Your Team Wisely

Let's break it down like your favorite 90s sitcom cast:

Big Banks (The Will Smiths of Banking)

- Well-known, widely available
- Lots of ATMs, digital tools
- May charge more fees

Credit Unions (The Uncle Phils of Banking)

- Community-based, not-for-profit
- Usually lower fees and better rates
- More personal customer service
- Must qualify for membership

Online Banks (The Issa Raes of Banking)

- No brick-and-mortar, all digital
- Lower overhead = fewer fees, higher savings rates
- Great for tech-savvy folks
- No in-person support

Black-Owned Banks (The Hidden Figures)

- Built for us, by us
- Support community reinvestment
- Smaller networks, but big impact

The key is not where *they* want you to bank—it's where *you* feel supported, empowered, and seen.

Checking Accounts: The Hub

This is where most people start.

A checking account is your financial inbox. Your job deposits here. You pay your bills from here. You swipe here. You Venmo here.

Things to look for:

- No monthly maintenance fees
- No minimum balance requirements
- Access to mobile banking
- Easy direct deposit setup
- ATM network or reimbursement

Pro Tip: Set up two checking accounts: one for bills and one for spending. That way you always know what's really yours to play with.

Savings Accounts: Your Financial Seatbelt

You don't save just because it sounds good. You save so you're not caught slipping.

A savings account should be:

- FDIC insured
- Separate from your checking (out of sight, out of swipe)
- Earning interest
- Linked for easy transfers

There are different types of savings accounts:

- **High-Yield Savings Accounts** – more interest, usually online
- **Money Market Accounts** – mix between checking and savings, higher balances required
- **Certificates of Deposit (CDs)** – lock in money for a period of time for higher return

Start where you are. $5 a week is better than nothing.

Overdrafts, Fees, and Bank Traps

Banks make billions off fees—*billions*. Overdrafts. Maintenance. Minimum balance violations. It's a hustle.

Avoid the traps:

- Opt out of overdraft protection (they charge you to "help")
- Keep a buffer in your account
- Set alerts for low balance
- Review your statements monthly

Don't let the bank rob you with a smile.

Direct Deposit and Automation: Your Money's GPS

Direct deposit isn't just convenient—it's strategy.

You can split your check:

- 70% to checking
- 30% to savings

That's saving without thinking about it.

Automate your bills too. That's fewer late fees, less stress.

Automate your life so you can focus on the big stuff.

Banking and Budgeting: A Power Duo

Banking is the engine. Budgeting is the map.

Use your bank tools:

- App notifications
- Spending reports
- Category breakdowns

Link your accounts to budgeting tools (like Mint, YNAB, or Empower) and track it like it's March Madness.

Know your trends. Adjust as you grow.

Banking and Credit: The Silent Relationship

Did you know your bank habits influence your credit indirectly?

- Consistent income shows up on applications
- Bank statements help with mortgage or rental approvals
- Secure credit cards come from banking institutions
- Loans often require account history

Your bank account is like a financial resume. Keep it clean.

Pros and Cons of Traditional Banking

Pros:

- Security
- Access to credit, loans, and services
- FDIC protection
- Financial recordkeeping

Cons:

- Fees
- Low interest on savings
- Predatory practices in some areas

Choose wisely. Use wisely. Review regularly.

Action Steps: Boss Up Your Banking

1. Audit your current bank account—do they treat you right?
2. Shop around—compare interest rates, fees, mobile tools
3. Open a high-yield savings account online
4. Automate your bills and transfers
5. Set up two checking accounts (bills + spending)
6. Review your statements monthly

It's not about having 10 accounts—it's about having the right accounts for *you*.

Final Word: The Bank Works for You—Not the Other Way Around

This isn't just about where your paycheck lands. It's about how your money moves. It's about controlling the flow. It's about making your money work smarter.

You don't need to be rich to bank like you got sense. You just need to be intentional.

So get organized. Get strategic. And get your banking system in order.

Because building wealth isn't just about how much you make—it's about what you *keep,* where you put it, and how it grows.

Chapter 8: Insurance – Protecting What You Build

You Worked Hard—Now Protect It

Let's get one thing straight: insurance is not just for rich folks, married folks, or "someday when I'm grown" folks. If you're out here building something—your health, your business, your family's future, your peace of mind—you need to protect it. Period.

Too many of us treat insurance like that dusty treadmill in the basement—good to have, but not something we think about 'til it's too late. Then something hits the fan, and we're passing the plate, setting up GoFundMes, or digging into savings that took years to build.

Insurance is the financial version of seat belts, airbags, and security alarms. It's not exciting. But it's essential.

So let's stop thinking of it as a luxury and start seeing it for what it really is: a shield for the wealth, wellness, and wisdom you're building.

Let's break it down.

What Is Insurance?

Insurance is a contract—a promise from a company to pay for certain losses or damages in exchange for a fee you pay (called a premium).

You're transferring the risk from you… to them.

That means instead of one big financial hit (like a car wreck or hospital bill), you pay small amounts regularly so if something does happen, the insurance company handles the heavy lifting.

Why We Avoid It (But Can't Afford To)

Let's be real:

- We don't understand the fine print
- We don't want to think about worst-case scenarios
- We assume it's too expensive
- We think we don't need it yet

But guess what? Insurance isn't for when things are *going right.* It's for when things go *left.*

And if we've learned anything from life, it's that it be goin' left—*quick.*

Types of Insurance You Need to Know

Let's talk about the ones that matter most.

1. Health Insurance – Protecting Your Body and Your Bag

Medical bills are the #1 cause of bankruptcy in America. Read that again.

Whether it's through your job, the ACA marketplace (Healthcare.gov), Medicaid, or a private plan—you *need* health insurance.

Key terms to understand:

- **Premium:** what you pay monthly
- **Deductible:** what you pay out-of-pocket before insurance kicks in
- **Copay:** flat fee for doctor visits
- **Coinsurance:** shared cost between you and insurer after deductible
- **Out-of-pocket max:** the most you'll pay per year

Even if you're young and healthy—accidents don't discriminate.

2. Life Insurance – Protecting the People Who Count on You

If someone depends on your income—kids, parents, spouse—you need life insurance.

It's not about you. It's about who you leave behind.

Term Life Insurance:

- Covers you for a set period (10, 20, 30 years)
- Cheaper
- Great for families and budget-conscious folks

Whole Life Insurance:

- Covers you for life
- Builds cash value
- More expensive, more complex

Pro Tip: Start with term. Get enough to cover:

- Income replacement
- Debt payoff
- College for kids
- Funeral costs

3. Auto Insurance – More Than Just a State Requirement

If you drive, you need car insurance. And not just the minimum liability.

Types of coverage:

- **Liability:** covers other people's damage if it's your fault
- **Collision:** covers your car if you hit something
- **Comprehensive:** covers theft, fire, floods, etc.
- **Uninsured motorist:** covers you if someone without insurance hits you

Bundle policies when possible to save money. Keep a clean record. And always know what your deductible is.

4. Renters/Homeowners Insurance – Protecting Your Space

Renter? Your landlord's insurance doesn't cover your stuff. A kitchen fire, a break-in, or even burst pipes could leave you empty-handed.

Homeowner? You need insurance to cover:

- The structure
- Your possessions
- Liability (in case someone gets hurt on your property)
- Temporary living expenses if you're displaced

Don't wait until disaster hits. Protect your sanctuary.

5. Disability Insurance – When You Can't Work

If you couldn't work for 3-6 months due to illness or injury—what's your plan?

Disability insurance replaces part of your income when you're unable to work. It's more important than you think, especially for freelancers, self-employed folks, and single-income families.

Short-term: a few months **Long-term:** several years or until retirement

It's the grownest of grown-folk moves.

6. Umbrella Insurance – For the Unexpected

Let's say you're in a major car accident, someone sues you, and your regular policy maxes out. Umbrella insurance covers the excess.

It's not for everyone—but if you have significant assets or are in a high-risk profession, it's worth looking into.

7. Business Insurance – If You're a Boss

Got a side hustle? A legit business? You need to protect it.

There are several types:

- General liability (slips, falls, lawsuits)
- Professional liability (bad advice, errors)
- Product liability

- Business interruption
- Workers' comp (if you have employees)

If you're building generational wealth—protect the business too.

Pros and Cons of Insurance

Pros:

- Peace of mind
- Financial protection
- Keeps your savings intact during crises
- Shows financial responsibility

Cons:

- Premiums can add up
- Can be confusing to navigate
- May feel unnecessary—until it's not

But the risk of not having it? That's way more expensive.

Action Steps to Get Covered Right

1. Review what coverage you *already* have
2. Identify any gaps (ex: no renters insurance, no term life, etc.)
3. Get quotes from 2-3 providers (use an agent or broker if needed)
4. Read the fine print—know what's *included* and *excluded*
5. Set annual check-ins to update policies as your life evolves

And always ask questions. Never sign something you don't fully understand.

Insurance in the Black Community – The Legacy Play

Life insurance isn't just about paying for a funeral—it's about creating wealth.

You can:

- Use life insurance proceeds to pay off your house
- Leave a college fund for your children
- Eliminate generational debt
- Create opportunities that didn't exist before

We've seen too many GoFundMes. Let's flip the script.

Let's create GoBuildMes. GoInvestMes. GoGrowMes.

Insurance can be the first seed in your family's financial garden.

Final Word: You Don't Just Build—You Guard It

You've worked too hard, prayed too long, and grown too much to let one emergency wipe it all out.

Insurance is not about fear. It's about wisdom.

It's the grown-up version of "Don't touch that stove." It's the money move you make when you care not just about what you have—but about *who* you're building for.

Protect your income. Protect your home. Protect your health. Protect your people.

Because wealth without protection? That's just potential waiting to be lost.

Let's rise.

Part IV: Growing the Bag

From Hustle to Harvest – This Is Wealth in Motion

You've done the healing. You've built the blueprint. Now it's time to level up and *grow the bag.*

Part IV is where we stop playing defense and start playing offense. This is where your money doesn't just sit—it moves, multiplies, and builds something bigger than you. We're talking about growing what you've got through saving, investing, entrepreneurship, and making long-term plays that put your family and your future on solid ground.

But this ain't just Wall Street talk—it's hood-smart, soul-rich, culturally relevant guidance that meets you exactly where you are. Whether you're new to investing or already flipping properties, this section is built to help you build—brick by brick, decision by decision.

In this part of the book, you'll learn:

- How to make your savings strategy match your lifestyle
- What real investing looks like (without the hype)
- How to build wealth through ownership—business, real estate, and beyond
- The mindset and moves to keep your money growing, even while you sleep

Because growing the bag is about more than making money. It's about making moves that matter. It's about learning how to plant, water, and protect the seeds of wealth so they bear fruit for generations.

You've been the hustler. Now it's time to become the investor, the owner, the architect of your financial future.

Let's grow the bag—with purpose, with pride, and with power.

Chapter 9: Investing – Making Your Money Work for You

Let's Flip the Script: From Hustling for Dollars to Having Dollars Hustle for You

Here's the truth nobody told us growing up: working hard will help you survive, but *investing* is how you build freedom.

Most of us were raised to think the only way to earn money was to trade time for it. Work a shift, get a check. Pull overtime, get a little extra. But we rarely saw money working in the background, multiplying, compounding, and building.

So we stayed grinding.

But guess what? Wealthy folks don't just work hard. They make their money work for them—while they sleep, travel, spend time with family, or start passion projects. They invest.

And now? It's our turn.

This chapter is about breaking down the mystery of investing in a way that makes sense to your real life, your culture, and your goals.

Let's build.

What Is Investing?

Investing is the act of using money to make *more* money.

You're putting your dollars into something—stocks, real estate, a business, etc.—with the hope that over time, it grows in value and produces income or profit.

That's it. That's the whole concept.

And here's the kicker: you don't need to be rich to invest. You get rich *because* you invest.

Why We've Been Left Out

There's a reason why many of us didn't grow up hearing about stocks, 401(k)s, or mutual funds at the dinner table.

- Our ancestors were locked out of land ownership.
- We were redlined out of real estate.
- We were excluded from early stock market access.
- We were told investing was risky, scary, or "not for us."

So we saved in jars. Kept money in envelopes. Bought material things instead of financial assets.

But now? The knowledge is out here. The doors are open. It's time to walk through.

Investing vs. Saving

Let's clear this up:

- **Saving** is for short-term safety.
- **Investing** is for long-term *growth.*

If you're stacking cash for a vacation, emergency fund, or car repair—that's saving.

If you're putting money into something that could grow over years or decades—that's investing.

You need both.

But only investing builds wealth.

The Power of Compound Interest (aka Financial Magic)

Compound interest is when your money earns money—and then *that* money earns money. It's like your cash had kids, and those kids had kids.

If you invest $100 a month and earn 8% annually, in 30 years you'll have over $140,000. And only $36,000 of that came from your pocket. The rest is growth.

That's why the earlier you start, the better. Time is your best investor's friend.

Types of Investments to Know

Let's break down the basics:

1. Stocks

Buying a stock means owning a small piece of a company. If the company grows, so does your piece.

Examples: Apple, Amazon, Nike

You can:

- Buy individual stocks
- Invest in mutual funds (group of stocks)
- Use ETFs (exchange-traded funds)

2. Bonds

You're loaning money to a company or government, and they pay you back with interest.

Lower risk, lower return. Good for balance.

3. Real Estate

Buying property (a home, rental, land) that grows in value or earns rent.

You don't have to be a landlord—you can invest in REITs (real estate investment trusts).

4. Retirement Accounts

These are your tax-friendly investing vehicles:

- 401(k) or 403(b): from your job
- IRA: individual retirement account
- Roth IRA: tax-free growth and withdrawals

These accounts often hold stocks, bonds, and funds.

5. Business and Entrepreneurship

Investing in your own hustle—starting or scaling a business.

High risk, but potential for high reward and ownership.

6. Index Funds

These are like mixtapes of the market—collections of companies you can buy into all at once.

They're diversified, low cost, and great for beginners.

Where to Start: Beginner Moves

1. Open a Roth IRA
2. Start with a low-cost index fund (like S&P 500)
3. Set up auto-contributions—$25 a month if that's all you got
4. Leave it alone and let it grow

Pros and Cons of Investing

Pros:

- Builds wealth over time
- Beats inflation

- Creates income without active work
- Allows generational transfer of assets

Cons:

- Risk of loss
- Requires patience
- Can be intimidating at first

But the biggest risk? Not investing at all.

Avoiding the Hype and Traps

TikTok investing advice? Red flag. Random crypto coin from your cousin? Red flag. Anything promising quick riches? You already know.

Stick to:

- Proven strategies
- Reputable platforms (Fidelity, Vanguard, Schwab)
- Long-term thinking

This is a marathon, not a money grab.

Investing in the Culture

You can invest in what you believe in:

- Black-owned ETFs
- Impact funds that support communities
- Real estate in your neighborhood
- Your own business or idea

Put your money where your heart is.

Action Steps to Start Investing

1. Learn the basics—read one article per week
2. Choose an investment platform (Fidelity, Vanguard, or a robo-advisor like Betterment)
3. Open a Roth IRA or brokerage account
4. Pick an index fund to start (like VTI or FXAIX)
5. Set it and forget it—automate your investing
6. Review annually, not daily

Legacy, Ownership, and Power

Investing is about ownership.

Owning stocks, land, businesses, and your time.

You don't have to come from money to build wealth. You just need intention, consistency, and time.

Let's grow the bag with purpose. Let's build the table—not just pull up a chair.

9.1: Why "Black People Don't Invest" Is a Lie

First Things First: Stop Playing with the Narrative

We've all heard it. At cookouts, in barbershops, on Twitter timelines, on cable news debates. "Black folks don't invest." "We don't trust the stock market." "We'd rather buy Jordans than stocks."

Let's be real—that whole idea? That's a bold-faced lie. Not just a half-truth or a misunderstanding—a *straight-up lie*.

The truth is, Black people have *always* invested. We've just been investing differently, in systems that didn't always respect, include, or value us. We invested in family. In education. In faith. In hustle. In community. In land when we were allowed. In businesses when the banks said no. In culture when nobody else could see the value.

This chapter is about telling the full story—not the edited, "blame-the-community" version that gets passed around when folks don't feel like looking at systemic oppression.

We invest. And we always have.

The Roots of the Lie

Let's get into why this myth exists in the first place.

1. Historical Exclusion

We were:

- Locked out of wealth-building programs like the GI Bill
- Redlined out of neighborhoods where home values grew
- Denied loans by banks, even with solid income
- Left out of early retirement and stock programs at work
- Used as experiments for bad investments (see: Freedman's Bank)

So when folks say "Black people don't invest," they're ignoring the reality that we weren't *allowed* to play the same game, with the same rules, on the same field.

But best believe—we still found a way.

2. Mistrust (and for good reason)

The Black community didn't just randomly decide not to trust financial systems. That mistrust was earned.

From shady lenders to predatory policies to stolen land and broken promises, we've seen too many people get burned.

So yeah—we're cautious. But cautious isn't the same as ignorant. It's protection.

3. Cultural Investment Looked Different

You know what Black people *do* invest in?

- Our kids' education

- Our churches
- Funeral policies
- Multi-generational households
- Supporting cousins' businesses

We've always put money into things that matter. It just didn't always look like Wall Street.

Now we're expanding that definition.

The Truth: We're Investing More Than Ever

The new stats are in, and they tell a different story.

According to recent studies:

- Over 60% of Black millennials are investing in the stock market
- Black women are the fastest-growing demographic of entrepreneurs
- More Black families are opening custodial accounts and teaching their kids about investing
- Fintech platforms like Acorns, Cash App Investing, and Robinhood have helped eliminate some of the gatekeeping

So the narrative is changing—and we're leading it.

Famous Black Investors (You May Not Know)

- **Reginald F. Lewis** – One of the first Black billionaires via leveraged buyouts
- **Robert F. Smith** – Tech investor and philanthropist who paid off Morehouse's class of 2019 debt
- **Daymond John** – Not just a fashion mogul, but a strategic investor on Shark Tank
- **Mellody Hobson** – President of Ariel Investments, one of the largest Black-owned investment firms

We're not new to this. We're just finally getting our flowers.

Breaking the Cycle: What's Changing?

1. **Access Is Easier** You can now start investing with $1. That's less than a bag of chips and a honey bun.
2. **Education Is Everywhere** Podcasts. YouTube. IG Lives. TikToks. Books. You name it, we got it. The knowledge gap is closing.
3. **Community Is Stronger** We're forming investment clubs. Sharing plays. Holding each other accountable. We're not just getting the bag—we're passing the blueprint.

Pros and Cons of Changing the Narrative

Pros:

- Empowers the next generation
- Counters financial stereotypes
- Attracts resources and support
- Builds confidence

Cons:

- Still fighting against deeply rooted media myths
- Requires consistent effort to educate and model

But let's be honest—we've flipped worse narratives before. This one's just next in line.

Action Steps: How to Invest Even If You're New to This

1. **Open a Brokerage or Roth IRA Account** Use platforms like Fidelity, Vanguard, or Charles Schwab
2. **Start Small and Consistent** Invest $25/month in a low-cost index fund. Let time do the work.
3. **Join a Community** Find an investment club, Facebook group, or book club focused on wealth
4. **Read One Article or Watch One Video Per Week** Build your knowledge like you'd build a playlist
5. **Teach the Babies** Open a custodial account for your kids, nieces, nephews, or godchildren. Show them what ownership looks like.

Final Word: The Lie Dies Here

The next time someone says, "Black people don't invest," correct them with confidence.

Tell them: "We've always invested. Now we're doing it in the market *and* the movement."

Because wealth isn't just a flex—it's a form of resistance. A tool for healing. A path to freedom.

And this generation? We're not just investing for ourselves. We're investing so the next generation doesn't start from scratch.

We're not asking for a seat anymore. We're buying the table.

9.2: How to Start Small and Grow with Confidence

Don't Let the Fancy Talk Fool You—You Can Start Where You Are

Let's set the tone right now: you don't need to be ballin' to start investing. You don't need to wait until your debt is gone, until your income hits six figures, or until you "feel ready."

The biggest wealth builders you know didn't start with thousands in the bank. Most of them started with a few dollars, a lot of faith, and a plan.

This chapter is about how *you* can do the same.

Starting small isn't weak—it's wise.

And when you combine that with consistency, confidence, and culture? That's a blueprint.

Let's get into it.

Step One: Flip the Mindset

First off, let's kill the shame.

You didn't learn this in school. You didn't grow up with this in the household. Nobody passed down a Roth IRA to you.

But guess what? You're here now.

And that makes you a cycle-breaker.

You don't need to have it all figured out. You just need to *start.* Starting small doesn't mean thinking small—it means building strong.

The Power of Micro Moves

Let's talk numbers.

If you invest $25 a month in an index fund that earns 8% annually:

- In 10 years, that's $4,500+
- In 20 years, it's $14,000+
- In 30 years, it's nearly $34,000

That's off of just $25 a month. That's lunch money. That's one dinner out.

That's Uber Eats canceled once a week.

Compound growth is like that cousin who keeps bringing more cousins to the cookout—you started small, but now it's a full-blown family reunion.

What to Do Before You Invest

Let's set the table before we serve the meal.

1. **Budget First** You need to know what's coming in and going out so you can see what's available to invest.
2. **Emergency Fund in Place** Have at least $500–$1,000 tucked away. If something breaks, you don't want to pull out of your investments.
3. **Pay Down High-Interest Debt** If you've got credit card debt at 20% interest, handle that first. Your investments can't grow fast enough to beat that.
4. **Know Your Why** Why are you investing? Retirement? Freedom? A family legacy? Knowing your reason keeps you focused when the market dips.

Where to Start: Easy Entry Points

Here's a no-frills list of starting options for beginner investors:

1. **Robo-Advisors** Platforms like Betterment or Wealthfront build and manage your portfolio automatically based on your risk tolerance.
2. **Index Funds** Low-cost, diversified investments. You buy one fund, and you're instantly investing in hundreds of companies.
3. **ETFs (Exchange-Traded Funds)** Like index funds, but trade like stocks. Good for buying the market as a whole.
4. **Fractional Shares** Can't afford a full share of Amazon? No problem. Platforms like Cash App, Fidelity, and Robinhood let you buy a slice.
5. **Retirement Accounts** Start with a Roth IRA if you qualify. Your money grows tax-free, and you won't pay taxes when you withdraw

it in retirement.

Keep It Simple

Here's the setup:

- Open an account (Fidelity, Vanguard, Charles Schwab)
- Link your checking account
- Set up automatic monthly deposits
- Choose one index fund (like VTI, FXAIX, or SWPPX)
- Don't touch it unless you're rebalancing once a year

You don't need a million moves. Just consistent ones.

The Confidence Equation: Knowledge + Action = Growth

Confidence doesn't come before you invest—it comes *after* you start. Every move you make builds trust in yourself.

- The first account you open
- The first deposit you automate
- The first article you understand

Confidence comes from showing up. Not from knowing it all.

Common Fears and How to Beat Them

Fear: I don't want to lose money Truth: The market goes up and down. But historically, it always trends up over time. You're playing the long game.

Fear: I waited too long to start Truth: The best time was yesterday. The second-best time is now.

Fear: I'll mess it up Truth: You don't have to be perfect. You just have to be consistent.

Pros and Cons of Starting Small

Pros:

- Less pressure
- Easier to build consistency
- Builds habits that last

Cons:

- Growth may feel slow at first
- Tempting to stop when life gets tight
- Requires patience and faith

But remember—trees don't rush their roots. They grow slow, then all at once.

Action Steps to Get Started Today

1. Choose a platform (Fidelity, Vanguard, or a robo-advisor)
2. Open an account (brokerage or Roth IRA)
3. Set a recurring deposit (start with $10–$50/month)
4. Pick one diversified fund (like VTI or FXAIX)
5. Set a date to review it every 6 months
6. Tell someone you trust so they can hold you accountable

How to Keep Growing Over Time

1. Increase your contributions as your income grows
2. Learn a little more each quarter (books, podcasts, newsletters)
3. Diversify as you learn (real estate, REITs, international funds)

4. Teach someone else what you know (teaching locks in knowledge)

This is a lifestyle now—not a phase.

Final Word: From Baby Steps to Big Moves

You don't need to know the whole plan. You just need to take the first step.

You don't need Wall Street credentials. You've got common sense, hustle, and the ability to learn.

You don't need a bag to get started. You grow the bag *by* starting.

So whether you've got $10 or $100, whether you learned from TikTok or your uncle, whether you're in your 20s or 50s—this is your moment.

You're not too late. You're not too broke. You're not too behind.

You're building.

You're growing.

You're investing in the one asset that matters most—*you*.

9.3: Stocks, Real Estate, ETFs, and Index Funds

Let's Break Down the Building Blocks of Wealth

Investing ain't just about jumping into the stock market and hoping for the best. It's about knowing the plays, understanding the positions, and moving like a seasoned coach with a long-term game plan.

This chapter is your sideline strategy. We're gonna walk through the big four asset classes that most people use to grow their wealth: stocks, real estate, ETFs, and index funds.

We're not just gonna define them—we're gonna decode them. With real talk, Black culture references, and steps that make sense whether you're new to the game or leveling up your playbook.

Let's go.

Section 1: Stocks – Owning a Piece of the Pie

What Are Stocks?

When you buy stock, you're buying a tiny piece of a company—like Apple, Amazon, Nike, or Netflix. It's called equity, and it means you're not just a fan of the brand—you're a part-owner. When that company grows, your piece grows with it.

Why It Matters

You earn when the stock goes up in value (called capital gains)

You may also earn dividends—little checks they send out to shareholders

Think of it like this:

You're not just buying Jordans—you own Nike. You're not just binge-watching shows—you own Netflix.

That's boss behavior.

Pros:

Easy to get started

High potential returns over time

You can own companies you believe in

Cons:

Prices go up and down (volatility)

Emotional investing can lead to bad decisions

Requires research or a solid long-term approach

How to Start:

Open a brokerage account

Start with a few companies you know and use

Don't put all your money in one stock—spread it around

Rule of Thumb:

If you can't explain what the company does or how it makes money, don't invest in it yet.

Section 2: Real Estate – The Original Wealth Play

What Is Real Estate Investing?

Real estate means owning land or property for the purpose of making money—either through rental income, appreciation (value increase), or flipping (buy low, sell high).

Why We Love It

For many in our community, real estate is the dream. Owning a home, building generational wealth, creating something tangible you can pass down.

Types of Real Estate Investments:

Residential: homes, apartments, duplexes

Commercial: offices, retail, storage units

Short-term rentals: Airbnb, VRBO

REITs: real estate investment trusts (more on this later)

Pros:

Tangible asset

Monthly cash flow from rentals

Tax breaks and equity growth

Cons:

Requires upfront money

Property management headaches

Market can crash (remember 2008?)

Ways to Start:

House hack: rent out a room in your own house

Buy a duplex, live in one side, rent out the other

Partner with friends/family for group investing

Buy REITs if you're not ready for physical property

Game-Changer Tip:

Get pre-approved even if you're not ready to buy right now. It gives you a target and shows you where your credit and finances need work.

Section 3: ETFs – The Smooth Blend

What Are ETFs?

Exchange-Traded Funds are like mixtapes of stocks. One ETF might contain pieces of 500 different companies, all bundled into one single investment.

Think of an ETF like a "greatest hits" album—you're not betting on one song (stock), you're getting the whole vibe.

Popular ETFs:

VTI (Total Stock Market)

SPY (S&P 500)

QQQ (Top 100 tech companies)

Pros:

Diversified automatically

Low cost

You can trade them like stocks

Cons:

Still exposed to market ups and downs

Doesn't pay off quick (this is a long game)

How to Start:

Choose a brokerage

Search for ETFs

Buy a small amount (you can get fractional shares)

Cultural Analogy:

ETFs are like the Verzuz battles—no matter who wins, you still get the best of both worlds.

Section 4: Index Funds – The Passive Powerhouse

What Are Index Funds?

Index funds are like ETFs' cousin—similar concept, slightly different in how they're managed.

An index fund follows a specific market index, like the S&P 500. That means your money is spread across the 500 largest U.S. companies—automatically.

Why They're Great for Beginners:

Super low fees

No need to pick winners and losers

Proven long-term growth

Pros:

Hands-off investing

Solid returns over time

Built-in diversification

Cons:

Not exciting (this is the grandma of investing—it's stable but not flashy)

You won't beat the market—but you'll be the market

How to Start:

Open an IRA or brokerage account

Choose a fund like FXAIX (Fidelity), VFIAX (Vanguard), or SWPPX (Schwab)

Set up auto-deposits and forget about it

Real Talk:

If you're not trying to babysit your money every day, index funds are your best friend.

Putting It All Together – Building Your Starter Portfolio

So you're ready to make your first real moves. Here's a simple starting lineup:

60% Index Funds

20% ETFs

10% Individual Stocks

10% REITs or a real estate fund

As your income grows and your knowledge expands, you can start adjusting the weights.

But this foundation? Solid as Auntie's potato salad.

Pros and Cons of Each Investment Type

Stocks

Pros:

High growth

Ownership

Brand loyalty

Cons:

Volatile

Requires research

Real Estate

Pros:

Tangible

Passive income

Tax breaks

Cons:

Expensive to start

Active management

ETFs

Pros:

Diversified

Low cost

Beginner-friendly

Cons:

Not super customizable

Index Funds

Pros:

Long-term stable growth

Low fees

Cons:

Not flashy

Slow growth compared to stocks

Action Steps

Decide your budget (even $50/month is enough to start)

Choose one platform (Fidelity, Vanguard, Charles Schwab)

Set up your account (Roth IRA for retirement or brokerage for general investing)

Pick one investment in each category:

Stock (Nike, Apple, Disney)

ETF (VTI or QQQ)

Index fund (FXAIX or VFIAX)

REIT (VNQ or SCHH)

Set it and forget it (auto-transfer every paycheck)

Schedule a quarterly review, just like your hair appointments or oil changes

Final Word: Ownership Is the New Flex

You don't have to be rich to own assets.

You just need a plan, some patience, and the right plays.

Stop being a consumer. Start being an owner.

Stop betting on other people's empires. Build your own.

You got the culture. You got the hustle. Now it's time to get the compound interest.

Chapter 10: Retirement Planning – Freedom Later Starts Now

Let's Talk About the Real Endgame

Retirement ain't just about golf courses, RVs, or sipping mimosas on a beach (though if that's your vibe, do you). It's about freedom. Choice. Peace.

It's about waking up and knowing you don't *have* to clock in. About knowing that your money is working so you don't have to break your back to survive.

And guess what? That freedom doesn't just magically appear at 65. You have to plan for it.

That's what this chapter is all about—creating a retirement game plan that fits your life, your culture, and your dreams. Because "later" starts *right now*.

Let's build your exit strategy.

Why Retirement Planning Matters (Especially For Us)

In the Black community, retirement often feels like a luxury—not a guarantee.

Many of us watched our parents and grandparents work until their bodies gave out. We saw folks retire with barely enough to survive—let alone travel, rest, or enjoy.

That ends with us.

We're flipping the script.

Because retirement isn't just about not working—it's about *having options*.

First Things First: What Is Retirement, Really?

Retirement is the phase of life where you stop actively working for income—and live off what you've saved, invested, and built over time.

It doesn't mean sitting still. You can retire and still:

- Start a business
- Travel
- Volunteer
- Mentor
- Work part-time (by *choice*)

Retirement is freedom funded.

When Should You Start Planning?

Short answer: yesterday.

Real answer: now.

The earlier you start, the easier it gets. Compound growth is real, and time is your secret weapon.

If you start investing $200/month at age 25, by age 65 you could have over $500,000. But wait until age 40 to start, and that number might be less than half.

Time matters. But even if you're starting late, it's *not too late.*

Know Your Retirement Number

You need a target.

Your retirement number is how much you need saved to retire comfortably. It depends on:

- Your lifestyle goals
- Where you'll live

- Healthcare costs
- Inflation

A good rule of thumb: aim to replace 70–80% of your pre-retirement income each year you're retired.

Example: If you make $60,000 now, you might need $45,000–$50,000/year in retirement. If you retire at 65 and live to 90, that's 25 years = $1.1–$1.25 million.

That number sounds big. But you don't have to save all of it—your investments will do the heavy lifting.

Retirement Accounts You Need to Know

Let's break down the tools in your retirement toolbox.

1. 401(k) or 403(b)

These are retirement accounts offered by employers.

You contribute money directly from your paycheck, *before taxes*.

Pros:

- Employer may match your contribution (free money)
- Grows tax-deferred
- Higher contribution limits ($23,000/year in 2025 if under 50)

Cons:

- Withdrawals taxed in retirement
- Early withdrawals = penalty (unless special circumstances)

2. Roth IRA

You contribute *after-tax* dollars, but your money grows tax-free—and you don't pay taxes when you withdraw in retirement.

Pros:

- Tax-free withdrawals
- Great for younger folks or those expecting to be in a higher tax bracket later
- Withdraw contributions (not earnings) anytime without penalty

Cons:

- Lower contribution limit ($7,000/year in 2025)
- Income limits apply

3. Traditional IRA
   Like a 401(k), but for individuals. Contributions may be tax-deductible.
   Pros:

- Flexibility if you don't have an employer plan
- Can roll over a 401(k) when changing jobs

Cons:

- Same early withdrawal penalties
- Income phaseouts for deduction

4. SEP IRA and Solo 401(k)
   For the entrepreneurs, freelancers, and side-hustlers.
   Pros:

- Higher contribution limits
- Great way to build tax-advantaged wealth outside of a job

Cons:

- More admin (especially Solo 401(k)s)
- Need self-employment income

Diversifying for Retirement

Don't just throw all your money into one account.

Balance between:

- 401(k) (pre-tax)
- Roth IRA (after-tax)
- Brokerage accounts (flexibility)

Each account has its own strengths, and mixing them gives you more control over your taxes in retirement.

Investing Inside Your Retirement Accounts

Opening a retirement account is step one.

But where that money goes *inside* the account matters too.

Don't let your contributions sit in cash. You need to invest them.

Common strategies:

- Target Date Funds (automatically adjust as you age)
- Index Funds (VTI, FXAIX, SWPPX)
- ETFs (SPY, QQQ, etc.)

Rule of Thumb:

- The younger you are, the more aggressive you can be (more stocks)
- As you near retirement, shift to more conservative (more bonds)

Social Security – Don't Rely on It, But Understand It

Social Security is a government program that pays you monthly income when you retire.

You qualify by working and paying into the system (via payroll taxes).

You can start collecting as early as age 62, but waiting until 67–70 increases your benefit.

It's helpful—but not enough to live on. Treat it like a side dish, not the main course.

Retirement and Healthcare

Healthcare is one of the biggest costs in retirement.

Medicare kicks in at 65, but it doesn't cover everything.

Plan for:

- Supplemental insurance (Medigap)
- Dental and vision
- Long-term care (nursing homes, in-home care)

Tip: Consider opening an HSA (Health Savings Account) if eligible. It's a tax-advantaged way to save for medical expenses.

Pros and Cons of Retirement Planning

Pros:

- Peace of mind
- Financial freedom
- Builds long-term wealth
- Reduces stress as you age

Cons:

- Takes discipline
- Can feel overwhelming at first
- Requires patience

But like a good gospel album—it only gets better with time.

Action Steps to Start Now

1. Check if your job offers a 401(k)—and enroll
2. Contribute at least enough to get the full employer match
3. Open a Roth IRA online (Fidelity, Vanguard, Schwab)
4. Set up automatic monthly contributions ($25–$100 to start)
5. Choose a Target Date Fund or Index Fund inside your account
6. Calculate your retirement number using online calculators
7. Increase contributions 1–2% each year as your income grows

Bonus: Talk to your parents or older relatives about their retirement plans. It'll help them—and you.

Cultural Reflection: Retirement Isn't Just for Other People

We've seen too many folks work forever because they had to.

Let's be the generation that retires *on purpose.*

Let's take vacations with our grandkids. Let's give back to our communities. Let's start foundations, support the arts, fund scholarships.

Let's not just *leave* work. Let's walk into a season of rest, joy, and power.

We deserve that.

We've earned that.

And it starts with a plan.

Final Word: Freedom Later Starts Right Now

Retirement isn't about age—it's about *agency.*

It's the day you stop hustling because you *want to,* not because you *have to.*

It's the result of all your sacrifices, all your smart moves, all your long nights.

And every dollar you invest today is a vote for that freedom.

So whether you're 25 or 55, employed or self-made, just starting or circling back—it's your time.

Start now. Start small. Just *start*.

Because your future self is already out there, waiting on you.

Chapter 10: Legacy Planning – Generational Wealth in Action

Let's Talk About What Really Lasts

Legacy ain't just about your name in lights, a street sign, or some fancy family crest. For our people, legacy is deeper. It's what you *leave behind*—not just in assets, but in mindset, memory, and movement.

It's about whether your grandkids are starting from scratch or standing on your shoulders.

This chapter is about making sure they're standing tall.

Because real generational wealth isn't just about passing down money—it's about passing down *game*.

Let's break it down.

What Is Legacy Planning?

Legacy planning is the process of organizing your finances, values, and resources in a way that ensures your family and community are protected and empowered after you're gone.

It includes:

- Estate planning (wills, trusts, beneficiaries)

- Life insurance
- Business succession
- Philanthropy
- Financial literacy for the next generation

It's the ultimate grown-folk move.

Why It Hits Different for Us

For Black families, legacy has always been layered.

We didn't always have land or life insurance to pass down, but we passed down recipes, church roots, family traditions, and neighborhood connections.

But now we're in a position to pass down more:

- Home equity
- Investment accounts
- Businesses
- Knowledge
- Power

We just gotta plan for it.

Let's Talk Wills and Why They Matter

A will is a legal document that outlines what happens to your stuff—your house, your money, your car, your jewelry, your grandmother's Bible—when you pass.

Without a will:

- The state decides who gets what
- Family drama can pop off (and you know how that goes)
- Your wishes may not be honored

With a will:

- You stay in control
- You name guardians for your kids
- You leave instructions for your assets

It ain't about being morbid. It's about being *mature.*

Trusts: Next-Level Protection

Trusts go beyond wills. They allow you to control when and how your assets are distributed.

For example:

- You can leave money to your kids but only give it to them when they turn 25 or finish college
- You can set up a trust that pays out annually instead of all at once

Types of Trusts:

- Revocable Living Trust (can be changed)
- Irrevocable Trust (more protection, but can't be changed)
- Special Needs Trust (for children with disabilities)

Pros:

- Avoids probate (court process)
- Keeps things private
- Helps prevent the money from being blown

Cons:

- More complex to set up

- Legal fees involved

But if you've got real assets and big vision—it's worth it.

Life Insurance: The Wealth Transfer Hack

Life insurance is one of the easiest, fastest, most impactful ways to leave your family with something real.

Term Life Insurance:

- Covers you for a set period (20–30 years)
- Affordable
- Great for young families

Whole Life Insurance:

- Covers your entire life
- Builds cash value
- More expensive

Why It's Powerful:

- Pays out tax-free
- Can wipe out debt
- Can fund college, business, or home down payments
- Helps avoid GoFundMe funerals

Every head of household should have *something* in place.

Real Estate and Inheritance

If you own property, you're already ahead of the game.

But make sure it's in order:

- Put your house in a trust
- Add transfer-on-death deeds where available
- Talk to your family about who will manage or inherit it

Black families lose billions in generational wealth due to unclear titles, probate issues, and family conflict.

Don't let your home become a headache.

Business Succession: Don't Let the Hustle Die With You

If you've built a business—whether it's a barbershop, beauty brand, tax service, or bakery—you need a plan for what happens when you're no longer in the mix.

Key Questions:

- Who will run it?
- Who owns what?
- How will it be passed down?

Put it in writing. Train the next generation. Don't let your empire fall apart because of silence.

Teach the Game: Legacy Is More Than Legal

What good is passing down wealth if the next generation doesn't know how to use it?

Legacy also means:

- Teaching your kids about money
- Having annual family financial meetings
- Writing down your story, your values, your why
- Leaving behind not just assets, but *instructions*

Start with:

- Showing them how to budget
- Explaining how insurance works
- Opening a custodial investment account for your children

This is the part where culture meets capital.

Pros and Cons of Legacy Planning

Pros:

- Protects your family from stress and confusion
- Transfers wealth efficiently
- Builds generational power
- Keeps your values alive

Cons:

- Can be emotionally tough to think about
- Requires time, effort, and sometimes legal help
- Can stir up family dynamics

But trust—doing nothing costs more.

Action Steps to Build Your Legacy

1. Write or update your will (use a lawyer or a trusted online platform)
2. Get term life insurance if you don't have it
3. Talk to your family about your wishes
4. Start a family legacy folder (include passwords, policies, deeds, etc.)
5. Meet with a financial planner or estate attorney if you have significant assets
6. Set a calendar reminder to review everything annually

Bonus Step: Write a legacy letter—something from the heart that your family can hold onto forever.

Final Word: Make the Story Bigger Than You

Legacy is not about perfection. It's about preparation.

It's about making sure your babies aren't starting over.

It's about your people knowing that you were thinking about them even when you weren't here.

It's about shifting the energy from "I hope we make it" to "We got it."

So don't just leave behind a couch and a couple of boxes.

Leave behind a plan.

Leave behind clarity.

Leave behind freedom.

Part V: Life Events and Financial Transitions

Because Life Be Lifein'—Here's How to Stay Ready

Money ain't just about math—it's about moments.

Big ones. Painful ones. Beautiful ones. Unpredictable ones.

Part V is all about the **real-life chapters** we don't always see coming—but we *have* to be ready for. Whether it's having a baby, losing a job, going through a divorce, caring for your parents, or even grieving a loved one, money is always in the room. And if you don't have a plan? That moment can turn into a mess.

In this section, we walk you through the financial side of major life events—step by step, with empathy and strategy. Because it's not just about surviving change—it's about being prepared for it so you can move with confidence and care.

This ain't your average financial advice. We're keeping it honest, culturally relevant, and grounded in the realities of our community.

In Part V, you'll learn:

- What to do financially when your relationship status changes
- How to navigate job loss, career pivots, and unexpected income drops
- The smartest ways to prepare for parenthood (even before the baby shower)

- How to handle financial caregiving for elders and aging parents
- Why your emergency plan matters more than ever—and how to build one
- How to grieve while still keeping your finances from falling apart

Because at the end of the day, *life will happen*.

But with the right tools, **you'll be ready**—not shaken.

This part of the book is your survival kit, your reset button, and your grown-folk guide to staying grounded no matter what life throws your way.

Let's navigate the transitions with grace, strategy, and power.

Chapter 11: When a Parent Dies – Grief, Paperwork, and What to Do Next

Let's Keep It Real: This One Hurts

Losing a parent hits different. It doesn't matter if you saw it coming or if it came out of nowhere—it changes you. Deep down.

And while your heart is cracked wide open, here come the phone calls, the funeral planning, the family drama, and a stack of paperwork that don't care nothing about your tears.

This chapter is here to walk with you through the fog.

Not just the emotional part—but the legal, financial, and practical parts too. Because unfortunately, when somebody passes, the system keeps moving. And if you don't have a roadmap, it can leave you feeling lost and overwhelmed.

Let's walk this road together.

First Things First: Give Yourself Permission to Grieve

Before we even talk about paperwork, let's sit with this:

You just lost your parent.

Maybe your first best friend.

Maybe your hardest critic.

Maybe the glue that held the family together.

Whatever your relationship was—complex, beautiful, distant, tight—it mattered. And so does your grief.

So cry when you need to.

Take a breath when it gets heavy.

And don't let anybody rush your process.

Immediate Steps in the First 24–72 Hours

Even in grief, some things can't wait. Here's what usually needs to happen right away:

1. **Notify close family and friends**
2. **Contact the funeral home** (they will transport the body and begin the death certificate process)
3. **Locate their ID and important documents**
4. **Secure the home and belongings** (lock up, turn off appliances, check the mail)
5. **If they had a will or trust, locate it**
6. **Contact employer if they were still working** (for benefits or final paycheck)

These first few days are tender. Don't try to do it alone. Let folks bring food. Let somebody else call the church. Let your cousin handle the playlist.

The Funeral: Cultural Ritual and Financial Reality

Let's be honest—Black funerals are more than a service. They're a celebration, a family reunion, and sometimes a whole production.

But they also cost money.

The average funeral can run $7,000–$15,000. Casket. Flowers. Programs. Obituary in the paper. Repast.

If your parent had life insurance, check with the funeral home to see if they'll accept an "assignment of benefits" while the claim is being processed.

If they didn't? You may need to:

- Pool family contributions
- Use savings or a credit card
- Set up a donation or crowdfunding page

Do what's best for your peace—not your ego.

And remember: the love is in the presence, not the presentation.

What to Gather: The Paper Trail Begins

You'll need documents to start handling business. Start a folder or box with:

- Death certificate (order at least 10 copies)
- Social Security number
- Birth certificate (if possible)
- Marriage certificate (if applicable)
- Will or trust documents
- Life insurance policies
- Bank account info
- Retirement and pension statements
- Property deeds or mortgage info
- Utility bills
- Driver's license or ID card
- Credit card and loan info

This may take time. Be patient with yourself.

The Estate: Who's in Charge and What Happens Next

If your parent had a will:

- The person named as executor will manage their estate
- The will must go through probate (court process) in most cases

If they didn't have a will:

- The court will appoint someone (usually a child or spouse) to serve as administrator
- The estate will be divided according to state law

Executor Duties May Include:

- Paying off debts and bills
- Canceling subscriptions
- Notifying creditors
- Distributing property to heirs
- Filing final tax return

Life Insurance and Benefits

If your parent had life insurance:

- Contact the company to file a claim
- Provide a certified death certificate and ID

Also check for:

- Employer-sponsored life insurance
- Veterans benefits
- Social Security survivor benefits (if a spouse or minor children are left

behind)

Banking and Bills

Close or transfer accounts once all checks and bills have cleared.

If the account was joint, the surviving party can usually keep it.

Cancel utilities, cell phone, cable, subscriptions, etc.

Contact credit card companies and notify the credit bureaus to prevent identity theft.

What Happens to Debt?

Here's the real talk:

- Debt does *not* pass down to you personally unless you were a co-signer
- The estate is responsible for paying any debt before heirs get anything

If there's more debt than assets, creditors may not get paid in full—and that's okay.

Do *not* let collectors bully you.

Handling Property and Real Estate

If your parent owned a home:

- You'll need to determine if there's a mortgage
- Decide whether to keep it, sell it, or rent it
- Transfer title through probate or trust

If they didn't leave a clear will or deed? It can get tricky. Get legal help if needed.

Keep paying property taxes and insurance while you figure it out.

Family Dynamics: Drama, Division, and Decisions

Let's not pretend—grief brings stuff to the surface.

Old beef. Hurt feelings. Folks showing up with expectations.

Your job is to stay rooted in:

- Clarity (what did your parent *actually* want?)
- Documentation (what does the will say?)
- Boundaries (what *will* you engage in?)

Call in a neutral third party if necessary—a lawyer, pastor, or mediator.

And protect your peace at all costs.

Pros and Cons of Taking the Lead

Pros:

- You ensure your parent's wishes are honored
- You gain clarity and closure
- You may prevent family confusion or fighting

Cons:

- Emotionally and mentally draining
- May create tension with other family members
- Time-consuming and detail-heavy

You don't have to do it perfectly. You just have to do it with care.

Action Steps (In Order)

1. Secure the body and notify family
2. Choose a funeral home
3. Get multiple copies of the death certificate
4. Locate the will, trust, and financial documents
5. Contact banks, insurance companies, and employers
6. Notify Social Security and other agencies
7. Start probate or trust administration process
8. Pay bills and debts from the estate
9. Distribute assets according to the will or law
10. Close out accounts, cancel ID, and keep records

Cultural Wisdom and Financial Healing

Losing a parent can open up old wounds.

But it can also plant new seeds:

- A vow to create your own will
- A commitment to break the silence around money
- A dedication to making sure *your* kids aren't left guessing

Grief teaches us what matters most.

And it reminds us to live—and plan—with intention.

Final Word: Your Parent's Legacy Is in Your Hands

This moment may feel impossible.

But step by step, you will get through it.

You will honor them.

You will find the strength to carry out what they couldn't say.

And in the process—you'll write the next chapter of your family's story.

With wisdom.

With clarity.
With love.

Chapter 12: Losing a Spouse – Navigating Finances Through Grief

Let's Be Honest: This is One of the Hardest Chapters to Write... and Live

Losing a spouse is like losing a part of yourself. The one you planned with. Laughed with. Argued with. Prayed with. Built a life with. And when they're gone, it's not just the silence in the house that hits—it's the decisions. The paperwork. The bills. The questions you don't feel ready to answer.

This chapter is here for that moment.

To help you breathe through the grief while handling the money. To give you a checklist when your mind is spinning. To walk with you like your favorite auntie or your older cousin who's been through it and still standing strong.

Let's walk through it. Gently.

Grief is Real, Raw, and Unpredictable

Before we talk money, let's talk heart.

You are grieving.

And grief ain't linear.

Some days you'll feel strong. Some days you won't wanna get out of bed.

Some days you'll hear their voice in the hallway or reach for them at night. It's okay.

Give yourself grace.

This ain't about rushing through the pain—it's about not letting the financial part make it worse.

First 48–72 Hours: What Needs Immediate Attention

1. Contact a funeral home and start arrangements
2. Request multiple copies of the death certificate (you'll need 10 or more)
3. Notify close family and friends
4. Locate important documents (marriage license, will, insurance policies)
5. If they were employed, contact HR for final pay and benefits
6. If military or veteran, contact the VA for honors and benefits

Don't try to do all this alone.

Assign roles to trusted family or friends:

- One person to handle calls
- One to manage meals or kids
- One to track paperwork

You're not weak for needing help. You're human.

The Funeral: Love, Tradition, and Budget

Funerals in our community are sacred. They're a whole event—homegoing services, repast, flower arrangements, the outfit, the gospel choir, the slideshow.

But they also come with cost.

- Average funeral cost: $8,000–$15,000
- Extras: obituary printing, church donations, limo rental, food for repast

If your spouse had life insurance, the funeral home may accept an assignment of benefits (they get paid directly when the check comes).

If not, you may have to:

- Use savings
- Ask family for support
- Start a fundraiser (church, community, GoFundMe)

Don't go into deep debt trying to impress people. Do what honors your loved one and preserves your peace.

What Documents to Gather

Start a folder (physical or digital) and collect:

- Death certificate (get certified copies)
- Marriage certificate
- Social Security card
- Birth certificate
- Driver's license or state ID
- Health and life insurance policies
- Will or trust documents
- Bank and credit card info
- Mortgage or lease papers
- Car titles and loans
- Investment or retirement accounts
- Military service records (if applicable)

This list may feel long, but you don't have to find it all in a day. Pace yourself.

Understanding the Will and Estate Process

If your spouse had a will:

- You (or the named executor) will file it with probate court
- The court will authorize handling the estate

If they didn't have a will:

- The court will appoint an administrator
- Assets may be distributed according to state law

If you owned things jointly (like your home), they may pass directly to you without going through probate.

If you're unsure—get a probate attorney for guidance.

Life Insurance and Retirement Accounts

Start the claim process as soon as possible. You'll need:

- Certified death certificate
- Policy number
- Your ID

Also look for:

- Group insurance through employer or union
- Pension or 401(k)/403(b) accounts
- Military survivor benefits

Tip: Keep a list of every company you contact. Write down who you spoke to, when, and what they said.

Banking and Bills

Check how accounts are titled:

- Joint accounts usually stay open for your use
- Individual accounts may need court approval to access

Start reviewing all monthly bills:

- Rent/mortgage
- Utilities
- Insurance premiums
- Credit cards
- Subscriptions

Call companies and let them know of the death. Some will freeze interest or offer support.

Consider forwarding mail to your address to keep track of accounts and prevent fraud.

Social Security and Survivor Benefits

If your spouse worked and paid into Social Security:

- You may qualify for survivor benefits
- Call 1-800-772-1213 or visit a local office to apply

You may also qualify for a one-time $255 death benefit (small, but helps cover basics).

If you have minor children:

- They may also receive benefits until age 18 (or 19 if still in high school)

Navigating Real Estate

If your spouse owned your home:

- Check if you're on the deed or mortgage
- Look into refinance or assumption options if you're not listed

If you rented:

- Talk to the landlord about transferring or ending the lease
- Some states allow grieving spouses time to adjust without penalties

If you owned property together:

- Transfer title via a survivorship affidavit or court process

What Happens to Their Debt?

Here's the truth:

- You are NOT automatically responsible for your spouse's debt
- Their estate is responsible for paying what's owed
- If you co-signed a loan or shared a credit card, you may still owe it

Don't rush to pay bills until you speak to a financial advisor or attorney.

Joint Accounts, Credit, and Identity Theft Protection

Close or update joint accounts once all transactions clear

Notify the three credit bureaus (Experian, Equifax, TransUnion) of the death

Keep an eye on your spouse's credit for fraudulent activity
Consider freezing their credit to prevent identity theft

Handling Insurance, Health, and Work Benefits

Health insurance:

- If you were covered under their job, ask about COBRA continuation or alternate plans

Pension:

- Check for survivor annuity options
- Some plans reduce payouts upon death, others continue with reduced benefits

Employer benefits:

- Final paycheck, unused PTO, stock options, etc.

File claims through HR and be prepared to submit documentation

Kids, Teens, and Grown Children

This is hard on them too.
If you have young kids:

- Keep routines consistent
- Let their school know what's going on
- Consider counseling or group support

Adult children:

- May need emotional guidance more than financial
- Involve them in decisions if appropriate

Share stories, write down memories, keep your loved one's presence alive

Emotional and Mental Wellness

You may feel:

- Numb
- Angry
- Guilty
- Relieved
- Lonely
- Overwhelmed

And that's all normal.

Seek grief support:

- Church or spiritual community
- Support groups (in person or online)
- Therapy (individual or family)

You don't have to carry it all alone.

Pros and Cons of Taking Financial Control After Loss

Pros:

- Prevents bills from piling up
- Protects your credit and your future
- Gives you a sense of clarity and empowerment

Cons:

- Can feel cold or rushed
- May stir up emotions or conflict
- Takes energy you may not have

You don't have to do it fast.

You just have to do it *eventually*.

Action Steps: First 30 Days

1. Order death certificates (10+ copies)
2. Notify employer, insurance companies, banks
3. Locate and review the will or trust
4. Start probate process if needed
5. Begin life insurance claims
6. Notify Social Security and apply for survivor benefits
7. List all monthly bills and income sources
8. Set calendar reminders to cancel or transfer accounts
9. Find a financial advisor or estate attorney if you need help
10. Breathe. Rest. Cry. Repeat.

Final Word: Healing, Hustle, and Honor

You are not alone.

This loss may shake you—but it doesn't have to break you.

Your healing will come in waves.

Your strength will return.

And in time, you will rebuild a new life, carrying their memory and the lessons they left you.

You will honor them—in how you live, how you love, and how you handle this business with wisdom and grace.

You are still standing.

And that's powerful.

Chapter 13: Annual Financial Checklist – Staying Ready So You Don't Have to Get Ready

Let's Be Real: Adulting is an Extreme Sport

Between work, kids, texts, your cousin's birthday cookout, and remembering to drink water, life gets busy. Financial planning? That can easily fall to the bottom of the list.

But here's the thing—money loves order. Wealth grows where there's clarity. And peace? Peace comes when you know your stuff is handled.

This chapter is your go-to financial maintenance plan. Your yearly tune-up. Your "get right" guide. Think of it like your spiritual oil change—because you can't ride smooth if your money's leaking.

We're about to walk through your **Annual Financial Checklist**, the one that keeps you ready—not rushing. So the next time life throws you a curveball, you're already set up to catch it.

Let's get organized.

Why You Need an Annual Financial Check-In

Most people think about money reactively. Something breaks. A bill comes due. A paycheck gets stretched. Then they panic and patch it up.

But real wealth building? That's proactive.

It's looking ahead, not behind.

And it's not about perfection. It's about progress. Having an annual review builds:

- Awareness of what's working
- Space to fix what's broken
- Confidence in your direction

It's adulting with intention.

When to Do It

Pick one month every year—maybe January (New Year's reset), April (tax season), or your birthday month.

Make it a tradition. Light a candle, play some Anita Baker or Nipsey Hussle, and give your finances the attention they deserve.

This isn't punishment. It's power.

The Checklist: What to Review Each Year

Let's break this down into sections, like rooms in your financial house. You'll walk through each one and check for leaks, dust, or upgrades.

1. Income Review

- Did your income increase, decrease, or stay the same this year?
- Did you start a new job, side hustle, or business?
- Is your income aligned with your lifestyle and goals?

Action Steps:

- Get your last 3 paystubs
- Review your W-2 or 1099 from last year
- Estimate your total annual income

Reflection: Are you earning what you're worth? If not, what's the plan to level up?

2. Budget Check-In

- Does your current budget reflect your real life?
- What categories are over or under?
- Are you consistently saving, investing, and giving?

Action Steps:

- Review 3 months of bank statements
- Adjust your budget based on reality, not hope
- Use a budgeting app or spreadsheet that works for your style

Reflection: Do you feel in control of your money or like your money controls you?

3. Emergency Fund Status

- Do you have 3–6 months of expenses saved?
- Is the money in a high-yield savings account?

Action Steps:

- Check your current balance
- Calculate your target number (monthly expenses x 3 to 6)
- Set up an auto-transfer—even if it's just $25/month

Reflection: Would you be financially okay if you lost income for 90 days?

4. Debt Inventory

- What's your current balance on credit cards, student loans, car loans, etc.?
- What's your interest rate on each?

Action Steps:

- List all debts in a spreadsheet or app
- Choose a payoff strategy: snowball (smallest first) or avalanche (highest interest first)
- Make a plan to pay extra on one target debt

Reflection: Is your debt moving you forward (like education or real estate) or holding you back?

5. Credit Health

- Do you know your current credit score?
- Do you have any late payments or collections?

Action Steps:

- Pull your free credit reports (annualcreditreport.com)
- Check scores through apps like Credit Karma or your bank
- Dispute any errors

Reflection: Is your credit helping you build or blocking your growth?

6. Investment Review

- Are you investing regularly?
- Are your investments aligned with your age and goals?

Action Steps:

- Log into your retirement and brokerage accounts
- Review your contributions, performance, and fees
- Rebalance your portfolio if needed (especially if you're nearing retirement)

Reflection: Is your money growing quietly in the background? Or is it sitting still?

7. Insurance Check-Up

- Do you have enough life insurance?
- What about health, auto, renters/home, and disability?

Action Steps:

- Review your current policies
- Compare coverage and shop for better rates if needed
- Update beneficiaries

Reflection: If something happened to you tomorrow, would your family be okay?

8. Estate Planning

- Do you have a will?
- Have you assigned a power of attorney and healthcare proxy?
- Are your accounts set with beneficiaries (TOD or POD)?

Action Steps:

- Create or update your will
- Fill out estate planning documents (you can start online or talk to an attorney)
- Organize important papers in one location

Reflection: Do your loved ones know your wishes? Or would they be scrambling?

9. Tax Prep

- Are you withholding the right amount from your paycheck?

- Did you keep good records of deductions (donations, business expenses, etc.)?

Action Steps:

- Review your last tax return
- Adjust your W-4 if needed
- Create a folder for next year's tax documents

Reflection: Are you planning for taxes—or letting taxes surprise you?

10. Goal Progress

- What financial goals did you set last year?
- What did you accomplish?
- What do you want to hit this year?

Action Steps:

- Write down 1 short-term, 1 mid-term, and 1 long-term financial goal
- Break each down into action steps
- Track your progress quarterly

Reflection: Are you moving with purpose—or just spinning wheels?

Bonus: Family Financial Meeting

If you have a spouse or kids, this is the time to bring them in. Talk about:

- Budget goals
- Big dreams (vacations, new house, legacy planning)
- What each person can contribute

Let the kids help pick a savings goal. Teach them what it means to invest.

Make it fun—pizza night and money talk.

Normalize the conversations we didn't grow up having.

Pros and Cons of Doing a Financial Check-In

Pros:

- Catches problems before they get big
- Keeps your goals visible
- Reduces stress and chaos

Cons:

- Takes time and focus
- Can stir up shame or overwhelm if things aren't great
- Requires vulnerability if done with others

But the peace of mind? Worth it every time.

Annual Financial Maintenance Mindset

This isn't about being rich—it's about being ready.

It's about:

- Walking into tax season like a boss
- Seeing your credit rise like gospel chords in a Sunday service
- Knowing your family is protected if life shifts

You're not just building a budget. You're building freedom.

Action Steps Summary

1. Pick your check-in month (and block time in your calendar)
2. Walk through each section of this checklist
3. Celebrate your wins
4. Write down your gaps and goals
5. Create a plan to handle 1 area per week or per month

Start small. Start scared. Start wherever you are.

Just start.

Final Word: You Ain't Gotta Get Ready If You Stay Ready

Your money should be a mirror—not a mystery.

When you do this check-in each year, you remind yourself that you're in control. That you don't have to wait for a crisis to get clear.

And that's what grown-up wealth looks like.

So pour your tea. Play your playlist. Light your candle. Grab your statements. And do this.

Because your future self is already clapping for you.

Chapter 14: Know What You're Paying For – Bills, Utilities, Subscriptions, and Leaks

Real Talk: That Money You're Looking for? It Might Already Be Leaving

Let's keep it a buck. Most of us have more money than we realize—it's just leaking out through little cracks we don't pay attention to.

$12.99 here.

$19.99 there.

Some "free trial" you forgot about is now charging you every month. Your cousin's still using your Netflix. You're paying for a gym membership you haven't stepped into since Obama was in office.

It adds up.

This chapter is about plugging those holes. Knowing what you're really paying for. And taking your power back over the day-to-day money leaks that rob you of peace, potential, and progress.

Let's get into it.

The Power of Awareness: Shine a Light On Your Spending

You can't change what you don't track.

Knowing where your money is going isn't about judgment—it's about clarity.

It's about:

- Making sure your money reflects your values
- Stopping invisible expenses from stealing your wealth
- Giving yourself permission to say "No" to stuff that no longer serves you

Think of this as a financial spring cleaning. And yes, we're gonna go through every drawer.

Section 1: Monthly Bills – The Non-Negotiables (or Are They?)

These are the essentials. But even essentials can be trimmed.

1. Rent or Mortgage

- Know when it's due and how much is automatically withdrawn
- Review your lease or loan details once a year
- Consider refinancing or negotiating rent if market conditions shift

2. Utilities (Gas, Electric, Water)

- Are you on a budget billing plan?
- Are there energy-saving programs in your area?
- Can you cut down use (LED bulbs, unplug unused items, weather-proofing)?

3. Phone and Internet

- When's the last time you called to ask for a better deal?
- Do you actually need unlimited everything?
- Are you paying for a rental modem you could replace for less?

4. Insurance (Car, Renters, Health)

- Are you shopping rates once a year?
- Are you bundling policies?
- Have your life circumstances changed (like driving less)?

5. Car Payment and Transportation

- Know the interest rate and balance on your car loan
- Could you refinance, downsize, or use public transit sometimes?

Section 2: Subscriptions – The Silent Budget Killers

This is where the real leaks happen.

Streaming Services

- Netflix
- Hulu
- Disney+
- Amazon Prime
- HBO Max
- Peacock
- BET+ (if you ain't watching Martin reruns every week, do you need it?)

Ask yourself:

- How many are you actually using?
- How many did you forget about?

- Can you rotate them instead of keeping all at once?

Other Subscriptions

- Music: Spotify, Apple Music, Tidal
- Apps: Meditation, Workout, Editing, Cloud Storage
- Beauty Boxes, Meal Kits, Magazines, and more

Action Step:

- Go through your bank and credit card statements for the last 90 days
- Write down every subscription
- Cancel anything you haven't used in the last 30 days

You can always rejoin later. Don't let $9.99 be what holds you back from hitting your bigger goals.

Section 3: Hidden Fees – The Sneaky Ones

These don't show up bolded on your bill—but they still bite.

1. Bank Fees

- Monthly maintenance fees
- Overdraft fees
- ATM charges

Solution: Switch to a fee-free bank or credit union

2. Credit Card Fees

- Annual fees
- Late payment fees
- Foreign transaction fees

Solution:

- Set up autopay for minimums
- Ask for a fee waiver
- Use no-fee cards

3. Delivery and Service Fees

- Uber Eats, DoorDash, Instacart—those $4.99s add up fast

Solution:

- Use pickup instead of delivery when you can
- Look into memberships if you order often
- Tip fairly but watch convenience creep

Section 4: Lifestyle Inflation – When Your Wallet Thinks You Got a Raise

Remember when you were cool eating home-cooked meals and watching TV One reruns?

Then you got a raise...

Now it's daily DoorDash, a $200 cell phone bill, and you forgot what leftovers even are.

That's lifestyle creep. And it will quietly ruin your savings.

Check yourself:

- Have your monthly expenses increased with your income?
- Are you happier—or just spending more?

Action Step:

- List the extra things you added over the last year

- Rank them: keep, cut, or pause

Just because you can afford it doesn't mean you have to keep it.

Section 5: Annual Expenses You Forgot You Pay

These hit you outta nowhere if you don't plan:

- Amazon Prime renewal
- Car registration and tags
- Property taxes
- HOA fees
- School fees, sports leagues
- Holiday spending

Solution:

- Create a "sinking fund"—a savings account just for yearly costs
- Divide the total by 12 and set up monthly deposits

Example: If Amazon Prime is $139/year, save $11.58/month. When it hits? You're coolin'.

Section 6: Sharing Expenses – Roommates, Spouses, and Situationships

Clear the air.

- Who pays for what?
- Is the bill in both names or one?
- Are you stuck paying for services after a breakup?

Action Step:

- Have a monthly check-in
- Use shared budgeting apps like Splitwise or Zeta

Don't be the one still paying Hulu for someone who ghosted you.

Pros and Cons of Doing a Full Expense Audit

Pros:

- You save money instantly
- Reduces money anxiety
- Increases control and confidence

Cons:

- Time-consuming
- May be uncomfortable if it exposes past financial decisions

But exposure leads to empowerment. You can't fix what you won't face.

Action Plan to Patch the Leaks

1. Set aside 2 hours on a Sunday or weekday night
2. Grab your last 3 bank and credit card statements
3. Highlight everything that is NOT essential
4. Cancel or pause all subscriptions you don't use
5. Call 3 companies to negotiate better rates
6. Track every bill's due date in a calendar
7. Automate what you can—so you never miss a beat
8. Recheck everything in 6 months

Bonus: Use cash for one month to really feel your spending. You'll be surprised what you skip.

Final Word: Respect Your Coins Like You Earned Every One (Because You Did)

You work too hard for your money to let it sneak out the back door.

You deserve financial clarity. You deserve peace. You deserve to know exactly what's coming in, what's going out, and what's just wasting space.

This isn't about restriction. It's about intention.

Because once you clean up the leaks?

You'll be amazed at what's left over to build your dreams with.

Part VI: Working with Professionals

Because You Don't Have to Do This Alone

Let's be real—handling your money, building wealth, protecting your legacy, investing, insuring, budgeting, saving... it's a lot. And just like you wouldn't cut your own hair before prom or perform your own surgery (God forbid), you don't always have to be the solo captain of your financial ship.

That's where *professionals* come in.

But in our community, there's often hesitation. Distrust. We've heard the horror stories—folks getting played by shady advisors, signing contracts they didn't understand, or just avoiding professional help altogether because nobody ever taught us how to choose the right people.

This part of the book is here to change that.

Part VI: Working with Professionals breaks down who's who in the money world—from financial advisors to insurance agents, estate attorneys to tax pros—and how to vet them like a boss. No confusion. No shame. Just clarity, confidence, and a whole lot of "let me put you up on game."

Inside this section, we'll cover:

- The difference between a fiduciary and a salesman (and why it matters)
- What questions to ask any financial professional before trusting them
- How to avoid scams, schemes, and slick talkers
- The role of Black professionals and how representation helps build

trust
- When it's time to DIY vs. delegate to a pro
- How to build your personal "money team" like a CEO

You'll learn how to protect yourself, ask better questions, and feel *good* about sitting across the table from someone who's supposed to help you.

Because real wealth isn't built alone—it's built in community, with a team you trust and a plan that makes sense.

Let's get you the help you need—and nothing less than what you deserve.

Chapter 15: Meeting With Advisors – Who's on Your Financial Team?

Let's Set the Record Straight: You're the CEO of Your Life

And like any good CEO, you need a team.

Not just folks who hype you up on Instagram or co-sign your shopping sprees, but real ones. Experts. Professionals who know the game and know how to help you win—financially, legally, generationally.

This chapter is your front office playbook. We're talking about building your financial dream team—the folks you want in your corner when it's time to level up, plan ahead, protect your peace, and secure the bag.

Because even Beyoncé don't run the empire by herself.

Let's find out who you need, what they do, how to pick 'em, and how to make sure they're playing *for* you and not *you*.

First Things First: Why You Even Need a Team

You can only YouTube your way through finances for so long.

Eventually, you'll hit a point where you need:

- Guidance
- Strategy

- Accountability
- Protection

Just like LeBron's got a strength coach, nutritionist, and business manager—you need experts who help you win in your lane.

Money touches every part of life. So having people who actually *know* what they're doing can help you:

- Save time
- Avoid costly mistakes
- Maximize opportunities
- Sleep better at night

Section 1: The Core 5 – Your Starting Lineup

Let's break down the top players you'll likely need in your financial life.

1. Financial Advisor

What they do: Help you plan, invest, grow, and protect your money. Real ones look at the big picture—not just your portfolio.

Ideal for:

- Building wealth
- Retirement planning
- Managing investments
- College saving plans
- Creating a roadmap for financial goals

Questions to Ask:

- Are you a fiduciary? (They're legally obligated to act in your best interest)
- How do you get paid? (Fee-only, commission, or both)
- What kind of clients do you usually work with?

Red Flag: If they can't explain a concept in plain English, they're not the one.

2. Certified Public Accountant (CPA) or Tax Preparer

What they do: Help you stay right with the IRS, reduce your tax bill, and find legit ways to keep more of your money.

Ideal for:

- Filing taxes
- Handling 1099/self-employment income
- Tax strategy
- Audit defense
- Business structure advice

Questions to Ask:

- How do you stay current on tax law changes?
- Can you help me plan for next year—not just file for last year?

Red Flag: If they only pop up around April and disappear, keep it moving.

3. Insurance Agent

What they do: Help you cover your life, health, car, home, and income.

Ideal for:

- Getting the right protection
- Understanding policies
- Avoiding being over- or underinsured

Types:

- Captive agent (sells for one company only)
- Independent agent (shops around for best policy)

Questions to Ask:

- What kind of policy do you have yourself?
- Can I get a breakdown of coverage and cost?

Red Flag: Pressure to buy more than you need—or making it hard to cancel.

4. Estate Planning Attorney

What they do: Help you protect what you've built and pass it on to your loved ones without drama.

Ideal for:

- Creating wills, trusts, and healthcare directives
- Avoiding probate
- Naming guardians for kids

Questions to Ask:

- Do you specialize in estate law?
- Can you help me update documents over time?

Red Flag: If they make you feel dumb for asking questions. Nope.

5. Real Estate Professional

What they do: Guide you through buying, selling, or investing in property.

Ideal for:

- First-time homebuyers
- Real estate investing
- Navigating loans and contracts

Questions to Ask:

- Are you a full-time agent?
- Do you work with clients like me?

Red Flag: Talking fast, pushing you to "act now," or ignoring your goals.

Section 2: Supporting Players You May Need

These folks might not be on speed dial—but when you need 'em, you really need 'em:

- Business Attorney (for contracts, trademarks, LLCs)
- Bookkeeper (to keep your records straight if you run a biz)
- Therapist (because money trauma is real)
- Financial Coach (for mindset and budgeting work)
- Grant Writer (for non-profits or education funding)

Section 3: How to Choose the Right People

Just because someone got letters behind their name doesn't mean they're the one for *you*.

Here's your vetting process:

1. **Check Their Credentials**

- Are they licensed or certified in their field?
- Google them. Check reviews. Look 'em up on FINRA, CFP Board, Better Business Bureau.

1. **Have a First Meeting**

- It should feel like a conversation, not a sales pitch
- Ask questions like you're hiring a babysitter for your money (because you are)

1. **Ask About Fees—Clearly**

- Are they hourly, monthly, commission-based, fee-only?
- No shame in asking. If they dance around the answer, bounce.

1. **Notice the Vibe**

- Do you feel respected?
- Are they talking *to* you or *at* you?
- Can they explain complex stuff in simple terms?

Section 4: When to Build Your Team

You don't need everyone at once. But here are signs it's time to bring somebody in:

- You just got married or divorced
- You had a baby
- You started or sold a business
- You got a raise or inheritance
- You're making more money than you used to
- You feel overwhelmed trying to "do it all"

Section 5: Red Flags and Green Lights

Red Flags:

- High-pressure sales tactics
- Not answering your questions
- Overcomplicating basic stuff
- Making guarantees they can't legally promise

Green Lights:

- They teach while they advise

- They disclose all fees and affiliations
- They empower you to make informed decisions
- They respect your background, your culture, and your goals

Section 6: Action Steps to Start Building Your Team

1. Write down your current money challenges (budgeting, investing, insurance, etc.)
2. Prioritize which pro would help the most
3. Ask friends, coworkers, or church members for referrals
4. Schedule 1–2 intro calls this month
5. Take notes during each call—what felt right or off?
6. Choose the pro that gives you peace, not pressure

Bonus: Google "[name of professional] near me" with the word "Black" or "culturally competent" if that's important to you.

Final Word: You're Still the Boss

Hiring an advisor doesn't mean handing over your power—it means sharpening it.

You're the executive. The headliner. The captain.

But even MJ needed Phil Jackson.

Your financial team should bring wisdom, support, and strategy—not stress, shade, or silence.

Ask questions. Demand clarity. And remember: you're building something real.

And you ain't gotta do it alone.

Chapter 16: Rebuilding Trust in Financial Institutions

Let's Keep It 100: The Mistrust is Real

If you grew up hearing things like "never trust the banks," "don't mess with the stock market," or "the system ain't built for us"—you're not imagining things.

That hesitation? It didn't come from nowhere.

From redlining to predatory loans, from the Freedman's Bank collapse to the 2008 mortgage crisis that hit Black families the hardest—our communities have *receipts*. History has taught many of us to protect ourselves, even if it means staying unbanked, stashing cash under the mattress, or avoiding credit altogether.

But here's the hard truth: staying outside the system has its own costs. And if we want to build legacy, create wealth, and make sure our next generation isn't starting from scratch—we have to find our way back in.

This chapter is about acknowledging the harm, confronting the truth, and *rebuilding trust*—on *our* terms.

Let's unpack the history, challenge the fear, and lay a foundation that protects *and* empowers.

Section 1: Why the Distrust Exists (And Is Justified)

You can't talk about rebuilding trust without first talking about why it was broken.

1. The Freedman's Savings Bank Collapse (1874)

- Created for newly freed Black Americans to build wealth
- Mismanaged by white trustees
- $3 million (in 1870s money) lost
- Over 61,000 depositors affected

It left a legacy of mistrust—and for many, that pain got passed down.

2. Redlining and Housing Discrimination

- HOLC maps labeled Black neighborhoods as "risky" for loans
- Denied generations of Black families access to homeownership
- Created wealth gaps that still exist today

3. Subprime Mortgage Crisis (2008)

- Black and Brown families were disproportionately targeted for predatory loans
- Many lost homes, equity, and retirement savings

4. Payday Lenders and Check Cashing Stores

- Fill the gap where banks are absent
- Charge outrageous fees and trap people in cycles of debt

So yeah… it makes sense why many of us side-eye financial institutions. They've earned that skepticism.

But here's where the story shifts.

Section 2: What's Changed and What's Still Broken

What's Improved:

- More regulation to protect consumers (Dodd-Frank Act)
- Rise of fintech apps focused on transparency
- Banks offering second-chance accounts
- More Black financial advisors, bankers, and credit unions

What's Still Broken:

- Racial wealth gap
- Access to capital for Black-owned businesses
- Lending discrimination
- Lower approval rates for Black borrowers
- Lack of culturally competent professionals

We've made progress, but we're not done. The game is still rigged in many ways. But you can learn to play it to your advantage without being played *by* it.

Section 3: The Cost of Staying Outside the System

Let's talk consequences.

When you don't engage with financial institutions, here's what you risk:

- No credit history (harder to buy a house, car, or get a business loan)
- Paying more for everything (cash-based life costs more in fees and missed opportunities)
- Missing out on investment growth
- Limited access to protection tools like insurance
- Legacy gaps for your children

Avoiding the system to stay safe can ironically keep us stuck.

Section 4: How to Rebuild Trust Without Losing Your Mind

It starts with information. Empowerment. And baby steps.

Step 1: Get Banked—But On Your Terms

- Choose a credit union or community bank
- Look for fee-free checking and savings
- Use online banks with strong reputations

Questions to Ask:

- Are you FDIC or NCUA insured?
- What are your monthly fees and overdraft rules?
- Can I access my account easily (app, ATM, customer service)?

Step 2: Understand Credit Without Fear

- Credit is not a trap—it's a tool
- Start with a secured credit card or credit builder loan
- Pay on time, keep balances low, and check your score monthly

Step 3: Use Financial Professionals You Trust

- Ask for referrals from your circle
- Interview advisors like you're hiring a contractor for your house
- Don't be afraid to walk away if the vibe ain't right

Step 4: Join a Black-Owned Bank or Credit Union

- Support institutions that support your community
- Many offer culturally competent financial education

Step 5: Get Financially Educated—Your Way

- Books, podcasts, YouTube, group chats, workshops at your church—pick your lane

Knowledge builds confidence. Confidence builds clarity. Clarity builds trust.

Section 5: Pros and Cons of Re-engaging

Pros:

- Build credit and access
- Protect your assets
- Increase wealth over time
- Create legacy plans
- Gain peace of mind

Cons:

- Systems can still be biased
- Takes time to find the right fit
- Requires vulnerability and paperwork

But the pros far outweigh the risks—especially when you're informed and empowered.

Section 6: What to Look For in a Trustworthy Institution

Ask yourself:

- Do they speak my language? (not just culturally, but clearly)
- Are their fees transparent?

- Do they invest in underserved communities?
- Are there people in leadership who look like me?
- Are their products designed with *me* in mind?

Check their track record. Don't just look at marketing—look at movement.

Section 7: Action Plan to Start Rebuilding

1. Open a fee-free checking account
2. Get a secured credit card and use it for one small bill monthly
3. Pull your free credit report and learn how to read it
4. Follow 2–3 Black financial educators on social media
5. Set up a money date with yourself every month
6. Start tracking where your money goes
7. Share what you learn with someone else

The healing is communal.

Section 8: Cultural Healing – From Fear to Freedom

Let's name it:

- Our grandparents weren't dumb for not trusting the system
- Our parents weren't wrong for warning us
- *But we now have new tools they didn't have access to*

Financial institutions aren't family—but that doesn't mean we can't work with them strategically.

Rebuilding trust isn't about blind faith. It's about **informed partnership**.

We don't need to worship the system. We just need to understand how to **use** it to protect, grow, and pass on wealth.

That's freedom.

Final Word: From Side-Eye to Strategy

You don't have to trust institutions with your *soul.*

But trusting them with a **strategy**? That's a different game.

We're done with being afraid. Done with avoiding. Done with being left behind.

We're moving forward—eyes open, paperwork tight, and mindset sharp.

Because the system may not be perfect. But with the right tools? We can outsmart it, outbuild it, and outlast it.

Chapter 17.1: Vetting Professionals Who Understand Your Culture

Let's Be Honest: Everybody Ain't for Everybody

You ever try explaining your family dynamic to someone who just doesn't get it?

Like telling a therapist that your mama still calls you by your full government name when she's mad—at age 35. Or trying to break down why your auntie's house is the unofficial community center and Thanksgiving battleground. That look they give you? Blank. Confused. Judgy.

Now imagine that same misunderstanding—but with your *money* on the line.

This chapter is about finding the right *fit*—financial professionals who don't just have the degrees and credentials, but also understand the cultural nuances that shape how you view, use, and build wealth.

Because cultural competency isn't a bonus. It's essential.

Let's get into it.

Section 1: Why Culture Matters in Financial Advice

Culture influences:

- How we talk (or don't talk) about money
- Who we support financially (grandma, little cousins, siblings)
- What we fear (debt, banks, IRS)
- What we value (community, legacy, staying out of the spotlight)

If your financial professional doesn't understand that? Their advice might sound good on paper—but it won't land.

It's like giving directions using street names when you only know landmarks.

Example: A traditional advisor might say, "Cut expenses by reducing family support." But if you're Black, Latino, Caribbean, or part of an immigrant family—family support *is* non-negotiable.

You need someone who gets that.

Section 2: What Cultural Competence Looks Like in Practice

1. They Ask About Your Family Structure

Not just spouse and kids—but aunties, cousins, play cousins, church family.

2. They Understand Financial Firsts

If you're the first in your family to earn six figures, buy a home, or open a trust—it hits different. They should honor that, not rush you.

3. They Respect Non-Traditional Values

Like choosing to take care of elders instead of investing more aggressively. Or choosing to give back to your community even if it slows your financial growth.

4. They Don't Shame Your Starting Point

You should never feel dumb, behind, or embarrassed. Period.

Section 3: Red Flags to Watch Out For

1. They Talk *At* You, Not *With* You

If you feel like you're in a lecture instead of a conversation? That's a no.

2. They Make You Feel Small for How You Grew Up

If they roll their eyes when you mention "cash under the mattress" or "grandma's word was law"—they're not for you.

3. They Don't Acknowledge Racial or Cultural Barriers

If they act like redlining, wage gaps, or economic discrimination didn't happen? That's a dealbreaker.

4. They Pressure You into Plans That Don't Align with Your Reality

"Just stop giving money to your family" might sound efficient—but it's often unrealistic and culturally insensitive.

Section 4: Green Flags That You Found the Right One

1. They Ask Good Questions About *You*

Not just about your money, but your story, your people, your dreams.

2. They Take Time to Explain Concepts Clearly

And without attitude. They meet you where you are.

3. They Recognize Cultural Strengths

Like resourcefulness, community support, creativity, and generational loyalty.

4. They Encourage Wealth *and* Wellness

They see you as a whole person—not just a portfolio.

Section 5: How to Find a Culturally Competent Pro

1. Ask Your People

Talk to friends, family, church members, sorority/fraternity bros and sisters. Who do they trust?

2. Search Identity-Based Networks

- Association of African American Financial Advisors (AAAA)
- BLX Internship Program (for aspiring Black/Brown financial planners)
- National Association of Black Accountants (NABA)
- XY Planning Network (filter by race, experience, fee model)
- CFP Board's search tool (check their bio for culture cues)

3. Don't Be Afraid to Ask Directly

- "What experience do you have working with clients from my background?"
- "How do you incorporate cultural values into your planning?"
- "What assumptions do you avoid when giving advice?"

Their answers will tell you *everything*.

Section 6: Vetting Like a Boss

Use this checklist on your first call:

- Do they listen more than they talk?
- Do they explain things without jargon?
- Do they ask about your family and responsibilities?
- Do they bring up legacy, not just retirement?
- Do they seem comfortable with your cultural references?
- Do they acknowledge systemic challenges or just ignore them?

If you feel safe, seen, and respected—you're in the right room.

Section 7: Action Steps – Your Cultural Fit Filter

1. Write down 3–5 values that shape how you view money (ex: generosity, privacy, security, faith, tradition)
2. Use those values to guide your conversations

3. Interview 2–3 professionals before committing
4. Ask real-life questions:

- "How would you advise someone who supports multiple family members?"
- "What's your take on tithing or giving while still building wealth?"
- "How do you help first-gen wealth builders set boundaries?"

1. Don't ignore the vibe. Trust your gut.

Section 8: Pros and Cons of Prioritizing Cultural Fit

Pros:

- You feel understood and empowered
- Advice aligns with your real life
- You avoid shame or confusion
- Builds long-term trust and safety

Cons:

- May take longer to find the right person
- Fewer options in some areas
- You may have to travel or work remotely (Zoom is your friend)

But finding the *right* person beats settling for the *available* one.

Final Word: You Deserve a Team That Gets You

You're not asking for special treatment.

You're asking to be seen.

To be advised by someone who understands the nuance of your life, your legacy, your goals—and your grind.

Because financial planning isn't one-size-fits-all.

It's custom. It's cultural. It's personal.

You deserve professionals who know how to speak your language—and respect your hustle.

Chapter 17.2: Asking the Right Questions Without Feeling Intimidated

Let's Keep It a Stack: It's Okay to Not Know Everything

Walking into a meeting with a financial advisor, a banker, or any money expert can feel like stepping into a different world. Like pulling up to a dinner party where everybody's speaking a language you didn't grow up with. You start second-guessing yourself.

"Am I asking a dumb question?"

"Do they think I'm broke?"

"Should I already know this?"

If that's you—breathe. You're not alone. We've all been there.

This chapter is about taking your power back. About asking the questions that matter. And doing it in a way that feels good, not awkward. Because you have *every right* to understand what's happening with your money.

Let's break it down so you can walk into any financial conversation with confidence, clarity, and cool.

Section 1: Why It Feels Intimidating in the First Place

Before we talk about what to ask, let's name what's really going on.

1. You Weren't Taught This

If money talk didn't happen at your dinner table, how are you supposed to know the lingo? This stuff wasn't in the textbooks at your high school.

2. Professionals Can Seem Unapproachable

Suits. Fancy terms. A big desk. It can feel like you're being talked *at*, not *to*.

3. Fear of Judgment

Nobody wants to feel dumb. Especially when talking about something as personal as your finances.

4. Cultural and Generational Gaps

If you're first-gen wealth-building, there's no blueprint. And sometimes these meetings feel like playing chess in a game you never learned the rules for.

But here's the truth: asking smart questions doesn't make you look uneducated. It makes you look intentional.

Section 2: The Mindset Shift – You're the Client, Not the Student

Imagine going to a barber or hairstylist and being too scared to say what you want. That don't make no sense, right?

Same thing here. You're paying (or planning to pay) this person to help you. You are the client. You get to:

- Ask questions
- Get clarity
- Set boundaries
- Walk away if it doesn't feel right

You're not auditioning. You're interviewing *them*.

Section 3: The Most Important Questions to Ask

Let's get practical. Whether you're meeting with a financial advisor, CPA, insurance agent, or attorney, here are some universal questions you can keep in your back pocket.

A. Credentials and Experience

- What licenses or certifications do you hold?

- How long have you been in this field?
- What types of clients do you usually work with?

B. Services and Approach

- What exactly do you help with?
- How do you tailor advice to someone like me?
- Can you walk me through how we'd work together?

C. Fees and Compensation

- How do you get paid?
- Is it hourly, flat rate, commission-based, or percentage of my assets?
- Are there any hidden fees I should be aware of?

D. Communication and Transparency

- How often will we meet or check in?
- Can I call or email you with questions between meetings?
- What happens if I want to pause or cancel our relationship?

E. Philosophy and Culture Fit

- What's your philosophy on building wealth?
- How do you handle clients who support extended family?
- How do you incorporate culture or values into your work?

Section 4: Questions That Sound Smart But Feel Natural

You don't need to sound like a Wall Street analyst. Keep it real. Here's how you might phrase things in your own voice:

- "Can you break that down like I'm five years old?"

- "What does that actually mean for *my* money?"
- "If this was your sister or brother, what would you tell them to do?"
- "Is this something I need now, or can it wait?"
- "What are the pros and cons of doing it this way?"
- "What's the worst-case scenario here?"
- "What's the fine print I should be reading between the lines?"

Use your voice. You don't have to code-switch for clarity.

Section 5: What to Bring to the Table

You'll feel more confident if you show up prepared. Here's a checklist:

- Recent pay stubs
- Monthly expenses or a rough budget
- Any debt balances (student loans, credit cards, car note)
- Investment or retirement account statements (if you have them)
- Questions written down ahead of time (so you don't forget under pressure)

And most important: bring your truth. If you're behind on something, say so. If you don't get it, say that. Real ones will respect your honesty.

Section 6: Pros and Cons of Asking Questions

Pros:

- You gain clarity
- You avoid future mistakes
- You establish your voice early in the relationship
- You build trust with someone who respects your curiosity

Cons:

- It may slow the conversation down (but that's okay)
- Some professionals may get defensive (that's a red flag, not your problem)

Remember: If someone gets annoyed because you're asking questions, they're not the one.

Section 7: Action Steps – Your Confidence Toolkit

1. Write down your top 3 money concerns
2. Write down 5 questions you want to ask during your meeting
3. Practice saying them out loud to a friend, partner, or in the mirror
4. Role-play a mock Q&A session (yes, for real—it works)
5. After the meeting, jot down how you felt: Seen? Rushed? Understood?

Use those notes to decide if that person belongs on your team.

Section 8: How to Bounce If It's Not a Fit

You don't owe anyone your loyalty after one meeting. If it ain't hitting:

Say this: "Thank you for your time. I'm going to explore a few other options before moving forward."

That's it. Keep it smooth. Keep it respectful. Keep it moving.

Section 9: Rebuilding Confidence After a Bad Experience

Maybe you trusted someone before and got burned. Maybe a past meeting left you embarrassed or confused.

You're not broken. That experience taught you what to look for—and what to avoid.

Now? You're wiser. Now? You're equipped. Now? You walk in the room different.

Final Word: You're Not Just Smart Enough to Ask... You're Smart Enough to Decide

You don't need to speak their language. You just need to know yours is worth listening to.

So ask the questions. Pause the conversation. Take notes. Follow up.

Because this is *your* money. *Your* legacy. *Your* peace.

And you've earned the right to understand every single thing you sign.

Part VII: Flipping the Script – 30 Stereotypes About Black Wealth

Unlearning What They Told Us and Reclaiming What We Know

You ever hear something so many times you start believing it—even if it ain't true?

"Black folks don't invest."

"Black people don't trust banks."

"We're bad with money."

"Rich means you sold out."

"If you're struggling, it's your fault."

Nah. That's the script *they* wrote for us.

But this part of the book? It's about flipping that script.

Part VII: Flipping the Script – 30 Stereotypes About Black Wealth is where we call out the lies, unpack the roots of those beliefs, and rewrite each one with truth, history, and real-life strategy. From media portrayals to generational trauma, this section digs deep into the messages we've internalized about money, success, and self-worth.

Each stereotype gets:\n

- **Broken down** with cultural and historical context
- **Debunked** with facts, examples, and common sense
- **Reframed** with affirming, liberating truths

- **Connected** to action steps that help us move differently

This isn't about shame. It's about *clarity*. About looking at where the messages came from—and choosing better for ourselves and our families moving forward.

Because Black wealth is not a myth. It's not just about having money—it's about healing, ownership, legacy, power, and joy.

So in this section, we're unlearning the lies, reclaiming the truth, and showing the world what it really means to move in abundance.

Chapter 17: The Stereotypes and the Truth

Let's Set It Off Right Now: We're Not the Problem—The Narrative Is

When it comes to money and the Black community, the conversation is full of contradictions and assumptions. One minute it's, "Black folks don't save." The next minute it's, "Black folks are too flashy." You'll hear, "Y'all don't invest," and then turn on the TV and see another show mocking Black wealth as new, gaudy, or irresponsible.

It's exhausting.

But here's what we know: if the only stories being told about us are rooted in trauma, dysfunction, or stereotype—then we have to become the storytellers ourselves.

This chapter? It's not just about naming the lies. It's about shining a light on the *truth*—and doing it with confidence, context, and cultural pride.

We're going to break down 30 of the most common stereotypes about Black people and money, and then we're going to flip them with facts, history, and strategy.

So let's get into it—point by point.

1. Stereotype: "Black people don't invest."

Truth: We've *always* invested—just not always through Wall Street. From susu savings circles to buying land, we've been creative and communal in our approach. The barriers to traditional investing (lack of access, discrimination, income inequality) are real, but the desire and discipline have *always* been there.

2. Stereotype: "Black folks only care about looking rich, not being rich."

Truth: That's called survival signaling. Dressing well or driving nice isn't always about flexing—it's about dignity, protection, and representation. Let's not confuse expression with irresponsibility.

3. Stereotype: "Black families don't talk about money."

Truth: We talk about it—we just don't always have the right language, tools, or safety to talk about it openly. But we *are* talking more now. And this book is proof.

4. Stereotype: "Black men waste money on sneakers and rims."

Truth: First of all, stop policing joy. Second, economic data shows that Black men spend more on experiences and self-care proportionally because society offers fewer rewards elsewhere. And those same men are also opening businesses, buying homes, and investing in crypto and real estate.

5. Stereotype: "Black women are shopaholics."

Truth: Black women are the fastest-growing group of entrepreneurs in America. Period. They're paying off debt, raising families, supporting communities, and holding it all together—with or without a partner.

- Media representation is lazy and rooted in anti-Blackness.
- Systemic oppression gets repackaged as "personal choices."
- Financial gatekeeping means our wins get ignored and our struggles get amplified.

But when you control the lens, you control the legacy.

Section: How to Flip the Script in Real Life

Action Steps:

1. Learn our real history—beyond the trauma, into the triumphs.
2. Challenge the assumptions when you hear them—from others *and* from yourself.
3. Normalize financial conversations in your circle.
4. Share stories of Black financial success—not just the celebrity ones, but the everyday ones.
5. Teach the youth early so they start with the truth, not the lie.

Section: Pros and Cons of Debunking These Lies

Pros:

- Frees us from shame and self-blame
- Builds community pride
- Gives us a more accurate starting point

Cons:

- You may face pushback from folks still trapped in the lie
- It takes time and consistency to change narratives

But liberation always takes time.

Final Word: Your Story Is Bigger Than a Stereotype

They said we don't invest. We are. They said we don't save. We do. They said we don't build legacy. We've been doing that—in church halls, in hair salons, at family reunions, on side hustles, with soul food and second chances.

This chapter is the mirror, the microphone, and the machete. We're seeing ourselves clearly. We're speaking the truth loudly. And we're cutting down every lie that's tried to box us in.

The truth is—we're more than the headlines.

We are the builders. The dreamers. The planners. The providers. The protectors.

And we're just getting started.

18.1: "Black People Don't Invest"

Let's stop repeating that lie.

"Black people don't invest" isn't just false—it's insulting.

Because it ignores our history. It ignores our hustle. It ignores the fact that we've *been* investing—in ways that aren't always counted, tracked, or given the respect they deserve. But we know. And now, we're saying it loud: We do invest. We always have.

Where the Myth Came From

This myth wasn't born in truth—it was born in erasure.

It came from a country that made our people the investment instead of the investor. From a financial system that was built on our backs, but never meant to serve our interests.

During slavery, we weren't allowed to own property, save money, or build assets. We were *property*.

After emancipation, we opened savings accounts in the Freedman's

Bank—only to have that bank collapse and steal the hard-earned money of thousands of newly freed Black families.

We tried again. We built thriving Black communities—Tulsa, Rosewood, and more. Places with businesses, land ownership, and banks.

And they were burned down. Literally.

So when people say, "Black folks don't invest," what they really mean is: "We never counted the ways you've invested."

They didn't count the aunties who sent kids to college on a postal worker's salary.

They didn't count the uncle who bought a rental property and passed it down.

They didn't count the family who put every spare dollar into the offering plate because they believed in community.

That's investing too.

How We've Always Invested

Let's redefine investment.

Investment is more than stocks and real estate. It's time, effort, and money poured into something with the hope that it grows.

We've invested in:

- **Education:** Black families will do whatever it takes to send their kids to school. We believe in learning as a way out and a way up.
- **Entrepreneurship:** From side hustles to storefronts, we've been business-minded. Even when loans weren't an option, we still launched something.
- **Community:** We tithe. We give. We build. We help each other even when we barely have enough. That's investing in each other's futures.
- **Culture:** Art, music, food, faith—we've built and maintained cultural capital that's shaped the entire world.

We've been investing all along. Just not always in ways that Wall Street sees.

What's Changing Now

We're not just investing with faith—we're learning how to invest with strategy.

We're in the market now.

More Black people are buying stocks, owning crypto, investing in real estate, and starting businesses. We're using apps. We're watching financial creators. We're attending workshops. We're building portfolios.

We're learning the language of money and teaching it to our kids.

We're saying, "I own this," and meaning it.

What used to feel out of reach now feels like a lane we belong in.

And the truth is—we always belonged here. The doors were just locked. And we picked up the tools and built our own.

Why the Stereotype Still Lingers

So if we're investing, why does this stereotype keep following us?

Because there's a difference between perception and reality.

We don't always talk about our investments.

Sometimes we're the only Black person in the room.

Sometimes we're learning in silence because we don't want to admit we're new to the game.

And sometimes, the system still doesn't want to see us win—so it tells the world we're not even playing.

But that's starting to shift. Because we're becoming louder. Sharper. More confident.

And the more of us that step into this space, the more undeniable our presence becomes.

Moving Forward

Investing doesn't mean you have to have six figures in the bank.

It means believing your money can work for you, even when you're sleeping.

It means planting seeds—no matter how small.

Here's how to start if you're just getting into the investment space:

- **Start with what you know.** You don't have to become a stock market genius overnight. Start with companies you use and believe in.
- **Use the tools.** Apps like Robinhood, Fidelity, and Public make investing accessible. You can buy partial shares for less than you spend on fast food.
- **Learn from people who look like you.** There are Black creators, podcasts, and educators breaking it down with love and clarity.
- **Talk about it.** Share what you're learning with your family. Make investing part of your everyday conversation.
- **Be consistent.** Investing isn't about getting rich quick. It's about building wealth slowly, steadily, and smartly.

Final Word

The truth is—we've always known how to stretch a dollar.

Now, we're learning how to grow it.

Don't let anyone tell you that Black people don't invest. We do.

We invest in our children, our communities, our culture, and now—our capital.

We're not catching up. We're catching fire.

18.2: "We Don't Talk About Money at Home"

Let's talk about something real. Something quiet. Something that sat at our dinner tables without ever being said out loud: money.

See, in many Black households, money wasn't a topic—it was a temperature. You felt it before you ever understood it. You saw it in the way your parents moved, in what they said—or didn't say—when a bill came in the mail, when the lights flickered, or when payday was just a little too far away.

We didn't talk about money because talking about money meant facing pain. Facing lack. Facing the pressure to do more with less.

It wasn't about not caring. It was about not knowing how. Or not feeling safe to say, "We're struggling." Or "This is how you open a bank account." Or "Let me show you what I learned the hard way."

Silence was survival. But silence also became tradition.

And tradition, when left unchecked, becomes a trap.

Many of us grew up in homes where questions like, "How much do you make?" or "What's a mortgage?" were off-limits. Where shame filled the space where strategy should've been. Where love was abundant—but financial literacy was scarce.

And that's not an indictment of our elders. That's a reflection of their reality.

They did what they could with what they had. They stretched paychecks, they kept food on the table, they gave us joy in spite of chaos. But they weren't given the tools to pass down. So they gave us what they could.

Now it's our turn to break that cycle.

To start talking about money—not in whispers, but in wisdom. Not just about what we don't have, but what we're building. Not just about bills, but about budgets, assets, equity, freedom.

Because when we normalize these conversations at home, we start changing the narrative.

The stereotype says we don't talk about money at home. But the truth is—we're starting to. At the kitchen table. In group chats. On podcasts. In barbershops and salons.

We're pulling the curtain back and letting our kids see us plan, not just provide. Letting our partners into the process. Learning together.

And the more we talk, the more we teach.

Let's keep that energy. Let's build new traditions rooted in transparency, trust, and truth.

Money talk isn't taboo. It's the beginning of transformation.

Let's rise.

18.3: "We Live Paycheck to Paycheck by Choice"

Here's the thing—they love to act like we're just bad at money. Like we're reckless, impulsive, lazy. Like living paycheck to paycheck is a lifestyle we woke up and chose.

But let's keep it all the way real—nobody chooses struggle.

Living check to check isn't about poor planning. It's about being underpaid, overburdened, and shut out of wealth-building systems for generations. It's about jobs that don't pay enough. Rent that's too high. Health care that drains your savings. Grocery bills that climb while your income stays flat.

It's about being the first in your family to make "real" money—and being the first they call when someone needs help. It's about stretching a dollar until it breaks, then blaming yourself for not being able to save it.

It's survival math.

And survival math doesn't leave much room for stock portfolios.

The stereotype says we're living check to check because we're irresponsible.

But the truth is—we've been navigating a rigged game with genius and grit. We've made miracles out of minimum wage. We've fed families on fumes. We've turned side hustles into stopgaps, and made it work when nothing else did.

Still, that shouldn't be our forever.

Now, we're moving from survival to strategy. We're budgeting with purpose. Creating side streams that lead to long-term gain. Saying no to the guilt that comes with saying no to everybody else.

We didn't choose the paycheck-to-paycheck life. But we can choose to write a new script.

With better tools. Better knowledge. And better boundaries.

18.4: "We Always Spend Before We Save"

This one hits a nerve.

Because it's not just something people say *about* us—it's something some of us say about ourselves. Jokingly. Shamefully. Casually. Like it's just a personality trait.

"Black folks always spend before we save."

Let's be honest—this narrative didn't pop up out of nowhere. There's a reason why it circulates in our communities, and why it gets weaponized outside of it.

But let's not get it twisted.

This isn't about being bad with money. It's about being *human* in a system that's made saving nearly impossible, while selling us a lifestyle that says if you don't have it, you're failing.

This stereotype is lazy. It blames behavior without exploring *why* that behavior exists.

So let's break it down.

It's Not That We Don't Want to Save

Nobody wakes up and says, "Let me blow my check and end up stressed about rent."

Most of us *want* to save. We know the value of a rainy-day fund. We've heard the messages—"Pay yourself first." "Stack for a storm." "Get your money right."

The *desire* is there.

But the reality?

Sometimes you're trying to save while still climbing out of past-due bills, student loans, back rent, family obligations, and inflation that makes a grocery run feel like a luxury.

Sometimes you're the first in your family to have a consistent income, and now you're helping everybody eat.

Sometimes that little bit of spending is the *only* thing that makes you feel human in a world that tries to grind you down daily.

So no—it's not just reckless spending.

It's stress spending. Survival spending. Seeking-joy spending.

And when you've gone generations without "extra," the idea of saving can feel like a dream—not a discipline.

What We're Really Dealing With

Let's name what's really at play here.

Scarcity mindset.

When you've lived with "not enough" for most of your life, you tend to grab what you can while you can. That might look like splurging today because you're unsure what tomorrow holds.

Lack of modeling.

If your parents didn't talk about savings accounts, compound interest, or emergency funds, you're starting from scratch. And that takes time.

Emotional spending.

We use spending to cope. To reward ourselves. To show love. To keep up. That doesn't mean we're shallow—it means we haven't been taught how to deal with those emotions any other way.

Paycheck pressure.

If your check is already short, and it's already spoken for before it hits your account, where is the savings *supposed* to come from?

This isn't about financial failure. It's about financial fatigue.

Let's Flip the Narrative

We're not doomed to this cycle. We're waking up from it.

We're learning that saving isn't about denying yourself—it's about buying your freedom.

We're realizing that saving doesn't require thousands—it starts with intention.

We're replacing "I can't afford to save" with "How can I make this work?"

We're leaning into tools, apps, systems, and accountability.

We're breaking the cycle—not because we're perfect, but because we're tired of being broke in spirit *and* in pocket.

Pros and Cons of Saving First

Pros:

- It reduces anxiety. Knowing you've got something set aside gives you peace of mind.
- It builds habits. The discipline to save transfers to other parts of life.
- It helps you say no to things that aren't aligned with your goals.
- It shifts your identity—from spender to planner.

Cons:

- It takes effort, especially if you're behind on bills or debt.
- It can feel slow, especially if you're only saving small amounts.
- It can create tension if people around you expect financial support.

But here's the truth—every dollar you save is a dollar that *works* for you later.

That's the kind of flex that doesn't need to be loud. Just consistent.

Action Steps to Start Saving Before Spending

Make it automatic.

Set up auto-transfers, even if it's small. Treat saving like a bill. Pay yourself like you pay Netflix.

Name your savings.

Don't just "save." Create categories—Emergency. Rent buffer. Travel. Business startup. When your savings has a *purpose,* it's easier to protect it.

Build small wins.

Save $5 a week. Then $10. Celebrate the habit—not just the amount.

Find your leak.

Look at where your money "disappears" every month. It's usually in food, subscriptions, convenience. Plug those leaks and redirect the drip.

Stack in silence.

You don't need to tell everybody you're saving. Move quiet. Let the balance speak for itself later.

Don't shame your past.

So what if you used to spend first? You're not who you were. Forward motion only.

Final Word

We don't always spend before we save. That's a narrative that kept us stuck.

But now? We're flipping it.

We're saving so we can spend with power.

We're making decisions with the future in mind—not just the feeling in the moment.

We're building—not just buying.

We're creating space between our money and our emotions. Between our desires and our discipline.

And in doing that, we're proving something bigger:

We're not just surviving. We're shifting.

18.5: "We Don't Know How to Budget"

Let's get one thing clear—we know how to budget. We've *always* known how to budget.

You can't make it through Black life in America without knowing how to stretch. How to make something out of nothing. How to make a dollar holler.

The problem isn't that we don't know how to budget. The problem is that we've been forced to budget in survival mode for so long, we haven't always had the room or tools to build one that works for *freedom*.

This stereotype—"Black folks don't know how to budget"—isn't about our skills. It's about a system that makes our money feel like it's always running out, no matter how smart we move.

Let's talk about it.

The Real Budgeting We Grew Up Watching

Some of us didn't grow up with spreadsheets or finance apps.

But we *did* grow up watching moms, aunties, and grandparents do miracle math in their heads. They knew which bill could wait, what day that check was coming, and how to flip the food stamps to stretch through the month.

We saw rent paid late so the lights could stay on. We saw the envelope of cash under the mattress for "just in case." We saw payday plans laid out with surgical precision.

That was budgeting.

It wasn't always pretty. It wasn't always enough. But it was real. It was reactive. And it was necessary.

Now, we've got the chance to take that wisdom and evolve it—out of survival and into strategy.

Why Budgeting Has Felt So Hard

It's not about discipline. It's about trauma.

If your money experience has always been tied to stress, shame, and scarcity, then budgeting doesn't feel like a plan—it feels like punishment.

It feels like restriction. Like being told what you *can't* do with your own money. Like constantly saying no to yourself, over and over again.

So a lot of us avoid it. Not because we're irresponsible. But because we're exhausted.

We don't need more judgment. We need more grace.

And we need new language around budgeting—language that honors where we've been, but also empowers where we're going.

Budgeting Isn't a Trap—It's a Tool

Let's flip the mindset.

Budgeting isn't about saying "no" to everything.

It's about saying "yes" *on purpose.*

It's not about being broke with a chart. It's about creating a vision for your money—and making sure every dollar supports that vision.

Budgeting is planning for joy. For peace. For that vacation. For that business idea. For that moment when you finally breathe easy.

A good budget isn't a cage—it's a passport.

Budgeting Our Way

We don't all need to use the same method. Budgeting can look different for different folks, as long as it fits your lifestyle and helps you stay consistent.

Some options:

- **Zero-based budgeting:** Every dollar has a job—nothing is left "unassigned."
- **Percentage-based budgeting:** Allocate percentages to needs, wants,

saving, giving, etc.

- **Envelope or cash method:** Use physical cash for spending categories you tend to overspend in.
- **Digital tracking:** Use apps or spreadsheets to monitor your flow.

Whatever system you choose, the goal is to know where your money is going—and to make it reflect your values.

The "We Don't Know" Myth Is Lazy

This stereotype paints us like we're reckless.

Like we don't *want* to manage our money.

Like we just wake up and blow the bag on purpose.

But that's not real life.

We're budgeting right now.

We're paying rent, sending money to family, keeping up with student loans, making our kids look fresh for school—all while still showing up to work with our heads held high.

That's skill. That's sacrifice. That's strength.

Now it's time to pair that strength with strategy.

Action Steps to Start Budgeting Without Shame

Start with what you actually spend.

Don't guess. Pull those bank statements. Look at the truth. It might sting—but it's step one.

Pick a method that fits.

Don't force what doesn't flow. Try a method for 30 days and adjust as needed.

Include joy in your budget.

You're not a robot. Budget for your mental health. For your fun. For your rest.

Make it visual.

Write it down. Use a whiteboard. Use an app. Seeing it helps you *own* it.

Give yourself grace.

You'll mess up sometimes. That's part of it. Keep going.

Make it a family thing.

Bring your partner or your kids into the conversation. Normalize money talk.

Pros and Cons of Budgeting

Pros:

- You feel more in control of your life
- You stop wondering "where all my money went"
- You can plan for short-term goals and long-term dreams
- You can make informed decisions, not emotional ones

Cons:

- Takes effort and time up front
- Requires facing some uncomfortable truths
- Can feel discouraging when money is tight
- May be hard to stick with if you're doing it alone

But here's the truth: budgeting is one of the most powerful tools we have to reclaim our time, our choices, and our futures.

It's not about how much you make—it's about how much you *move with intention.*

Final Word

The idea that we don't know how to budget is outdated, played out, and false.

We've been budgeting since before we knew what to call it.

Now we're doing it on our terms. With our tools. For our freedom.
We're not just counting coins—we're crafting blueprints.
We're building lives that make room for both responsibility and rest.
Let them keep talking.
We'll keep budgeting—and building.

18.6: "We Only Care About Material Things"

Let's go ahead and drag this tired lie out into the open.

"They don't care about wealth, just Jordans and jewelry. Just flash. Just stuff."

You've heard it. Probably more than once.

Maybe you've even said it, jokingly, about your own people.

But let's slow that down.

This isn't about Black folks loving nice things—that's universal. This is about how our love of style, status, and self-expression gets pathologized. When other communities show off wealth, they're called successful. When we do it, we're called superficial.

So let's get into it.

We don't only care about material things. But yes—we've used material things as a language, a form of protest, and a way to reclaim dignity in a system designed to deny us value.

And there's history behind that.

Why We Show Our Worth

Let's look back at the roots.

When you grow up in a world that tells you you're less than, you start finding ways to *show* that you matter. To yourself. To the world. To your peers.

In our culture, clothing, sneakers, chains, hair, cars—these aren't just things. They're symbols. They're armor. They're identity.

When your ancestors were stripped of names, land, rights, and freedom, being able to say, "I look good today," is more than vanity—it's resistance.

When you've been told your skin, your hair, your culture isn't enough, sometimes the flyest fit feels like power.

This isn't about being shallow. It's about surviving with style in a world that never expected you to shine.

Let's Talk About What We Really Value

We value family.

We value community.

We value faith, education, music, resilience, entrepreneurship, and joy.

We value Black excellence, not just Black designer labels.

We value the hustle because we've *had* to hustle.

And yes, some of us use things to tell the story of that journey. But that doesn't mean we *only* care about things.

We care about legacy. About impact. About breaking generational cycles. That's why more of us are investing, buying homes, getting insurance, and starting businesses.

It just doesn't always make the highlight reel.

The Media Loves to Zoom In On Our Spending

Why is it that when a Black athlete buys a luxury car, it's reckless—but when a white CEO buys a yacht, it's aspirational?

Why is it that when we wear name brands, we're accused of being broke—but when others do it, they're "living the dream"?

Because they want to judge how we express wealth without ever examining why we had to express it that way in the first place.

We weren't raised around family trusts and wealth managers.

We were raised around payday loans, layaway plans, and the thrill of buying something *new* for once.

When you've gone without for so long, the feeling of finally having—of being able to buy what you want, when you want—is emotional.

That doesn't make us wasteful. That makes us human.

Are There Pitfalls to Watch Out For? Absolutely.

Let's keep it a hundred.

There *are* traps in chasing material validation:

- You can go broke trying to look rich.
- You can mask financial insecurity with "drip."
- You can spend out of pressure, not passion.
- You can confuse looking successful with *being* successful.

But those aren't uniquely Black issues. That's capitalism. That's social media. That's generational pressure dressed up as ambition.

The real flex isn't just buying stuff. It's knowing you have *options.*

Freedom. Liquidity. Assets. Peace of mind.

That's what we're after now.

Pros and Cons of Material Spending

Pros:

- Boosts confidence, especially when rooted in self-expression
- Reflects joy, creativity, and individuality
- Can be a motivator or milestone ("I bought this because I earned it!")
- Cultural connection and shared pride

Cons:

- Can distract from long-term goals if unbalanced
- Can be fueled by trauma or insecurity
- May create pressure to keep up with unrealistic standards

- If financed, can lead to debt traps or unstable cash flow

There's nothing wrong with loving nice things. But there *is* something wrong with letting them define you—or derail you.

Balance is the key. And balance comes with budgeting, self-awareness, and goals that go deeper than the surface.

Action Steps to Rethink Our Relationship With "Stuff"

Redefine the reward.

Instead of buying a $400 bag just to flex, ask: what else could this money do for me? Could it fund a side hustle? Cover an extra debt payment? Start an investment?

Create a joy budget.

Set aside money *on purpose* to enjoy the things you love. No shame. Just structure.

Be real about your "why."

Are you buying this for you—or for the 'Gram? Would it still matter if nobody saw it?

Replace the rush.

The dopamine hit from shopping fades fast. Find other ways to feel fulfilled—rest, relationships, purpose.

Talk about it.

Have real conversations in your family and friend circles about how we spend, why we spend, and what it's costing us or earning us.

Build both.

It's not either-or. You can build wealth *and* enjoy your life. You just have to be intentional about when and how.

Final Word

The idea that Black people only care about material things is not just false—it's lazy.

It ignores our depth.

It ignores our love for self-expression.

It ignores the systems that told us we were nothing—and our decision to *look like something* anyway.

But now? We're shifting.

We're not just dressing the part. We're owning the part.

We're not just shining on the outside. We're building wealth on the inside.

The gold chain is cool. But the trust fund hits different.

The fresh kicks are dope. But the paid-off mortgage? That's legacy.

We don't just care about things.

We care about freedom.

We care about progress.

We care about making sure the next generation doesn't have to choose between "looking rich" and *actually* being free.

18.7: "We're Financially Irresponsible"

Let's take this one head-on.

"They're just irresponsible with money."

That phrase has been weaponized against Black folks for generations. Said by systems, supervisors, schools, politicians, and sometimes even whispered within our own communities.

But here's the thing—they confuse *struggle* with *irresponsibility.*

They confuse *doing the best you can with what little you have* with making poor decisions.

They see the outcome—but they don't understand the context.

So let's set the record straight.

We're not financially irresponsible. We've just been navigating one of the most financially hostile environments in modern history—and we're still standing.

What They Don't See

They don't see that you were paying off someone else's student loan while trying to cover your own.

They don't see that your credit score took a hit because you co-signed for your cousin's car—and they disappeared with it.

They don't see that when you got your first "real" job, you were the bank, the babysitter, the bail fund, and the backup plan for half your family.

They don't see that your late payment wasn't neglect—it was prioritizing rent over a hospital bill, food over a minimum credit card charge.

What they call irresponsible, we call impossible math.

What they call bad decisions, we call hard choices with no good options.

We've been financially overextended, not financially ignorant.

There's a difference.

The Generational Weight We Carry

Being the first generation with access to income, credit, or higher education doesn't come with a guidebook.

We were told to go to college—then saddled with debt and zero financial coaching.

We were told to get a job with benefits—but not taught how to manage the benefits once we had them.

We were encouraged to "get that bag"—but not shown how to protect, grow, or multiply it.

And while other families were transferring wealth and wisdom, many of us were starting from zero. Or from behind.

So yeah, we made mistakes. But don't confuse lack of instruction with lack of intelligence.

We weren't irresponsible. We were *uninformed and over-pressured.*

Now we're learning. And now that we know better, we're moving better.

The Cost of That Label

Calling us financially irresponsible does more than just misrepresent us—it causes real harm.

It makes lenders more likely to deny us.

It gives employers and landlords a reason to judge our credit.

It makes us second-guess ourselves. Feel ashamed. Stay silent. Stop asking questions.

It makes us believe we're the problem—when we're actually the solution.

That label is heavy. And it's time we put it down.

The Truth About Our Financial Growth

Look around.

We're starting investment clubs.

We're buying land and property.

We're budgeting with apps and using tools our parents never had access to.

We're talking about money out loud, sharing resources, raising our kids with more knowledge than we got.

We're still helping family, still giving back, *and* still managing to save, build, and rise.

That's not irresponsibility. That's resilience.

Pros and Cons of Owning Our Financial Journey

Pros:

- Reclaims power over our money story
- Breaks cycles and re-educates our households
- Builds community through transparency

- Helps others grow through shared experience

Cons:

- Requires unlearning deep-rooted habits
- Can bring guilt from past mistakes
- May be met with skepticism from others used to the "old" version of us
- Takes time, patience, and consistency

But growth doesn't require perfection. Just progress.

And every decision to pause, learn, or rework your plan is a responsible one.

Action Steps to Move With Confidence

Track, don't judge.

Look at your spending—not to shame yourself, but to see your patterns clearly.

Set up systems, not just goals.

Use automatic savings, payment reminders, and weekly check-ins to keep you accountable.

Learn one thing at a time.

Don't try to master everything at once. Pick a topic—budgeting, investing, insurance—and build from there.

Talk to someone you trust.

Financial literacy is a team sport. Don't go it alone. Talk to a friend, mentor, or advisor who respects where you've been and supports where you're going.

Forgive your financial past.

You are not your overdraft fee. You are not your credit score. You are not your student loan balance. You are the person *learning* and *leading* forward.

Final Word

Let them say what they want.

But we know the truth.

We're not financially irresponsible—we're financially reborn.

We've been hustling through systems that were never designed for us to win.

And still, we're winning.

We're reclaiming our narrative.

We're building our literacy.

We're investing in ourselves, our families, and our futures.

We're not reckless—we're resourceful.

We're not wasteful—we're wise.

And most of all?

We're ready.

18.8: "We Can't Handle Credit"

This one hits hard because it's personal.

"They can't handle credit."

You know the vibe. The side-eye when you apply for a loan. The weird look when you ask about a better interest rate. The assumption that if you have a credit card, it's already maxed out.

This isn't just about money—it's about trust. Or more accurately, the *lack* of trust the system has in us—and the lack of tools we were given to trust ourselves with credit in the first place.

Let's talk about how this myth got started, how it's been used against us, and how we're taking the narrative back.

Because we *can* handle credit—we've just been handling it in a minefield.

The History Behind the Mistrust

Credit wasn't designed for us. That's not opinion—that's fact.

In the early years of credit scoring and loan approvals, Black folks were denied even when we met the qualifications.

We were "redlined" out of neighborhoods, given higher interest rates, and steered into predatory loans that were designed to fail.

So we learned two things early:

1. Credit was risky.
2. The game was rigged.

Some of us avoided it completely. Others were forced to rely on it because our cash didn't stretch far enough.

And when you're using credit just to survive—buy groceries, fix a car, keep the lights on—you don't get to use it strategically.

That's not mishandling credit. That's *credit trying to handle us.*

What We Didn't Learn—But Should've

Most of us didn't learn how credit works at home or in school.

We weren't taught:

- How your credit score is calculated
- The difference between interest rates and APR
- How paying the minimum keeps you in debt
- How utilization and on-time payments matter more than balance size
- That your credit report has errors you can dispute

It's not that we couldn't handle credit—it's that no one showed us how to *work it like a system.*

They told us credit was dangerous, and in some ways it was. But the real danger was not having the full picture.

Now we're learning. And learning is the first step to power.

Credit Isn't Bad—It's a Tool

Let's reframe.

Credit isn't a trap. It's a tool.

It's not evil—it's emotional.

It's not about flexing—it's about leveraging.

Good credit gives you options. It opens doors. It can help you buy a home, start a business, finance education, or survive an emergency without wiping out your savings.

But only if you treat it like a relationship—not a lifeline.

And relationships take understanding, respect, boundaries, and maintenance.

Real Talk: We've Been Improving

Let's give ourselves some credit—literally.

More Black millennials and Gen Z are checking their scores, disputing errors, opening secured credit cards, and using credit-building apps.

We're out here refinancing, consolidating, and raising scores like it's a sport.

We're helping each other. Sharing tips. Rewriting family patterns.

We're not perfect. But we're aware. And aware people *don't stay stuck.*

Pros and Cons of Engaging With Credit

Pros:

- Gives you access to big moves (home, business, education)
- Saves money on interest with better scores
- Shows lenders you're responsible and reliable
- Opens doors for partnerships, rentals, and more

Cons:

- Can lead to debt if unmanaged
- Easy to overuse if you're not tracking
- Missed payments can haunt you for years
- Emotionally triggering if tied to past trauma

The key isn't avoidance—it's education.

And we're finally getting that education for ourselves and passing it down.

Action Steps to Handle Credit Like a Pro

Check your credit reports.

Go to annualcreditreport.com and pull your reports. Look for errors. Know what's on there.

Use secured credit cards if you're rebuilding.

They report to credit bureaus and help you build positive history.

Pay on time—always.

Set reminders. Automate. Even the minimum counts toward your score.

Keep balances low.

Try not to use more than 30% of your limit on any card.

Don't close old accounts.

Longer credit history = better score. Keep old cards open with small purchases and regular payments.

Ask questions.

Credit shouldn't be mysterious. Ask a professional, mentor, or friend. No shame in learning late—it's worse to stay in the dark.

Final Word

Saying we can't handle credit is a weak excuse for not giving us the tools to thrive.

We've handled worse.

We've handled being counted out.

We've handled whole systems designed to break us.

So best believe—we can handle a credit card.

We just needed the manual.

And now that we have it?

We're building scores, buying homes, opening LLCs, and teaching our kids what a FICO score is *before* they graduate.

We're not credit risks.

We're credit ready.

18.9: "We Don't Plan for Retirement"

Let's go ahead and kill this one now.

"They don't plan for retirement."

Nah. What we *didn't* plan for was being the first generation to even *have* the chance to retire.

Our grandparents didn't retire. They worked 'til their hands gave out, their backs gave out, or their jobs pushed them out.

Our parents maybe had pensions if they got in early enough—teachers, postal workers, military, factory jobs. But even then, a lot of them were still working part-time in their 60s and 70s, not because they wanted to—but because they *had* to.

Retirement? That wasn't something we saw modeled. It was something we were told to "hope for." Something we might get if we were lucky, or faithful, or if Social Security held out.

But let's be real: planning for retirement requires more than prayer. It requires information, access, and vision.

And now that we're getting that? We're making moves.

Why We Weren't Planning for It Before

Planning for retirement doesn't happen in a vacuum. It happens in context.

And for a lot of us, the context was:

- Living check to check
- Carrying student loan debt
- Supporting family members
- Being the first in the household to earn a stable income
- Watching older relatives *never* retire

When you're just trying to survive the *month,* it's hard to think about 40 years from now.

Retirement planning sounds like a luxury when your rent is due, your kid needs braces, and your mama just called you for help with her bills.

So no, we weren't ignoring retirement. We were *prioritizing survival.*

But now, we're starting to shift.

We're starting to build margin. Starting to dream about life beyond the grind. And that shift is powerful.

The Retirement Game Wasn't Built For Us—But We're In It Now

Let's not forget: Black folks weren't included in most wealth-building policies of the 20th century.

The GI Bill, redlined housing programs, early 401(k) rollouts—all those systems skipped over us or gave us the worst version of the deal.

But the game has changed.

Now, with access to online education, financial tools, and employer-sponsored retirement plans, we're catching up fast.

We're opening Roth IRAs.

We're maxing out 401(k)s when we can.

We're asking questions.

We're learning how compound interest works.

We're not just working for the check—we're working for *choice* later in life.

That's retirement planning.

What Retirement Looks Like for Us

Let's be clear: retirement doesn't mean sitting on a beach for 30 years sipping something cold (although, let's be honest, that *does* sound nice).

For a lot of us, retirement looks like:

- Not having to *depend* on your kids
- Being able to take care of aging parents without going broke
- Traveling when you want to, not just when you can afford to
- Choosing to work—not being forced to
- Living out the dreams you've delayed for decades
- Giving back, mentoring, starting something new

It's not about quitting life. It's about living it *on your terms.*

That's what we're planning for now.

Pros and Cons of Retirement Planning

Pros:

- Peace of mind knowing you won't have to scramble at 65
- Ability to make decisions based on passion, not paycheck
- Builds generational modeling—your kids *see* the plan
- Allows you to walk away from unhealthy jobs without fear

Cons:

- Takes time to understand retirement options and tools
- Feels overwhelming if you're starting late
- Requires sacrifice now for reward later
- Can feel lonely if no one else in your circle is thinking long-term

But just because you didn't start early doesn't mean you're too late.

Today is the best day to start.

And every dollar you put toward retirement is a dollar buying your future freedom.

Action Steps to Start Your Retirement Plan (Even if You Feel Behind)

Open an account.

If you have a job with a 401(k), *use it*—especially if there's a match. If you're self-employed or don't have a plan at work, open a Roth IRA or traditional IRA. Just get started.

Automate it.

Set up an automatic deposit, even if it's small. Don't wait until you "have more." Start with what you can.

Educate yourself.

Look up videos or books on compound interest. Learn about the difference between pre-tax and post-tax retirement accounts.

Talk to someone.

A good financial advisor or planner can walk you through a plan based on your goals, timeline, and income.

Include retirement in your budget.

Treat it like a bill. Because it *is*—you're paying your future self.

Ignore the noise.

You don't need to invest like your coworker or your cousin. Move at *your* pace, with *your* plan.

Final Word

The myth says we don't plan for retirement.

But the truth?

We're just the first ones in our families with the tools, time, and tenacity to do it differently.

We're not waiting on the system to save us.

We're not hoping we'll "figure it out later."

We're building futures with intention.

We're showing up at HR offices asking about match contributions.

We're helping each other open Roth accounts.

We're dreaming in decades, not just pay periods.

We don't just retire from jobs.

We retire into freedom.

18.10: "We Don't Own Anything"

They love to say it.

"Black folks don't own anything."

They say it on the news. They say it in boardrooms. They say it in banking reports and real estate articles.

But what they really mean is: "We've made it almost impossible for y'all to own—and now we're gonna blame you for it."

Let's be real.

We don't lack the mindset to own. We've lacked the *access*. We've lacked the resources. We've lacked the inherited wealth, the forgiving lending terms, the inside info, the family co-signers, the trust funds.

But we've never lacked the *desire*.

This myth—this tired lie—isn't about our inability to build wealth. It's about the barriers that were deliberately placed in our way for centuries. And how, despite those barriers, we still find ways to own, build, and rise.

We Used to Own More—Until They Took It

Let's start there.

We *did* own things. Land. Businesses. Entire neighborhoods.

From Black Wall Street in Tulsa to Rosewood, to Seneca Village in New York—Black folks were building thriving communities. Ownership was happening.

And what happened?

Violence. Fires. Destruction. Government takings. Legal loopholes. Eminent domain. Highway construction. Backdoor deals.

They didn't just burn homes—they burned *wealth*.

Then came decades of redlining, loan denials, shady appraisals, and systemic undervaluing of Black assets.

So if we don't own at the same rate now—it's not because we didn't try.

It's because ownership, for us, came with obstacles that others never had to clear.

What Ownership Really Means

Let's break this down.

Ownership isn't just about houses or property.

It's about power. Control. Stability. Freedom.

It means you're not at the mercy of rising rent or a sudden eviction notice.

It means your kids have something to inherit other than debt and stress.

It means your voice carries more weight when your name is on the deed, the LLC, the lease, or the asset.

And it's not just about what you own—it's about *owning yourself* too.

Your time. Your choices. Your direction.

That's what we're chasing when we talk about ownership.

Not just things. But *authority over our lives.*

We Are Owning More Than Ever

The numbers don't lie.

More Black people are buying homes, starting businesses, investing in the stock market, and creating digital assets than ever before.

We're creating group economics through investment clubs.

We're building ownership digitally—through content, IP, brands, and tech.

We're claiming land in rural areas, developing real estate in cities, and funding projects together on our own terms.

Is it where we want it to be yet? No.

But we're not just consumers anymore—we're producers, founders, and buyers.

Ownership is in our future because it's already in our *movement.*

Why the Stereotype Hurts

This myth isn't just disrespectful—it's dangerous.

It convinces our youth that ownership is too far out of reach.

It tells us we should just be renters, borrowers, laborers—*never* landlords, lenders, or leaders.

It plays on our trauma. It shames us for past losses. It convinces us that we're behind, so we might as well stop trying.

That's psychological warfare.

And the antidote? Knowledge, exposure, action, and *community.*

Because ownership is possible. But it starts with mindset and a map.

Pros and Cons of Pursuing Ownership

Pros:

- Builds generational wealth
- Creates long-term stability and power

- Increases your financial confidence and literacy
- Gives you more options and freedom

Cons:

- Requires capital and credit (which have been historically harder to access)
- May come with unexpected costs and responsibilities
- Takes time—ownership is a marathon, not a sprint
- Can be isolating if no one in your circle is doing it too

But the pros? They build legacy. And that's what we're here for.

Action Steps to Step Into Ownership

Start where you are.

You don't have to buy a house tomorrow. Start by understanding what's possible. Read. Watch videos. Ask questions.

Repair your credit.

A better credit score = better loan terms = less money wasted.

Buy what makes sense.

Don't chase a big house to impress. Buy land, a duplex, a starter home—whatever fits your life and your goals.

Own your business.

Whether it's a side hustle or full-time grind, get your LLC. Separate your finances. Protect your brand. Build equity.

Invest in stocks or REITs.

Ownership doesn't always mean physical property. You can own part of Apple, Nike, or real estate through fractional investing.

Pass it down.

Create wills. Set up trusts. Talk to your kids. Ownership isn't real if it dies with you.

Final Word

The myth says we don't own anything.

But look around.

We're reclaiming land. Rebuilding businesses. Restarting conversations.

We're creating trust funds where there used to be trauma.

We're putting names on deeds that were once left off on purpose.

We're teaching our kids that ownership isn't for *other people*—it's for *us*, too.

We may not have been handed much.

But what we build from here? That's ours.

18.11: "We're Afraid of Banks"

Let's talk about trust. Or more specifically—the lack of it.

"They don't like using banks. Don't trust the system. Don't want to open accounts. Don't know how to handle money."

That's the stereotype.

But it's not fear—it's *experience*.

When they say "Black people are afraid of banks," what they're really ignoring is a history of banks being afraid of us—or better yet, working *against* us.

It's not paranoia. It's memory.

And that memory didn't start with overdraft fees. It started with broken promises and stolen savings.

Let's break it down.

The Trauma Is Real

The fear didn't come from nowhere. Let's start with the **Freedman's Savings Bank**.

After slavery ended, Black Americans were told, "Come here, deposit your earnings, and we'll help you build wealth." Thousands did. Over $3 million in deposits at a time when that money could've built legacies.

But the bank was mismanaged—invested in risky white-owned ventures, fraud ran rampant, and it collapsed in 1874.

People lost *everything*.

We're talking about formerly enslaved people who saved pennies and dollars from sharecropping, labor, and military service—only to be robbed blind by the very system they were told would protect them.

That wound never healed.

Then came decades of redlining, loan denials, predatory lending, and banks flat-out refusing to serve Black neighborhoods.

So no, it's not "fear" that keeps some folks from trusting banks.

It's *generational financial PTSD*.

We've Always Saved—Just Differently

Before we had access to traditional banking, we created our own systems.

We saved in cash—under mattresses, in envelopes, in lockboxes.

We used **sou-sous** and **tandas**—rotating savings circles passed around in trusted communities.

We kept money with Big Mama, not Bank of America.

Because sometimes, the system that's supposed to protect you feels more like a setup.

And when you don't see anyone in your family going to the bank for help—but you *do* see them getting denied for loans or hit with hidden fees—it shapes how you move.

But here's the shift: we're not just protecting money anymore. We're learning how to *multiply* it.

And that means facing the system with new tools—and new boundaries.

We're Not Afraid. We're Strategic.

Black folks are using banks more than ever.

We're comparing interest rates.

We're opening high-yield savings accounts.

We're using credit unions, fintech apps, digital wallets, and Black-owned institutions that *understand our history* and respect our present.

We're not running from banks.

We're choosing the ones that work *for* us.

That's not fear. That's discernment.

That's financial maturity.

That's healing in motion.

Pros and Cons of Banking (Especially When You're Black)

Pros:

- Safer than cash for storing large sums
- Helps you build financial history for credit, loans, and homeownership
- Gives access to online bill pay, direct deposit, and automatic savings tools
- Allows you to invest, budget, and track money efficiently

Cons:

- Fees (monthly maintenance, overdraft, ATM) can sneak up
- Discriminatory practices still exist in some institutions
- May feel intimidating if you've had a bad experience or were never taught how banks work
- Some banks still offer less access or support in Black communities

But here's the real: banking isn't optional anymore—it's a gateway.

It's how you get paid faster. How you apply for mortgages. How you show a paper trail when starting a business.

So instead of fear, we need *frameworks*.

Action Steps to Bank with Confidence (Not Fear)

Start with transparency.

Choose banks that show you their fees upfront. No surprises. No fine print traps.

Support institutions that support us.

Look into Black-owned banks and credit unions. They were built with *us* in mind.

Automate your peace.

Set up alerts, auto-savings, and balance notifications so you stay in control of your flow.

Use digital tools.

Apps like Chime, Ally, or local credit unions offer modern features with fewer fees.

Keep receipts—literally.

Always check statements, keep proof of deposits, and don't be afraid to ask questions.

Learn how it works.

Understanding interest, overdrafts, account types, and loan terms is power. The knowledge is out here—grab it.

Build relationships.

The bank isn't just a place—it's a tool. Get to know your banker. Ask about options. Advocate for yourself.

Final Word

The lie is: "We're afraid of banks."

The truth is: we're cautious with systems that have *already* failed us.

And rightfully so.

But we're not running from wealth—we're learning how to build it *safely*.

We're not avoiding banks out of fear—we're engaging with intention.

We're finding tools that fit our lives.

We're using what we need—and skipping what doesn't serve us.

We're replacing shame with strategy.

And most of all?

We're making sure the next generation knows they *can* trust the process—*when they've been taught how to vet the system.*

Because it's not about banking for the sake of it.

It's about building freedom. Security. Leverage. Legacy.

18.12: "We Only Use Cash"

You've heard it. Maybe you've even said it with pride.

"I don't do cards—I'm a cash person."

And then they flip that into a stereotype:

"Black folks only use cash because they don't trust the system. They don't understand credit. They're stuck in outdated financial habits."

Let's pause right there.

Because this isn't about not understanding money—it's about understanding it *too well.* It's about knowing that cash doesn't bounce. That if you can't swipe it, you can't overspend it. That once you hand it over, it's gone—and there's no surprise bill next month.

We don't "only use cash" out of ignorance.

We do it because for generations, *cash was control.*

Where the Cash Habit Came From

You have to understand where we're coming from.

When banks denied us loans, we paid in cash.

When we didn't trust lenders or couldn't get approved, we bought used cars with cash.

When our parents said, "Don't get a credit card, it'll ruin your life," they weren't trying to keep us small—they were trying to keep us *safe.*

They'd seen what debt did to families. They'd lived through times when credit meant stress, collection calls, and being treated like a criminal for falling behind.

Cash wasn't just money—it was *freedom from the system.*

And that made sense back then.

But now? We're evolving.

We're learning that while cash is powerful, credit and digital money management are part of the new wealth-building playbook.

And we're smart enough to hold both truths.

The Strengths in the "Cash-Only" Mentality

Let's give props where they're due.

Using cash can:

- Help people stay on budget
- Prevent overspending and debt
- Provide a real, tactile sense of how much you actually have
- Protect you from digital fraud or banking glitches

This is especially real for elders, immigrants, and folks who've been burned before.

Cash means *you know what's yours.*

No overdraft fees. No account freezes. No interest.

That's not dysfunction. That's discipline.

But Here's Where the Shift Is Happening

The economy has changed.

A lot of things are now easier, safer, and more efficient with digital tools:

- Building credit history

- Booking travel
- Applying for loans or apartments
- Shopping online
- Getting rewards, points, or cash back
- Protecting large sums

You can't put a down payment on a home with a shoebox full of hundreds. You can't prove income from under-the-table cash when applying for a business loan.

In other words—*you can't build future freedom if all your transactions live in the past.*

We need cash *and* credit. Physical dollars *and* digital discipline.

This isn't about abandoning our roots. It's about expanding our reach.

Pros and Cons of Being a Cash-Only Mover

Pros:

- Prevents overspending
- Helps avoid credit card debt
- Easy to manage in the moment
- No monthly interest or surprise charges

Cons:

- No credit-building benefit
- Can't track spending over time without a system
- Harder to rent, apply for mortgages, or qualify for loans
- Risk of theft, loss, or lack of recourse

In short: cash keeps you grounded—but credit moves you forward.

And the goal is not to *choose* between them—it's to know *how and when* to use each one to your advantage.

Action Steps for Moving From "Only Cash" to Full Financial Power

Open a checking account with no fees.

Start small if needed. Just having a record of your transactions can help build a foundation.

Use a secured credit card.

If you're nervous about credit, this is the gateway. You use your own deposit as collateral and build history without risk.

Create a "hybrid budget."

Use cash for day-to-day spending (like food and gas), but digital tools for bills, subscriptions, and recurring expenses.

Track your habits.

Use a journal, app, or spreadsheet to see where your money goes. Whether it's digital or cash, you can't manage what you don't monitor.

Teach the youth both.

Let them know the importance of credit *and* the beauty of cash control. Balance is the goal—not bias.

Don't let fear run the show.

Your money story deserves new chapters. What protected you before might limit you now.

Final Word

The stereotype says we only use cash because we don't know any better.

But the truth is, we've been *surviving with cash* because for a long time, it was the only thing that didn't fail us.

That's not ignorance—that's intuition.

Still, survival is no longer the goal.

Now it's about strategy. Growth. Leverage.

We can still hold on to the discipline that cash taught us.

But we're also building credit that opens doors.

We're creating paper trails that lead to mortgages, business funding, and generational wealth.

We're not cash-only anymore.

We're cash-wise, credit-conscious, and financially evolving—on purpose.

18.13: "We Depend Too Much on Government Assistance"

Here we go with another tired stereotype that folks love to throw around when they want to talk about Black folks and money.

"They're always on welfare."

"They live off the government."

"They don't want to work—they just want handouts."

Let's pause that right there.

This isn't just a lazy lie—it's a deeply rooted, politically weaponized, and racially charged myth that's been used for decades to paint Black people as dependent, lazy, and unmotivated.

But the truth?

Black folks aren't the majority of welfare recipients.

Black folks didn't invent government assistance.

And Black folks, more often than not, are *working while receiving assistance*—because the system is broken, not because we are.

This chapter is about setting the record straight. Because using a system you've paid into, or that exists to keep people afloat during hard times, is not failure. It's survival. And survival should never be shamed.

Where the Lie Came From

Let's go back to the 1970s.

That's when the media started pushing the image of the "welfare queen"—a term rooted in anti-Blackness and misogyny. They portrayed her as a Black woman, driving a Cadillac, collecting checks, living large off the government.

It was propaganda. And it worked.

Suddenly, welfare reform became code for cutting support to Black families—even though the majority of government assistance recipients have always been *white*.

But that image stuck.

Even today, you'll hear people talk about "those people" who "just want free stuff"—as if the system hasn't been playing us from the jump.

As if Black folks haven't worked *every kind of job* in this country, from unpaid slavery to essential frontline roles.

We don't depend on government assistance.

We *qualify for it*—often because the very systems we work in pay us the least and exploit us the most.

The Real Numbers

Facts over feelings.

Black folks make up about 13% of the U.S. population.

Yet, contrary to the stereotype, we are *not* the largest demographic on public assistance. That's been white Americans for decades.

But the media doesn't show white rural poverty.

It doesn't show working-class white families depending on SNAP or WIC.

It zooms in on Black faces in waiting rooms. It tells half-truths with full agendas.

So if you've internalized that narrative—even a little bit—it's time to unlearn it.

Using Support Is Not Shameful

Let's make this plain: using government assistance doesn't make you weak. It doesn't mean you're lazy. It doesn't mean you don't want better.

It means the cost of living is high. Wages are low. And sometimes you need help to make it through.

We've got folks working 40+ hours a week and still qualifying for housing assistance, food stamps, or Medicaid.

That's not because they're irresponsible.

That's because the system was built to *require hustle* without reward.

Assistance is a tool—not a lifestyle.

It's a net when life drops you.

It's not where you stay. It's what keeps you from sinking.

And anybody who's ever had to wait in line for a check or benefits knows—it's *not* fun. It's not easy. It's not glamorous. It's humbling.

But it's also sometimes *necessary.*

Generational Patterns and Structural Barriers

Let's be honest. If your community has faced:

- Job discrimination
- Redlined neighborhoods
- Underfunded schools
- Mass incarceration
- Predatory lending
- Medical racism

...then it makes sense that public support systems would play a bigger role.

We're not choosing struggle. We're navigating it.

And when the world tells you to "pull yourself up by your bootstraps"—but your family never had boots—assistance is sometimes the only thread you've got.

But that doesn't mean we aren't working, building, growing, or dreaming.

Pros and Cons of Using Government Assistance

Pros:

- Helps provide stability during hard times

- Allows families to feed their kids, stay housed, and access healthcare
- Creates a buffer while you pursue work, education, or entrepreneurship
- Gives breathing room for mental, emotional, and financial recovery

Cons:

- Can be stigmatized by society, employers, or even family
- May discourage long-term planning if benefits disappear when income increases slightly
- Systems are often difficult to navigate and full of red tape
- Does not always address the root causes of poverty

But the biggest con isn't about the people who use assistance.

It's the *system* that keeps people needing it.

Action Steps to Use Assistance as a Step, Not a Stop

Know your rights.

Understand the programs available to you—SNAP, WIC, TANF, Medicaid, housing vouchers, student grants. You paid into this system. You're *entitled* to support.

Use it to build.

While receiving assistance, look for opportunities to learn, skill up, or stabilize. Use the breathing room to dream bigger.

Plan for the exit.

Have a plan for when your income rises—so you don't get caught off guard when benefits decrease. It's not fair, but it's predictable.

Don't let shame win.

You are not your EBT card. You are not your subsidy. You're a human being doing what it takes to move forward.

Teach others.

Normalize conversations around temporary support and long-term goals. Help someone else apply, advocate, or ask the right questions.

Vote with your dollars and your ballot.

Advocate for fair wages, healthcare, and housing. Government assistance should be a bridge, not a trap.

Final Word

The myth says we're dependent.

But the truth?

We've been resourceful.

We've been resilient.

We've used the little help we got to carry families, raise generations, and survive systems that were never built for our success.

We're not waiting on handouts—we're demanding equity.

We're not content with the bare minimum—we're building toward abundance.

We're not ashamed of using help—we're ashamed that so many of us *have to.*

But even in that? We rise.

With food stamps or pay stubs. With Medicaid or mutual aid. With public housing or a starter home.

We rise.

Because dependence is not the story.

Part VIII: The Future Is Ours

This isn't just about fixing what's broken—it's about building what's next.

Part VIII is where the blueprint becomes the legacy. It's where we shift from surviving systems to designing our own. It's where we reclaim control, reimagine success, and redefine what wealth looks like—not just in bank accounts, but in mindset, family, and freedom.

The chapters in this section aren't just about money—they're about *movement.* From estate planning to teaching the next generation, from entrepreneurship to philanthropy, this is where we plant seeds that grow beyond our lifetime.

No more waiting for permission. No more second-guessing our place in the conversation.

We're owning our narratives, leveraging our gifts, and putting systems in place that our children's children can benefit from.

The future isn't something we hope for—it's something we *prepare* for.

It's time to stop playing defense and start playing offense.

Chapter 18: Setting Your Kids Up Right

Let's keep it real—we're not just trying to make it for *us.* We're trying to build something *they* can stand on. Our kids. Our nieces and nephews. Our god babies. Our little cousins who are watching everything we do.

We want to be the generation that breaks cycles, builds bridges, and sets the next one up to *win.*

That means teaching more than just "save your money" or "don't spend it all in one place." It means giving our kids game early—the kind of game most of us had to learn the hard way.

This chapter is all about that. How do you put your kids on the path to financial confidence, literacy, and freedom? What does it look like to set them up right?

Not just when they're 18. But when they're 8. When they're 3. When they're still watching you figure it out.

It's time to pass the baton—not with pressure, but with purpose.

The Cultural Gap We're Closing

In many Black households, money wasn't talked about. We were told to mind our business when grown folks were talking. We didn't see budgets being made. We didn't hear about investing or insurance. Bills got paid in silence—or in stress.

So how could we be expected to start strong when we were handed no roadmap?

That ends with us.

We're breaking the silence. We're talking about credit, budgeting, ownership, and legacy at the dinner table, in the car, at bedtime.

We're letting our kids ask questions. We're showing them receipts and balance sheets. We're pulling back the curtain.

Because what they don't know can hurt them. And what they *do* know can change the game.

Teaching Through Example

Let's be honest: your kids are watching you even when you think they aren't.

If you always stressed around payday, they pick that up. If you never use your debit card because it stays in the red, they notice. If you celebrate budgeting like it's a win (because it *is*), they'll learn that saving is powerful.

Money mindset is inherited way before money is.

So setting your kids up right starts with *your* healing. Your habits. Your language. Your posture around money.

Normalize saying:

- "I can't afford that right now" (without shame)
- "Let's save for it together"
- "Here's how I budgeted for that"

When kids see money talked about with confidence and calm, they won't grow up afraid of it. They'll grow up ready to *use* it with wisdom.

Age-Appropriate Game

For toddlers and little kids (ages 2–6):

- Use play money in games
- Let them "pay" for things at the store

- Talk about needs vs. wants with toys and snacks

For grade school kids (ages 7–12):

- Give a small allowance and help them split it (spend/save/give)
- Start a savings jar or digital savings tracker
- Let them earn money for tasks or goals

For teens (ages 13–18):

- Open a joint teen checking account
- Teach them how to use a debit card and track spending
- Talk about credit, taxes, and part-time job income
- Show them how to create a budget

For college-age and young adults:

- Teach about compound interest and investing
- Help them open a Roth IRA (if they're earning income)
- Walk through their first credit card together
- Discuss student loans with full transparency

We don't have to dump every financial concept on them at once. But we *do* need to start.

Start with what they can handle. And build from there.

Make Financial Literacy Normal, Not Formal

We're not talking about sitting your kid down with a 90-minute PowerPoint on mutual funds. We're talking about weaving money lessons into everyday life.

Grocery shopping? Talk about unit prices. Eating out? Discuss tipping and taxes. Getting a birthday check? Break it down: save some, spend some, bless somebody else.

Financial literacy isn't a subject. It's a *skillset.* And we build it in the everyday moments.

Make it normal. Make it matter.

Pros and Cons of Financial Parenting

Pros:

- Kids grow up confident around money
- They avoid common pitfalls
- They learn from your wins *and* your mistakes
- You build a legacy of knowledge, not just dollars

Cons:

- It takes time and patience
- You might have to unlearn your own money shame first
- Not every lesson will stick right away
- Some conversations may feel uncomfortable or unfamiliar

But let's be clear: the discomfort is temporary. The growth is generational.

Action Steps to Set Your Kids Up Right

Start talking. Don't wait for the perfect moment. Create it.

Let them see you manage money. Show them budgeting apps. Let them help you count out cash. Include them in financial decisions where appropriate.

Give them controlled autonomy. Let them make money mistakes while the stakes are low. A $10 lesson at age 10 is better than a $10,000 mistake at 25.

Invest in tools. Books, apps, games, workshops, youth savings accounts—use what's out there.

Be honest. If you messed up financially in the past, say that. If you're learning too, say that. Vulnerability builds trust.

Celebrate money wins. Not just grades or sports. Celebrate savings goals, smart spending, and giving back.

Talk legacy. Help them dream big. Talk about owning land, starting businesses, investing. Let them know it's possible—because it is.

Final Word

Setting your kids up right isn't about being perfect. It's about being *present.*

It's about being honest. Being open. Being intentional.

It's not about handing them a trust fund. It's about handing them *tools.*

Tools to navigate a system that's complex. Tools to rise above what we inherited. Tools to build what we weren't handed.

You don't need a six-figure salary to change your child's financial future. You need the will to start the conversation.

Let's raise a generation that's financially fluent. Let's raise kids who aren't afraid of money—who understand it, command it, and use it to create change.

Because the real wealth isn't just in what we leave them. It's in *what we teach them to build for themselves.*

Chapter 19: Building a Culture of Financial Literacy

Let's talk about culture—not just music, not just food, not just the style and swag we bring to the world. Let's talk about the culture around *money*.

Because here's the truth: financial literacy isn't just a class, a checklist, or a workshop. It's a *culture*. And cultures aren't built in a day.

They're built in barbershops, at kitchen tables, on the church steps, in group chats, during holiday dinners. They're shaped by what we talk about, what we model, what we normalize.

We can shift how we think about money—but only if we shift how we *live* around money.

This chapter is all about how to build that culture. The kind of culture where money isn't feared, avoided, or flexed irresponsibly—but respected, talked about, planned for, and passed down.

Not just in families, but in neighborhoods, churches, schools, and social circles.

Because a financially literate *community* is stronger than a financially wealthy individual.

What Is a Culture of Financial Literacy?

It's when talking about credit scores is as normal as talking about your favorite shows. It's when parents and kids talk budgets the same way they talk sneakers. It's when group chats include convos about stock moves, side hustles, or savings wins.

It's when we treat money like a tool, not a taboo. It's when we clap for debt payoffs like we do for new cars. It's when our spaces feel safe enough to say, "I don't know what that means, but I want to learn."

A culture of financial literacy is built on *openness, curiosity, and consistency.*

Why Our Culture Around Money Needs a Reset

For generations, Black folks have been left out of the financial conversation.

We weren't given wealth education in school. We weren't offered the same loan rates. We didn't grow up hearing about trusts, portfolios, or passive income.

Instead, we heard:

- "Don't tell nobody your business."
- "Just pay your bills and stay out of debt."
- "Money is the root of all evil."

What we really needed to hear was:

- "Let's learn together."
- "Here's how compound interest works."
- "You deserve to build wealth and rest."

Our culture was built to *protect* us—but now we need a culture that also *equips* us.

We can honor where we came from while updating how we move.

Culture Lives in Conversation

The best thing we can do? Start talking.

Talk to your friends about your savings goals. Ask your homegirl if she's ever tried investing. Break down your budget with your kids. Talk to your uncle about his retirement plan.

Make these conversations regular, relaxed, and real. No judgment. No flexing. Just growth.

Let's stop making money convo feel like a lecture and start making it feel like family.

Culture Lives in Community

Churches can hold money talks after service. Barbershops and salons can host workshops. Basketball teams can teach teens about budgeting and NIL deals.

Culture shifts when people gather with a shared mission. And financial literacy should be a community mission.

We can throw baby showers and talk about 529 plans. We can celebrate birthdays and open custodial accounts. We can watch the game and talk stock apps during halftime.

Money is *everywhere.* Let's stop acting like it ain't.

Pros and Cons of Creating a Financial Literacy Culture

Pros:

- Normalizes conversations that build generational wealth
- Builds accountability and shared learning in communities
- Reduces shame and secrecy around financial struggles
- Inspires kids early to value education and ownership

Cons:

- Can feel awkward at first if you weren't raised that way
- Some people will resist or clown you for being "too deep"
- You may feel like the only one doing it in your circle
- Requires patience and consistency to create change

But here's the thing: every movement starts with somebody saying, "We can do better."

That somebody might be *you*.

Action Steps to Build Financial Literacy Culture in Your World

Be the first to speak up. Don't wait for someone else to start the convo. Be the brave one.

Lead with love, not shame. Help people learn without making them feel behind.

Bring it where people already gather. Don't expect folks to come to a seminar at 7 p.m. on a Tuesday. Bring the convo to the cookout, the Bible study, the break room.

Share your wins and your stumbles. Both are valuable. Show people the real.

Use your platform. If you've got a social media presence, a classroom, a business, or a pulpit—talk money. Plant seeds.

Create rituals. Money Mondays. Financial Fridays. First-of-the-month check-ins. Make it routine.

Pass it down. Teach the kids. Involve them. Let them grow up with language you never had.

Final Word

You don't need a finance degree to teach people about money. You don't need to be rich to talk wealth. You just need to care.

Because culture isn't what we say. It's what we *do consistently.*

So if we want a future where our kids know how to build, protect, and pass down wealth, we have to start creating spaces where money talk isn't weird—it's *welcome.*

We build culture with our voices, our habits, and our courage.

Let's create a world where budgeting is cool. Where credit is power. Where investing is normal. Where financial freedom is expected—not exceptional.

Let's build that culture. Let's rise.

Chapter 20: The Book Club Blueprint – Learning Together, Growing Together

Let's keep it a buck—talking about money alone can be tough. But talking about it in community? That's where the real transformation happens.

This chapter is your blueprint for using something simple and powerful—a book club—to spark generational change. Because when we read together, we grow together. And when we grow together, we win *together*.

A book club focused on financial literacy isn't just a gathering—it's a movement. It's group therapy. It's family reunion energy with a purpose. It's where game gets passed around like a hot plate at Sunday dinner.

Whether you're starting one in your church, your friend group, your school, your barbershop, or just your living room, this chapter will help you make it real.

Why Book Clubs Work for Us

We've always learned in circles.

From barbershop banter to kitchen-table truth-telling to late-night porch convos, our culture has always used *community dialogue* to break things down.

Book clubs let us:

- Create safe space for financial conversation

- Hold each other accountable
- Share resources and real-life application
- Bring different ages and life stages to the table
- Build emotional and intellectual connection

We don't just read the book. We *live* it.

What to Read

You don't need a PhD in finance to pick the right book. Choose something that speaks the language of real life.

Look for books that:

- Are culturally relevant
- Break down concepts simply
- Include real-life stories or case studies
- Inspire action and discussion

And yes—that might be the very book you're holding right now.

You can also switch it up: read books about mindset, legacy, entrepreneurship, credit, or investing. Or focus on one topic per season.

The key is: pick a book that gets people *talking* and *doing*.

How to Start Your Book Club

Step 1: Find Your People

Invite folks who are hungry to grow. Doesn't have to be 20 people. Start with 3. Real ones only. No flexing. No shaming.

Step 2: Choose a Frequency

Weekly? Biweekly? Monthly? Pick what works for your people. Keep it consistent.

Step 3: Pick a Time and Place

Virtual or in-person—just make it sacred. This is *study hall meets revival* energy.

Step 4: Set a Vibe

Food? Music? Icebreakers? Set the tone. Make it feel like culture, not classroom.

Step 5: Assign Pages and Roles

Break the book into chapters. Assign a leader for each meeting who helps guide discussion. Maybe someone keeps notes. Another person brings the questions. Share the work.

Step 6: Build Real Conversation

Don't just recap. Reflect. Ask: How does this apply to *you*? What would you do differently after reading this?

Step 7: Track Progress

Celebrate who paid off a debt. Who opened an account. Who taught their kid something new. Every win matters.

Step 8: Stay Flexible

Life be lifin'. Let people catch up if they fall behind. Keep it real and relaxed.

What to Talk About

Some folks are shy. Some don't know where to start. Here's how you warm it up:

- What part of this chapter hit you the hardest?
- Did this bring up anything from your past?
- What's one small step you can take this week?
- How do we teach this to our kids, cousins, or crew?
- Who do you want to invite to the next meeting?

Money talk is emotional. Be gentle. Be curious. Be open.

Pros and Cons of Running a Book Club

Pros:

- Shared accountability
- Real growth through shared experiences
- Builds community around empowerment
- You learn more by teaching and sharing
- Creates a multiplier effect in your family and community

Cons:

- Takes consistency and coordination
- Some folks may drop off or ghost
- Discussions can get sidetracked if there's no structure
- Group dynamics can be tricky—not everyone is ready to grow

But when it works? It's magic. It's movement. It's legacy in real-time.

Action Steps to Build Your Book Club

- Pick a start date and invite at least 3 people
- Choose your first book and break it into manageable chunks
- Create a group chat or email thread for reminders
- Set expectations (show up, be respectful, keep it 100)
- Make it fun: themes, food, raffles, music, giveaways
- At the end of each book, ask: what's next?

Keep growing. Keep building. Keep showing up.

Final Word

The truth is, we were never meant to do this alone.

We were meant to build together.

And a book club ain't just about reading pages. It's about turning those pages into *practice.*

It's where new habits are born. Where community rises. Where confidence takes root.

You want to build a legacy? Start with a table. Invite people to sit down. Open a book. And start talking.

Because when we talk money, we change mindsets. When we change mindsets, we change behaviors. And when we change behaviors?

We change the future.

One chapter at a time.

Chapter 21: Tools for the Journey – Books, Podcasts, Websites, and Apps

Here's what nobody tells you: trying to learn about money without the right tools is like trying to bake a sweet potato pie without measuring cups, a rolling pin, or an oven. You might have the ingredients—a little knowledge, a little motivation—but without the right tools? It's not gon' cook up right.

The tools matter.

And the good news? You don't need to be rich to get access. You just need to be intentional. Because there are books, podcasts, websites, and apps made just for people like you—Black folks who want to learn how to manage their money, build wealth, and leave something behind.

In this chapter, we're laying out a full toolbox. Real talk, real resources. This is your guide to what's worth your time, what speaks your language, and what will help you take the next step—wherever you are.

Why You Need a Toolkit

You don't go to the gym without gym shoes. You don't run a marathon without training.

So why do we expect ourselves to build financial freedom with no blueprint, no game plan, and no guidance?

This chapter is about building your *financial gym bag*.

And just like in the gym, some tools work better for different people.

Your favorite podcast might not be your sister's favorite. One app might help you budget. Another might help you invest. A certain book might speak to your spirit. Another might go over your head.

That's okay.

You build the bag that works for *you.*

Let's break it all the way down.

Books That Break It Down

Books let you sit with the information. Highlight it. Re-read it. Process it on your time.

Look for books that speak your language. That understand your cultural context. That don't shame you for what you don't know.

Books should educate, empower, and equip.

Categories to look for:

- Budgeting for beginners
- Understanding credit
- Black wealth and historical context
- Investing for newbies
- Generational wealth and estate planning
- Mindset and money trauma

You don't need a PhD in economics to get the game. You just need authors who know how to break it down.

Podcasts That Hit

Podcasts let you learn on the go—in your car, at the gym, washing dishes. No pressure, no classroom.

Find hosts that keep it real, speak with clarity, and bring on guests who tell the truth. You want shows that teach you something new, but also leave you feeling *seen.*

Whether it's Black entrepreneurs, financial therapists, everyday people getting out of debt, or money pros who come from where you come from—there are voices for you.

Pro tip: Subscribe to 3. Rotate depending on your mood—inspiration, strategy, or storytelling.

Websites Worth Visiting

Not all information online is created equal. Some blogs and sites are straight fluff. Some are full of technical jargon. Others are goldmines.

Here's what to look for:

- Clear, plain-language explanations
- Tools like calculators and templates
- Updated info on laws, tax rules, or investing options
- Cultural sensitivity and representation

Bookmark sites that offer:

- Budgeting worksheets
- Investment glossaries
- Estate planning guides
- Comparison tools for accounts, credit cards, or insurance

And if it feels shady or full of pop-ups? Bounce.

Apps That Put Power in Your Pocket

Your smartphone can be a distraction—or a discipline tool. It all depends on what's downloaded.

These apps can help you:

- Track your spending

- Set savings goals
- Monitor your credit
- Learn how to invest
- Automate payments

Choose apps that are easy to use, secure, and flexible. Test a few out. Keep the ones that feel like a good fit.

And yes, the *free* versions often work just fine.

How to Use Your Toolkit

Start with one category. Books, podcasts, apps—pick one. Don't overwhelm yourself.

Set a schedule. Maybe one podcast a week. Or 10 minutes a day in a budgeting app. Or a chapter each weekend. Consistency > intensity.

Apply as you go. Don't just learn. *Do.* If a book teaches you about sinking funds, open one. If a podcast teaches you about compound interest, start an account.

Share with your people. Drop the link in your group chat. Screenshot the tip. Read a chapter with your kids. Normalize this.

Stay curious. Ask yourself: What's next? Where's my growth edge?

Pros and Cons of DIY Financial Tools

Pros:

- You learn at your own pace
- You can choose what fits your style
- Low cost (often free)
- Gives you language to ask better questions when you meet with professionals

Cons:

- Some tools have a learning curve
- It's easy to get overwhelmed by too many options
- Not all tools are culturally inclusive
- Self-discipline is required to keep going

This ain't magic. It's movement. And movement takes momentum.

But once you start? It compounds.

Action Steps for Building Your Personal Toolkit

- Pick one book to read by the end of the month
- Subscribe to one podcast that drops weekly episodes
- Download one money app that tracks spending
- Bookmark one financial education website
- Schedule 30 minutes a week to engage with these tools
- Share your favorite with one other person

You don't need every tool on Day 1. But you need *a tool.*

And once you've got that hammer? That screwdriver? That chisel?

You can start building.

Not just budgets. Not just bank accounts.

But freedom.

Final Word

Let's stop pretending like we have to figure it all out from scratch.

The tools are already out here. Somebody built the app. Somebody wrote the book. Somebody started the podcast.

All you gotta do is pick it up.

You don't have to go broke to learn how to build wealth. You just need the right resources, a little consistency, and a whole lot of *why.*

Your phone? It's a financial coach. Your bookshelf? It's a generational classroom. Your earbuds? They're piping in multi-million dollar game.

You are not alone on this journey. You just need to know what to pack. The destination is freedom. And this chapter? That's your suitcase.

Chapter 22: Car Chase

This is soooo random, but I always wanted to write a book with a car chase!

Any time someone tells me about a book—whether it's a mystery, romance, financial guide, or even a cookbook—I always ask with a smile:

"But does it have a car chase?"

So YES, this book even has a Car Chase.

It's my way of asking: is there movement? Is there action? Is there something that makes it exciting? That gets your heart racing, your eyes wide open, and your foot pressing gently on the gas?

So yes—this book absolutely has a car chase.

But not in the Fast & Furious way (although, if Vin Diesel wants to narrate the audiobook, let's talk). No, this car chase is the one you're already in... right now. It's the wild, high-speed pursuit called Name, Image, and Likeness. It's financial freedom. It's legacy. It's doing something different so the next generation doesn't have to start from scratch.

You're the driver.

You've got talent, visibility, and momentum.

The engine's running, the opportunity is real, and the road ahead is wide open.

But let's talk about your dashboard for a second.

Are you watching your fuel—aka your budget? Because too many folks run hot with new money and burn through it before the season ends.

Is your check engine light on? That might be that contract you didn't fully read. Or the taxes you haven't set aside. Or that cousin who keeps asking for "just a little help."

Are you checking your rearview mirror? Because behind you are people trying to catch up—maybe even catch you slipping. The IRS, compliance offices, scammers, and old spending habits don't just disappear when the money comes in.

And what about your GPS? Are you actually headed toward something—like long-term wealth, entrepreneurship, or financial freedom—or are you just taking exits that look cool in the moment?

This car chase isn't about speed. It's about control.

It's about knowing when to shift gears, when to pull over and get help, and when to hit the gas.

Yes, people are going to zoom past you on social media. They'll flash deals, big purchases, and rented lifestyles. But what they won't post are the breakdowns, the burnout, and the "out of gas" moments that come when you drive with no plan.

So here's your moment to shift. To get in the driver's seat with clarity, confidence, and a clean dashboard.

This book is your manual. Your map. Your mechanic in the glovebox.

Because life moves fast. Money moves faster. And trust me—there's no worse feeling than realizing you had the keys to your own success, but never learned how to drive it.

So yeah, this book has a car chase.

And you? You're the one steering. Let's make sure you know where you're going.

Chapter 23: What Is the Market, the Economy, and Everything Else You See on TV?

You've probably heard things like:

"The market is crashing!" "The S&P 500 is on a hot streak!" "The Fed raised interest rates again!" "Inflation is out of control!"

It's enough to make you want to change the channel.

But guess what? Once you understand what all this means, you'll see it's just like a game. The financial world has teams, scores, momentum, injuries, coaches, rules, and streaks — just like sports.

Let's break it all down so you can start playing to win.

What Exactly Is the Stock Market? The stock market is where people buy and sell shares of companies. Buying a share means you own a small piece of a business like Nike, Apple, or Amazon.

Sports analogy: It's like being part of a franchise. You're not just a fan — you're a partial owner of the team. When the team wins and grows in value, so does your share.

What Causes the Market to Go Up or Down? The stock market moves based on supply and demand. If more people want to buy, prices go up. If more people want to sell, prices go down.

What changes that supply and demand? News, earnings reports, interest rates, political events, and even tweets.

Sports analogy: Think of it like player hype. A good performance (great earnings) drives up value. A scandal or slump? The price drops fast.

What's the Difference Between the Stock Market and the Economy? The market is the scoreboard — investors' expectations about the future. The economy is the actual game — jobs, production, consumer spending, etc.

Sports analogy: The market is fantasy football. The economy is the actual football game. Sometimes the fantasy points and the real game align — and sometimes they don't.

Is the Market Risky? Can I Lose All My Money? Yes, there's risk. If you invest in one stock, it could crash. But if you invest in hundreds of companies through an index fund or ETF, your risk drops big time.

Sports analogy: Betting on one player is risky. Building a whole roster gives you protection. If one player flops, your team can still win.

What's the Best Way to Invest? For most people, the best play is:

- Index funds or ETFs (which include hundreds of companies)
- Roth IRA or brokerage account
- Long-term mindset
- Stay consistent

Sports analogy: It's like running the offense — simple, repeatable, and hard to stop. You don't need trick plays. Just execute the fundamentals.

When's the Best Time to Start? Now. Always now.

Sports analogy: The best athletes don't wait until playoffs to train. They build in the offseason. The earlier you invest, the stronger your financial "season" will be.

What's the S&P 500? It's a list of the 500 biggest U.S. companies, and it's used as a scoreboard to measure how the market is doing.

Sports analogy: Think of it as the AP Top 25 of business. If most companies in the S&P 500 are "winning," the market is doing well.

What's a Bull Market vs. a Bear Market? Bull Market = Prices rising, people feeling confident Bear Market = Prices falling 20% or more, people panicking

Sports analogy: A bull market is a winning streak — everything's clicking.

A bear market is a slump — the team's struggling, fans are frustrated.

Should I Sell When the Market Drops? No. Selling during a drop locks in your losses.

Sports analogy: You don't bench your franchise player after one bad quarter. You ride it out, adjust, and stay focused on the long game.

How Much Money Do I Need to Start? You can start with $50, $100 — whatever you've got. Many platforms let you buy fractional shares of big stocks.

Sports analogy: You don't have to start as the star. You just need to get on the roster. Reps build results.

Can I Make Fast Money in the Market? Sure — but it's gambling. Not investing.

Day trading = playing hero ball. Investing = running the system.

Sports analogy: Anyone can hit a half-court shot once. But champions win with consistent layups, defense, and smart plays.

What's an ETF? An ETF (Exchange-Traded Fund) is a bundle of investments (like stocks or bonds) that you can buy or sell like one single stock.

Sports analogy: It's like drafting an entire all-star team with one pick. You don't have to guess which player will shine — you get them all.

Is Investing Only for Rich People? Absolutely not.

Investing is for anyone who wants to build wealth. You don't need to start big — you just need to start.

Sports analogy: Great careers begin in high school gyms, not in pro arenas. Start where you are.

What's the Difference Between a Stock and a Bond? Stock = ownership in a company Bond = loan to a company or government

Stocks can grow more but are riskier. Bonds are steadier but slower.

Sports analogy: Stocks are like shooting guards — high-scoring, high risk. Bonds are like veteran defenders — low flash, but reliable.

What's Diversification? Diversification means spreading your money across lots of different investments — not putting all your eggs in one basket.

Sports analogy: You don't build a team with only point guards. You need size, speed, shooters, defense — balance is the key to winning.

Why Do People Say "Buy Low, Sell High"? Because that's how you make money: buy when prices are low, sell when they're higher.

But most people do the opposite — they panic when prices drop and buy when hype is high.

Sports analogy: You don't trade away your superstar when they're cold — you trust they'll bounce back.

How Do I Know What to Invest In? Start simple:

- Index funds like S&P 500
- Total Market ETFs
- Low fees
- Wide diversification
- Reinvest dividends
- Stay long term

Sports analogy: You don't have to shoot from half-court. Just run the offense, take high-percentage shots, and play disciplined ball.

What Happens in a Recession? A recession is when the economy slows down for several months. Jobs get cut. People spend less. Businesses tighten up. The market might drop — but it's usually temporary.

Sports analogy: A recession is a rebuilding year. No playoffs this season, but you use it to regroup and reload for the next run.

Do I Need a Financial Advisor? Not to start. You can use apps like:

- Fidelity
- Vanguard
- Schwab
- M1 Finance
- Public
- Betterment

But if your NIL money grows, or your situation gets complex, a good financial advisor can be your coach.

What's the #1 Rule of Investing? Start early. Stay consistent. Don't panic.

Sports analogy: The best players aren't perfect — they're dependable. They show up to every practice, stick to the playbook, and never get rattled by one loss.

What's a Dividend? A dividend is a cash payout some companies give to their shareholders — a bonus just for being on the team.

Sports analogy: It's like getting a check even when you're on the bench. You don't have to do anything extra — just hold the stock and let it pay you.

How Often Should I Check My Investments? Once a month. Maybe once a quarter.

Sports analogy: Checking your account every hour is like staring at the scoreboard during warmups. Focus on playing the game — not watching every score change.

What's a Stock Split? When a stock gets expensive, companies sometimes split the shares to make them more affordable.

If you owned 1 share at $100, now you might own 2 shares at $50.

Sports analogy: It's like switching jersey numbers — the look changes, but your role on the team stays the same.

What's a Market Correction? When the market drops about 10% from a recent high, that's a correction.

It's normal and healthy — just part of the game.

Sports analogy: A correction is like a team huddle at halftime after a rough second quarter. Not a meltdown. Just time to refocus.

Should I Invest if the Market Is Going Down? Yes. That's often the best time to invest — everything's on sale.

Sports analogy: It's like getting your favorite sneakers at 30% off. Same product. Just a better deal.

Can I Lose All My Money in the Market? If you put everything into one stock? Yes. If you invest in diversified funds or ETFs? Very unlikely.

Even during crashes, the total market has always bounced back.

Sports analogy: One player can get injured. But a deep bench? That keeps you in the game.

What's a Mutual Fund vs. an ETF? Both are baskets of stocks or bonds.

Mutual funds: trade once per day, may have higher fees ETFs: trade like stocks all day, usually cheaper and more flexible

Most beginners stick with ETFs.

Sports analogy: Mutual funds are like old-school coaches — still useful, but a bit slower. ETFs are today's fast-paced game — lean, simple, efficient.

What Are Interest Rates and Why Do They Matter? Interest rates are the cost of borrowing money.

When the Fed raises rates, loans (like car loans, mortgages, business loans) get more expensive. That slows spending — which can hurt company profits — and cause the market to drop.

Sports analogy: It's like your coach making you run extra sprints. The whole team slows down. But sometimes it's necessary to build long-term stamina.

What's Dollar-Cost Averaging? It means you invest the same amount of money on a regular schedule — no matter what the market's doing.

For example: $200/month into your Roth IRA, every month.

This strategy helps you buy more shares when prices are low and fewer when prices are high — averaging it out over time.

Sports analogy: It's like showing up to lift every week — no matter how tired you feel or how good last week was. The consistency is what wins.

Final Thoughts: Learn the Game. Play it Smart. Build Your Legacy. The market isn't magic. The economy isn't a mystery. It's just a different version of a game you already understand.

Diversify your portfolio like you build a team. Invest consistently like you train in the offseason. Don't panic during slumps. Stay calm during hype. Play the long game.

Because money, like sports, rewards discipline, patience, and preparation.

So put in your reps. Stick to the game plan. And build a financial legacy that outlasts the spotlight.

Let's rise.

Chapter 24: Don't Become the Stereotype – Become the Blueprint

Let's get something straight right out the gate. You were never meant to be a stereotype. You were born to be the blueprint.

A lot of us grew up hearing the lies before we ever saw the truth. Lies like: "Black folks don't invest." "We don't save." "We blow money on shoes, not stocks." "We live for the moment, not the legacy."

And after a while, if you hear it enough, you start to believe it. Or worse—you start to live it. But that stops here. That stops with you.

Because this chapter isn't just a call-out. It's a call-up.

It's time to stop living down to the lies and start living up to the legacy.

Where Stereotypes Come From (And Why They Stick)

Stereotypes don't come from nowhere. They get shaped by history, media, trauma, and misunderstanding. They stick because they're easy. They give people shortcuts to judgment. But they never tell the whole story.

Yes, some of us struggle with money—but so does every group. Yes, some of us didn't learn about wealth—because we were locked out of it for generations. Yes, some of us fall for get-rich-quick schemes—because we never got taught slow-build strategies.

But that doesn't define us.

We are more than our pain. More than our paycheck. More than their projections.

The Cost of Playing the Stereotype

Every time we live down to the stereotype, it costs us:

- Financial independence
- Family legacy
- Personal peace
- Power and positioning
- Representation

You can't pass down what you never built. And if we don't shift the narrative, somebody else will keep writing it for us—wrong.

We become the punchline in someone else's story.

But when you decide to become the blueprint? Everything changes.

What Does It Mean to Be the Blueprint?

Being the blueprint means you become the example. You show what's possible. You walk different. You talk different. You plan different.

You're not waiting for a handout. You're designing a handoff. You're not just talking about generational wealth. You're building it brick by brick.

And no, it's not flashy. It's not always sexy. It doesn't look like the highlight reels.

But it's *real.*

It's:

- Creating a budget and sticking to it
- Teaching your kids about credit before they get a card
- Choosing life insurance over likes
- Investing $100 instead of blowing it
- Setting boundaries with money and people

Being the blueprint means your life becomes a masterclass. Not in perfection, but in *intention.*

Pros and Cons of Becoming the Blueprint

Pros:

- You shift your family tree
- You gain confidence and clarity
- You become a resource for your community
- You sleep better knowing you have a plan
- You stop reacting and start strategizing

Cons:

- It takes discipline
- You may outgrow some people
- Folks might not get it at first
- You'll need to unlearn old habits

But here's the thing: the cons are temporary. The pros? They outlive you.

Action Steps to Become the Blueprint

Audit your habits: Where are you reinforcing a stereotype? Where can you pivot?

Learn consistently: Read, listen, ask. Grow every month.

Build community: Don't walk this alone. Create your squad of builders.

Model for the youth: Let the kids see you budget, save, say no, and plan.

Document your plan: Write your will. Create your goals. Make it real.

Share your wins: Not to flex, but to inspire. Normalize wealth moves.

Subvert the Narrative

Remember when they said we only care about material things? Show them a life insurance policy.

When they said we don't talk about money? Host a family finance night.

When they said we're bad with credit? Show your credit score like it's your GPA.

When they said we don't invest? Teach them what a Roth IRA is.

Flip every stereotype into strategy.

You Already Got the Juice

Think about this:

- We built culture with nothing but rhythm and soul.
- We flipped pain into poetry, struggle into song, and hardship into hustle.

So don't tell me we can't build wealth. We just need to be given the playbook—or better yet, write our own.

You are not behind. You are not broke. You are not dumb with money.

You are equipped. You are evolving. You are enough.

Final Word

They made you think you were the cautionary tale. But really? You're the example. You're the evidence. You're the energy.

So don't become the stereotype. Become the blueprint.

Let them say: "Oh, you know [insert your name]? Yeah, they're the one who started budgeting and got everybody on track."

"They're the reason our family got out of debt." "They made financial freedom look fly."

Let your name be spoken in rooms as a reference for what's possible.

Be the one who breaks the pattern. And starts the legacy.

Chapter 25: Helping Without Hurting – How to Support Loved Ones Without Going Broke

You Love Them. But You Can't Save Them All

Let's talk about one of the hardest parts of coming into money—especially when you're young, successful, and the first in your family to earn like this.

Helping a single mom who's always held it down? You want to. Helping your dad who's always struggled but showed up for your games? Feels like the least you can do. Supporting a friend who's stuck or down bad? They were with you before the glow-up.

You want to be loyal. You want to be generous. You don't want to seem selfish.

But if you're not careful, you'll drown while trying to save everyone else.

This chapter is about doing it differently. About helping without hurting. About giving with boundaries, not guilt. About building a future where you don't have to say, "I used to have money…"

Start With This Truth: You're Not Their Retirement Plan

If you're the first in the family to "make it," people will look to you for support. Sometimes it's asked for. Sometimes it's expected silently. Either way, you need a plan before you get pulled into financial chaos.

You are not your family's emergency fund. You are not the government. You are not a bottomless pit of money.

Even if you choose to help—it has to be structured.

Option 1: The Monthly Budget Strategy

Let's say you want to help Mom with groceries, bills, or rent. Instead of saying "yes" every time she calls, you set a monthly family support budget.

Example: You decide $500 a month is what you can afford to help with consistently without sacrificing your own savings, investments, or goals.

Here's how that looks:

- $200 goes toward groceries or utilities
- $200 is paid directly to her landlord or mortgage company
- $100 goes on a pre-loaded debit card for other needs

Once you hit that $500 for the month, you're done.

If someone asks for more? You say: "I already hit my family support budget for the month. We can revisit it next month, but I can't go over that."

You're not being cold—you're sticking to your boundaries.

Option 2: The Lump Sum Strategy

Maybe you don't want to deal with monthly requests. Maybe you want to give a little breathing room up front.

That's when you decide to give a one-time gift, and that's it.

Example: You come into a large check or bonus. You decide you can spare $2,000 to help Mom with overdue bills or car repairs.

You say: "This is a one-time gift. I love you and wanted to do something meaningful. But after this, I won't be able to give more right now."

Then you send it. You don't revisit. You don't fall into guilt. You protect your plan.

And here's the most important part: you don't keep reloading the gift. This isn't a subscription service. It's one-time support—done with love and limits.

If It's More Than One Person...

What if you're trying to help your mom and your dad and your siblings and your childhood best friend who's "just tryna get back on their feet"?

Same rules. Set a total monthly or annual support budget, and divide it—if you want.

Example: You decide to budget $6,000 for family/friend support per year. That's $500/month total.

- Mom gets $300
- Dad gets $100
- Your best friend gets $100

That's it. You don't add more. You don't loan more. You don't get drawn into guilt. If one person's situation changes, it doesn't automatically mean your budget does.

Your financial plan comes first. Everyone else fits within that plan—or not at all.

Say It Early, Say It Often

If you don't say how and how much you're willing to help, people will assume it's unlimited. And assumptions are where resentment and entitlement grow.

Have the conversation. It might be awkward, but it's worth it.

You say: "I love you, and I'm proud to be in a place to help. But I'm setting a boundary. I've got a budget for support, and once I hit that number, I can't go past it. It's not personal—it's me protecting my future."

And when they say "but just this one time..." You hold the line.

How to Avoid Enabling

Helping becomes enabling when:

- They stop trying to help themselves
- They start expecting it
- They guilt you when you say no
- You give money that solves the same problem over and over again
- You feel resentment instead of peace

To avoid enabling, try this:

- Pay the bill directly, don't give cash
- Offer help with job searching, not just money
- Suggest financial literacy resources
- Make the help temporary, not open-ended

If they need $200 for rent every month, what they really need is a plan, not a handout. You can love someone without being their financial crutch.

If They Get Mad, That's Okay

Boundaries make people uncomfortable—especially if they're used to you saying "yes."

They may accuse you of changing. They may say, "You forgot where you came from." They may try guilt or shame.

Let them.

Because the goal isn't to win everyone's approval. The goal is to build something that lasts—for you and for the people you'll be able to help down the line the right way.

You can't pour into others if your own cup is empty.

Final Thoughts: Help With Strategy, Not Emotion

You're not heartless for saying no. You're not selfish for setting limits. You're not wrong for wanting to keep what you earned.

If you choose to help family or friends, do it:

- With intention
- With a clear budget
- With hard boundaries
- Without shame

Because the best gift you can give isn't a check. It's the example of financial strength, discipline, and long-term thinking.

If they love you, they'll understand. And if they don't now... they will when you're still standing strong ten years from now while others are broke and bitter.

That's real love. That's real leadership. That's legacy.

Chapter 26: Every Household Needs a Game Plan

Think of your financial future like a championship season. You wouldn't go into a big game without a playbook, right? You need strategy. You need roles. You need a team that can win in different situations.

That's exactly what a portfolio is. It's your financial lineup. It's a mix of different players—investments—each with their own strengths, risks, and jobs to do. When you build a smart portfolio, you're giving yourself the best shot at long-term success.

So, What's in a Portfolio?

A portfolio is your mix of money moves. It includes things like:

- Stocks (your offensive players – high-scoring, high-risk)
- Bonds (your defense – stable, dependable, protects the lead)
- Cash (your bench – ready when you need quick subs or timeouts)
- Real estate, ETFs, mutual funds (your utility players – all-around options)

Just like you wouldn't play a whole basketball game with only point guards, you don't want your financial team made up of one type of investment.

You need balance. You need different players. That's where diversification comes in.

Why Diversification Is Like Having a Strong Team

If you put your entire financial future into one stock or one type of investment, it's like betting the whole season on one player. What if they get injured? What if they have a bad game? You're cooked.

Diversification is spreading out your risk. It's like building a full roster—scorers, defenders, role players—so if one guy has a bad night, others can step up.

When the market gets rough (and it will), your diversified portfolio helps you stay in the game.

Different Portfolio "Teams" – Conservative, Moderate, Aggressive

Depending on your goals, age, and mindset, you're going to want a different type of portfolio "team." Let's break it down.

Conservative Portfolio – Play Defense First

This is the type of lineup you build when protecting the lead matters more than running up the score.

You're stacking your team with safe, slow-moving players: mostly bonds, with a few stocks sprinkled in.

It's like playing zone defense, controlling the tempo, limiting fast breaks. You're not trying to blow anyone out—you're just trying not to lose.

Who's it for?

- People close to retirement
- People who need their money soon
- Anyone with a low risk tolerance

Pros:

- Less volatile
- Easier to sleep at night
- Steady, predictable returns

Cons:

- Less upside
- May not beat inflation
- Not ideal for young folks building wealth

Moderate Portfolio – Balanced Offense and Defense

This is your two-way team. A good mix of offense (stocks) and defense (bonds).

You've got players who can score, but you're not ignoring protection. It's like a team that can grind out close games and still run when they need to.

Who's it for?

- People with 5–10 year goals
- Those who want growth but hate chaos
- Anyone building wealth and playing it smart

Pros:

- Balanced risk and return
- Can handle market swings better
- Suitable for most people in the middle of their career

Cons:

- Can feel slow when the market's hot
- Still risky in downturns
- Requires patience

Aggressive Portfolio – Go For the Win

This is your fast-paced, high-scoring team. Mostly made up of stocks, it's built to run the floor, attack constantly, and take big swings.

It's not for the faint of heart—but over time, this strategy usually puts the most points on the board.

Who's it for?

- Younger people
- People who won't need their money for 10+ years
- Risk-takers who understand the long game

Pros:

- Huge upside potential
- Great for early wealth building
- Takes full advantage of compounding over time

Cons:

- Big mood swings (a.k.a. market drops)
- Emotionally tough to stick with
- Not for short-term goals

How to Choose Your Strategy – When to Attack, When to Hold Back

Just like in sports, you change your game plan depending on the situation. You don't full-court press up 30 points in the fourth quarter. You don't play conservative if you're down 10 with two minutes left.

Same with investing.

Be more aggressive when:

- You're in your 20s and 30s
- You don't need the money for at least 10 years
- You're focused on building, not protecting
- You can handle the emotional swings of the market

Be more conservative when:

- You're close to needing the money (within 5 years)
- You're about to retire
- You're risk-averse and losing money keeps you up at night
- You've already won financially and just want to protect your lead

Your Portfolio Changes With Your Season

Your investing strategy should evolve just like your life does.

Early in your journey? You're trying to grow, build, and take some smart risks. That's your aggressive portfolio phase.

Mid-life? You're balancing growth with protection. That's your moderate stage.

Later in life? You've built your lead—now it's about not blowing it. That's when you go conservative.

The key is to know where you are in the game and adjust your lineup accordingly.

Final Thoughts – Build a Dynasty, Not a One-Season Wonder

A good coach knows it's not just about winning one game—it's about building a program that lasts. Your portfolio is your program.

Don't get distracted by hype plays. Don't panic during a losing streak. Don't chase risky trades just because someone else hit big.

Stick to the fundamentals:

- Diversify your roster

- Match your strategy to your season
- Adjust over time
- Play the long game

Because when you look back after 10, 20, 30 years… you'll be glad you didn't go for just highlight reels. You built something solid.

You didn't just play the game. You owned the league.

Chapter 27: Compound Interest

When it comes to building wealth, most people think it takes a lot of money. But the truth is, it takes time and consistency more than anything else. One of the most powerful forces in all of finance is compound interest—and the earlier you start using it, the more it works in your favor.

Albert Einstein allegedly called compound interest the "eighth wonder of the world." He supposedly said:

"He who understands it, earns it. He who doesn't, pays it."

Whether or not Einstein actually said it doesn't matter—because the principle is absolutely true. Compound interest can make your money grow exponentially over time, or it can work against you if you're borrowing and building debt.

In this chapter, you'll learn what compound interest is, how it works, how to make it your financial superpower, and how to avoid being crushed by it through credit cards, loans, or missed opportunities.

What Is Compound Interest?

Compound interest is interest that earns interest. You make money not just on your original investment (called the "principal"), but also on the interest that investment earns over time.

Unlike simple interest, which only pays on the principal, compound interest grows faster and faster over time because every year, you're earning interest on a bigger number.

It's like a snowball rolling downhill—slow at first, but eventually unstoppable.

Example:

If you invest $1,000 at 10% annual interest:

- Year 1: You earn $100. Now you have $1,100.
- Year 2: You earn $110 (10% of $1,100). Now you have $1,210.
- Year 3: You earn $121. Now you have $1,331.

Over time, the gains get bigger—not because you added more money, but because the growth builds on itself.

Why Compound Interest Matters for You (Especially Now)

You have something most people don't: youth. And when it comes to compound interest, the earlier you start, the more powerful it becomes.

Even small amounts can turn into huge sums if you give them time.

Let's compare two people:

One starts investing $200/month at age 18 and stops at age 28. They invest for just 10 years—$24,000 total.

Another waits until age 28 to start and invests $200/month until age 65. They invest for 37 years—$88,800 total.

Assuming an 8% return, the person who started earlier ends up with more money—even though they invested less—because their money had more time to grow.

Time Is More Valuable Than Timing

A lot of people try to "time the market." They wait for the right moment to invest. But when it comes to compound interest, time in the market matters far more than trying to time the market.

The best time to start was yesterday. The second-best time is today.

The longer your money stays invested, the more compound interest can do its magic.

Rule of 72 – The Shortcut to Doubling Your Money

Want to know how long it takes to double your money with compound interest? Use the Rule of 72.

Just divide 72 by your expected annual return.

Examples:

- 72 ÷ 6% = 12 years to double
- 72 ÷ 9% = 8 years to double
- 72 ÷ 12% = 6 years to double

So if you earn 9% annually, your money will double about every 8 years. That means $10,000 becomes $20,000 in 8 years… $40,000 in 16 years… and $80,000 in 24 years. Without you adding a single extra dollar.

The Compounding Timeline – Why Waiting Hurts

Every year you wait makes it harder to catch up. Let's look at three people who all invest $100/month at 8% return:

- Start at age 18: ~$351,428 by age 65
- Start at age 28: ~$164,870 by age 65
- Start at age 38: ~$74,336 by age 65

Waiting just 10 years can cost you hundreds of thousands of dollars. That's the power of compound interest. It rewards early starters and punishes procrastinators.

Where Can You Use Compound Interest?

You don't need to be a Wall Street trader to benefit from compounding. Here are common accounts that allow compound interest to work for you:

- Roth IRA – Tax-free growth and withdrawals in retirement
- Traditional IRA or 401(k) – Tax-deferred growth
- High-yield savings accounts – Low growth, but still compound
- Investment accounts (brokerage accounts) – Stocks, ETFs, mutual funds
- HSA (Health Savings Account) – Triple tax benefit if used properly

Start small. Stay consistent. Let time do the heavy lifting.

Compound Interest Can Hurt You Too

So far we've talked about compound interest working for you. But it can also work against you—especially when you're dealing with debt.

Credit cards, payday loans, and high-interest loans compound your debt, not your wealth.

Let's say you owe $5,000 on a credit card at 22% interest. If you don't pay it off quickly, that balance can balloon. You end up paying thousands more than you borrowed.

The same snowball effect that makes investments grow can turn debt into a financial disaster.

Protect Yourself: Avoid the Trap of Reverse Compounding

To make compound interest work for you, not against you:

- Pay off credit cards in full each month
- Avoid payday loans or high-interest borrowing
- Don't finance things you don't need

- Invest early and regularly—even small amounts matter
- Automate savings and investment to stay consistent

The goal is to earn compound interest, not owe it.

The Mindset Shift: Think Like an Investor, Not a Spender

Here's the bottom line: when you get extra money, you'll be tempted to spend it. That's natural. But every dollar you spend today is a dollar that won't grow tomorrow.

Think like an investor. Ask:

- Will this help me grow long-term?
- Am I giving this dollar a job, or am I letting it disappear?
- Can I invest this now so I don't have to work as hard later?

Compound interest is like planting a tree. You won't get shade immediately—but in a few years, you'll be thankful you did.

How to Get Started – Action Steps

- Open a Roth IRA – It's tax-free growth, and you can contribute up to $6,500/year (as of 2025) if you have earned income.
- Set up recurring contributions – Automate $50, $100, or more monthly.
- Choose a low-cost index fund – S&P 500 or Total Market index funds are great for starters.
- Leave it alone – Resist the urge to withdraw. Let it compound.
- Check once a year – Rebalance if needed, but don't obsess.
- Increase contributions as your income grows – Pay yourself first.

Final Thoughts: Make Compound Interest Your Teammate

You understand what it means to play the long game. You show up, you grind, and the results come later. Compound interest works the same way.

It rewards patience, discipline, and consistency.

The money you invest now has the power to buy your freedom later—freedom to choose your job, support your family, travel, give back, and retire early.

So don't just hustle for today. Put some of it to work for the future you.

Compound interest doesn't need you to be rich to start. It just needs you to start.

Chapter 28: How to Buy a Personal Home

Buying your first home isn't just a financial decision—it's a life-changing move. It's proof that stability, ownership, and legacy are possible, even if no one around you ever had it. Maybe you grew up in apartments. Maybe your family never owned property. Maybe people told you owning a home was "doing too much." But here's the truth:

Homeownership is one of the most powerful ways to build generational wealth.

And it's not just for "them." It's for *us*, too.

This chapter is your step-by-step guide to going from renting to owning—on purpose, with preparation, and without being played.

Why Buying a Home Matters

Let's keep it real: buying a home is hard work. But it's worth it. When done right, a personal home can:

- Build equity as the value increases
- Provide stability in neighborhoods and schools
- Be passed down or sold to support future goals
- Shield you from rising rent
- Become a base for business, family, and future planning

Homeownership isn't just about the house—it's about the power, pride, and peace that comes with it.

Before You Even Look at Homes

1. Check Your Credit

Your credit score will determine what kind of loan you qualify for, how much you'll pay in interest, and how smooth your approval process will be.

Goal: Aim for at least a 620 for FHA loans, and 700+ for better rates.

2. Pay Down Debt

Lenders look at your **debt-to-income ratio**—how much you owe versus how much you make. Lower debt = more loan options.

3. Build an Emergency Fund

Before you sign any mortgage, make sure you have 3–6 months of living expenses saved. Homeownership brings surprise expenses—roof leaks, broken appliances, etc.

4. Save for a Down Payment

The bigger your down payment, the lower your mortgage. But you don't need 20% to buy a house.

- FHA loans: As little as 3.5% down
- VA loans: 0% down (if you qualify)
- Conventional loans: Usually 5%–20%

Plus: You'll need money for closing costs (2%–5% of the home price).

The Homebuying Process, Step by Step

Step 1: Get Pre-Approved for a Mortgage

Don't go house-hunting without knowing what you can afford. A lender will review your credit, income, debts, and savings.

Pro Tip: Don't just get "pre-qualified." Get **pre-approved**—it's stronger and shows sellers you're serious.

Step 2: Set Your Budget (Not Just the Bank's Budget)

Just because the bank says you can afford a $400,000 home doesn't mean you should. Factor in:

- Mortgage payment
- Property taxes
- Insurance
- Utilities
- Maintenance
- HOA fees (if any)

Only commit to a monthly payment you can handle **comfortably**.

Step 3: Choose the Right Real Estate Agent

Find an agent who understands **you**, your community, your goals, and your budget. Don't just work with your cousin's friend if they're not aligned with your vision.

Ask them:

- Do you specialize in first-time homebuyers?
- Are you familiar with programs that help people in my situation?
- Can you walk me through this entire process step by step?

Step 4: Start House Hunting

Make a list of **must-haves** (3 bedrooms, safe neighborhood, good schools) vs. **nice-to-haves** (a pool, updated kitchen).

Visit multiple homes. Don't rush. Trust your gut—but trust your budget more.

Step 5: Make an Offer

Once you find a home you love (and can afford), your agent will help you submit an offer. Be prepared to negotiate. You may need to offer more if the market is competitive.

Earnest money: A small deposit (usually 1%–3%) that shows you're serious. It's applied to your down payment or closing costs.

Step 6: Home Inspection & Appraisal

Inspection: Hire a licensed home inspector to check for issues (plumbing, foundation, roof, etc.).

Appraisal: Your lender will send someone to confirm the home is worth the price you're paying.

If issues are found, you can:

- Ask the seller to fix them
- Ask for a credit to fix them yourself
- Walk away if it's too risky

Step 7: Final Approval & Closing

Your lender reviews everything one last time (credit, income, etc.) and issues a "clear to close."

At **closing**, you'll:

- Sign a lot of documents
- Pay your down payment and closing costs
- Get your keys

Welcome to ownership.

The Pros of Buying a Home

- **Stability:** No more worrying about rent hikes or being forced out.
- **Equity Growth:** Every mortgage payment brings you closer to full ownership.
- **Customization:** Want to paint the walls purple? Go for it—it's your house.
- **Potential Tax Benefits:** You may deduct mortgage interest or property taxes.
- **Generational Wealth:** Your kids or future heirs inherit not just money—but security.

The Cons to Be Aware Of

- **Upfront Costs:** Down payments and closing costs can be steep.
- **Maintenance:** You're responsible for all repairs. There's no landlord to call.
- **Lack of Flexibility:** Selling a home takes time. If you move often, this could be a drawback.
- **Market Risk:** Home values can fall during recessions or local downturns.
- **Insurance & Taxes:** These often increase over time, affecting affordability.

Tips For First-Time Buyers in the Culture

- **Look into down payment assistance programs.** Cities, states, and nonprofits offer grants and loans to first-time and lower-income buyers.
- **Buy with intention.** Don't stretch just to impress. Buy what fits your life and financial plan.
- **Don't skip the inspection.** Even if the house looks good, always check under the hood.
- **Budget for more than just the mortgage.** Furniture, repairs, yard tools—it adds up.
- **Think long-term.** A home can be a blessing or a burden depending on how you manage it.

Key Questions to Ask

- What is the monthly mortgage including taxes and insurance?
- How much should I expect to spend on maintenance each year?
- Can I comfortably afford this home on one income if needed?
- Am I buying in an area that's growing in value or declining?
- What's my backup plan if I lose income or need to move?

Final Word: Buy Smart. Buy Strong. Buy for the Future.

Homeownership isn't just about keys and contracts—it's about claiming space in a world that hasn't always welcomed us.

It's about building equity, planting roots, and creating something that outlives you. It's about saying, **"This is ours."**

You don't have to do it all today. But when you're ready, step in with knowledge, power, and a team around you that's just as committed to your legacy as you are.

Chapter 29: How to Buy a Car

For a lot of folks, buying a car is the first major financial decision they make. And let's be honest—**it's easy to get got.**

Whether it's a slick-talking salesperson, sky-high interest rates, or a car that looks good on the outside but is falling apart underneath, the car-buying game is full of traps. But when you know the rules, you don't just play the game—you win it.

This chapter will walk you through how to buy a car wisely, whether you're buying new or used, from a dealership or a private seller, financing or paying cash.

Let's make sure your next ride moves you forward—not backward.

Step 1: Know Your "Why"

Before you start scrolling through dealership websites or hitting up Craigslist, ask yourself:

- **Why do I need this car?** (Commute? Family? Rideshare driving?)
- **How often will I drive it?**
- **What kind of maintenance can I handle?**
- **How long do I plan to keep it?**

Knowing your "why" helps you avoid buying more car than you need—or less car than your life requires.

Step 2: Set a Real Budget

Forget what the dealership tells you. They'll ask, "What monthly payment are you looking for?" But that's the wrong question.

You need to know the full cost:

- Purchase price
- Interest over time
- Insurance
- Gas
- Maintenance
- Tags, taxes, and registration

Rule of Thumb:

Your car (including the loan and insurance) should cost no more than **15%–20%** of your take-home pay.

If your monthly take-home pay is $3,000, aim for no more than $450–$600/month total for the car and all its costs.

Step 3: Decide How You'll Pay

Cash

- No payments, no interest, no stress.
- Great for cheaper used cars.
- If you've got the savings, this is the simplest way.

Financing

- A loan from a bank, credit union, or dealership.
- Monthly payments over 3–7 years.
- Interest rates depend on your credit score.

Pro Tip:

Shop for a loan BEFORE you shop for the car. That way, you know what you can afford—and avoid letting the dealership "find you financing" (which often means higher interest rates).

Leasing

- Like renting a car for 2–3 years.
- Lower monthly payments, but you don't own the car.
- Usually has mileage limits and fees for wear and tear.

Unless you're a business owner writing off the lease, leasing usually isn't a wealth-building move.

Step 4: Know Your Credit Score

Your **credit score affects your interest rate.**

- 750+ = Excellent (lowest rates)
- 700–749 = Good
- 650–699 = Fair
- Below 650 = High risk (high interest)

A low credit score can cost you thousands over the life of a loan. If your credit is struggling, focus on improving it before buying—or buy a cheap used car in cash and build credit while you drive.

Step 5: New vs. Used?

New Car Pros:

- Warranty included
- Lower maintenance (at first)
- Latest features

New Car Cons:

- **Loses value fast** (20%–30% just by driving off the lot)
- Higher purchase price
- Higher insurance

Used Car Pros:

- Lower price
- Slower depreciation
- Lower insurance

Used Car Cons:

- May need repairs sooner
- Shorter or no warranty
- Unknown history if not certified

Smart Strategy:

Buy a used car that's 2–4 years old. Let someone else take the depreciation hit, while you still get a reliable ride.

Step 6: Do Your Research

Don't buy anything you haven't researched thoroughly.

Sites to use:

- Kelley Blue Book (kbb.com) – to check fair prices
- Edmunds.com – car reviews and comparisons
- Carfax.com – vehicle history reports
- Autotrader, Cars.com, Facebook Marketplace – to shop

Look up:

- Reliability
- Gas mileage
- Average maintenance costs
- Common issues

Ask: "Can I afford to maintain this car for the next 5 years?"

Step 7: Don't Skip the Test Drive (and Inspection)

Drive it how you'll actually use it—on the highway, in traffic, uphill. Listen for weird sounds. Check how it brakes and accelerates. See if you fit comfortably.

If buying used: Always get a **pre-purchase inspection** from a trusted mechanic. It might cost $100—but it could save you thousands.

Step 8: Make the Deal Work for YOU

If at a dealership:

- Never say you "love" the car. It kills your negotiating power.
- Know the value of the car before you arrive (use KBB).
- Negotiate the **price**, not the monthly payment.
- Walk away if the deal doesn't feel right. There will be other cars.

If buying from a private seller:

- Meet in a public place
- Check the title and VIN
- Make sure there are no liens or legal issues
- Bring someone with you for safety

Step 9: Don't Forget the Extra Costs

Once you buy the car, you'll still need to budget for:

- **Insurance:** Shop around and get quotes beforehand.
- **Sales tax:** Varies by state—don't forget it at closing.
- **Registration and tags:** Required by your DMV.
- **Maintenance:** Oil changes, tires, brakes—plan ahead.
- **Gas:** Hybrid or electric might save you money long-term.

The Pros of Buying a Car

- Freedom and flexibility
- No relying on Uber or others
- Long-term savings if you choose wisely
- A tool for work, family, or business
- Asset (if paid off) you can leverage or sell

The Cons of Buying a Car

- Depreciation—value drops fast
- Ongoing maintenance costs
- Car loans can trap you if you overpay or finance too long
- Insurance and repairs add up
- Emotional purchases can lead to long-term regret

For the Culture: Drive Smart, Not Just Flashy

Let's be real—car culture is big in our communities. From candy-painted Impalas to luxury foreign whips, the car has always been more than transportation—it's been a statement.

But **don't let the statement cost you your savings**.

Your car should fit your lifestyle and your long-term financial goals. Owning a nice car and being broke behind the wheel is not the move.

If you're gonna flex, **flex smart.**

Final Word: Own the Road, Don't Let It Own You

Buying a car is one of the most common ways people fall behind financially. But it can also be one of the smartest moves if done right. Don't rush. Don't get played. Don't overspend trying to impress people who don't pay your bills.

Move with strategy.

Drive with purpose.

And remember: *the best car is the one that gets you where you're going—financially, physically, and spiritually.*

Chapter 30: Home and Auto Insurance

We talk a lot about building wealth, but part of that game is *protecting* what you build. That's where insurance comes in. It's not flashy. It's not exciting. But it's essential. Because whether it's your house or your car, one unexpected event could set you all the way back if you're not covered right.

Let's break down how home and auto insurance actually work, what deductibles mean, and how to pick a policy that doesn't just sound good—but actually *is* good.

What Is Insurance?

Insurance is a contract between you and a company. You pay them a little each month (called a premium), and in return, they agree to cover you for big, unexpected losses—like a car accident, house fire, theft, storm damage, or liability lawsuits.

It's like paying a security guard to watch your stuff. If nothing happens? Cool—you're safe. If something *does* happen? That guard steps in to protect you from major losses.

Home Insurance: More Than Just the House

When people hear "homeowners insurance," they think it's just about the building—but it covers a lot more than that.

Dwelling Coverage

This is the core of your home insurance. It covers the physical structure of your house: walls, roof, floors, built-in appliances, etc.

If your home is damaged by a covered event (like fire, lightning, hail, or wind), this kicks in to repair or rebuild it.

Property (or Personal Property) Coverage

This covers the stuff inside your house—your clothes, furniture, electronics, kitchenware, jewelry, and so on.

Make sure this part is high enough to actually replace your valuables if you had to start from scratch.

Liability Coverage

If someone gets hurt on your property and sues you? This is your protection. It also covers damage your kids or pets might cause to other people's property.

Loss of Use Coverage

If your house gets so damaged you can't live in it during repairs, this helps pay for hotel stays or temporary housing.

Auto Insurance: Keeping You Covered On the Road

Auto insurance works similarly—but tailored for your car and what happens on the road.

Liability Insurance

This is usually *required* by law. It covers damage or injuries you cause to others in an accident. If it's your fault, liability pays for their medical bills and car repairs—not yours.

There are two parts:

- **Bodily Injury Liability**: Covers medical costs for people you hurt.
- **Property Damage Liability**: Covers damage you cause to someone else's car or property.

Collision Coverage

This covers damage to *your* car if you crash into something (or someone), no matter who's at fault.

Comprehensive Coverage

This covers your car for non-collision incidents: theft, vandalism, fire, falling trees, broken windows, hail damage—you name it.

Uninsured/Underinsured Motorist Coverage

If someone hits you and *they* don't have enough (or any) insurance? This covers your costs so you're not stuck paying.

What's a Deductible?

A **deductible** is the amount you pay out of pocket before your insurance starts helping.

If your deductible is $1,000 and a tree falls on your house causing $10,000 of damage, you pay $1,000 and your insurance pays $9,000.

High Deductible vs. Low Deductible

High Deductible

- You'll pay less in monthly premiums.
- But when something happens, you pay more out of pocket.

Low Deductible

- You'll pay more each month.
- But your insurance kicks in quicker with smaller expenses.

Which one is better?

It depends on your financial situation.

If you have a strong emergency fund, a **high deductible** might make sense to save on premiums.

If you don't have cash ready for emergencies, go for a **lower deductible**—even if the monthly premium is higher.

Pros and Cons of Home and Auto Insurance

Pros

- Protects your biggest assets: your home, car, and future income.
- Gives peace of mind—less stress if the worst happens.
- Helps prevent financial disasters from lawsuits, theft, or natural disasters.

Cons

- Can be expensive—especially if you over-insure or have low deductibles.

- Policies can be confusing if you don't read the fine print.
- Claims can raise your premium over time.

How to Pick a Good Policy

Step One: Shop Around

Don't just go with the company your cousin recommends or the first quote you get. Compare at least three.

Step Two: Know What's Covered

Not all policies are equal. One may exclude flood damage or only offer actual cash value (which depreciates your stuff).

Make sure you understand:

- What's covered
- What's excluded
- The limits of coverage
- The deductible
- How claims are handled

Step Three: Look for Discounts

Bundling home and auto with the same company? You might get a discount.

Good driving record? Security system? Loyalty discount? Ask about all of it.

Review It Every Year

Just like you don't wear the same outfit every day, you shouldn't keep the same insurance plan forever.

Life changes. You move. You buy new stuff. You get married. Your kids start driving.

Review your policies every year and adjust:

- Are your coverage limits still enough?
- Did you buy expensive electronics or jewelry this year?
- Has your driving record improved (which might lower your rate)?
- Did your home value change?

Final Thoughts: Insurance Is a Safety Net, Not a Scam

A lot of people think, "I've never used it, so why pay for it?"

That's like saying, "I've never had a fire, so why own a fire extinguisher?"

When life hits hard, insurance keeps you from going broke. It protects what you've built and gives you room to recover.

Make it part of your financial routine:

- Budget for premiums
- Set your deductibles based on your savings
- Pick policies that fit your actual needs
- Review them yearly
- Don't be afraid to switch if you find better coverage

Because financial literacy isn't just about making money. It's about keeping it—and protecting what's yours.

Chapter 31: Investing in Real Estate – Building Wealth Beyond the Block

For generations, we've been told that real estate is the cornerstone of wealth—and in many ways, it's true. But for many in *The Culture,* the road to owning property has been filled with redlining, inflated interest rates, lack of representation, and misinformation. Still, we've found a way to make a way. Whether it was your grandmother owning the family home outright or your cousin flipping rentals—real estate has always been one of the most powerful paths to economic freedom. This chapter breaks it all down, plain and simple.

Why Real Estate Still Matters

Unlike some investments that feel abstract or out of reach, real estate is *tangible.* You can walk into it. Live in it. Rent it. Improve it. Pass it down. It's one of the few asset classes where ownership often feels real, especially in communities where land was historically taken or never offered.

But real estate isn't just about emotions—it's about economics. When done right, it can:

- Generate passive income
- Appreciate in value over time
- Offer tax advantages
- Build generational wealth

Let's break it down further.

The Pros of Real Estate Investing

1. Cash Flow

Rental properties can bring in monthly income that exceeds your expenses. That's money in your pocket every month—passively.

2. Appreciation

Over time, real estate tends to increase in value. A house bought for $150,000 today could be worth $250,000 in 10 years. That increase in value builds your net worth.

3. Leverage

You can use other people's money (the bank's) to buy an asset. That means with a relatively small down payment, you can control a large property and benefit from its full value growth.

4. Tax Benefits

Owners can deduct mortgage interest, property taxes, maintenance, depreciation, and other expenses. Real estate often reduces your taxable income.

5. Tangible Asset

You can see it. Touch it. Improve it. Rent it. Live in it. Pass it down. That's different from stocks or crypto, which can feel invisible or unpredictable.

6. Legacy & Equity

Owning a property in the right area means you've got a valuable asset that can support your family for generations.

The Cons of Real Estate Investing

1. Upfront Costs

It takes money to get started. Down payments, closing costs, inspections—it adds up quickly.

2. Time & Effort

You might deal with tenants, maintenance, vacancies, late-night calls, and unexpected repairs. It's not always "passive."

3. Market Risk

Housing markets can crash. Neighborhoods can decline. You might buy at the wrong time or price.

4. Liquidity

You can't sell a house in 24 hours if you need cash. It takes time to sell, and there's no guarantee you'll get what you want.

5. Debt Risk

Taking on a mortgage is a big responsibility. If you lose your job or a tenant bounces, the mortgage is still due.

Types of Real Estate Investing

- **Primary Residence** – Your home. Often the first and most important investment.
- **Rental Properties** – Single-family homes, duplexes, or multi-units rented out for monthly income.
- **House Hacking** – Living in one part of a home (like a duplex) and renting the other to cover your mortgage.
- **Fix and Flip** – Buying undervalued homes, improving them, and selling for profit.
- **Short-Term Rentals** – Airbnb-style properties rented by the night or week.
- **REITs (Real Estate Investment Trusts)** – Stocks you can buy that let you invest in real estate without owning property directly.

Action Steps to Get Started

Step 1: Get Your Money Right

- Build an emergency fund (3–6 months of expenses)
- Pay down high-interest debt
- Improve your credit score (aim for 700+ for the best loan rates)

Step 2: Educate Yourself

- Read real estate books
- Follow real estate investors of color on YouTube, Instagram, or podcasts
- Join local real estate meetups or Facebook groups

Step 3: Choose Your Strategy

- Are you buying a home for your family?
- Do you want to rent it out?
- Do you want to flip houses?
- Know your goal before you buy.

Step 4: Get Pre-Approved

- Talk to multiple lenders
- Understand your loan options (FHA, conventional, VA, etc.)
- Know how much you can afford—not just what they say you qualify for

Step 5: Start Looking

- Work with a real estate agent who understands your goals and your background
- Look in up-and-coming areas
- Check school districts, job growth, and development plans

Step 6: Run the Numbers

- Can you rent it for more than it costs you?
- Factor in taxes, insurance, repairs, and vacancies
- Use tools like BiggerPockets calculators or Excel

Step 7: Protect Your Investment

- Get landlord insurance
- Create a lease agreement with legal support
- Consider forming an LLC to hold rental property

Tips for the Culture

- **You don't need to start big.** Buy a duplex. House hack. Partner with someone. Start where you are.
- **Ownership equals power.** Don't let fear or lack of knowledge keep you from building equity.
- **Land is legacy.** Whether it's one property or ten, real estate can become part of your family's future.
- **Don't get hustled.** Do your research. Know your numbers. Vet every deal, every lender, every contractor.
- **Work with professionals who understand you.** Your lender, realtor, and attorney should speak your language—literally and culturally.

Final Word: The Block Is Watching

Real estate isn't just about profit—it's about presence. When we own, we shift power. We stabilize neighborhoods. We keep grandma's house out of probate court. We raise kids with roots. We plant seeds for the next generation.

Real estate won't solve every problem, but it gives you options. And in this world, **options = freedom**.

So if you've ever dreamed of buying back the block—or just buying your first home—know this: **you can.** And when you do, you're not just investing in property. You're investing in power, purpose, and *The Culture*.

Chapter 32: The Other Big Expenses

What Life Hits You With When You Least Expect It

Let's keep it real: life costs money.

And not just rent and food. We're talking about those **big-ticket moments**—the milestones, emergencies, and surprises that can either build your legacy or break your budget if you're not ready.

In many of our communities, we weren't always prepared for these expenses because nobody talked about them. Nobody planned for them. So when they showed up, they hit like a financial storm.

This chapter is about naming those major money moments and helping you get in position before they show up—so you can move with power, not panic.

1. Having a Baby

Babies are beautiful—but they're not free.

Costs to consider:

- Prenatal care and delivery (especially if uninsured or underinsured)
- Hospital bills
- Diapers, formula, clothes, crib, car seat
- Childcare (can be $800–$2,000+ per month)
- Lost income if one parent takes time off work

Tip: Before the baby arrives, start a "baby fund." Look into employer leave policies, Medicaid, WIC, and free parenting resources in your community.

2. Childcare and Education

From daycare to college, raising kids requires real resources.

Costs to expect:

- Preschool or daycare
- After-school programs
- School supplies, tech, extracurriculars
- College tuition or trade school
- Out-of-state fees or dorm costs

Tip: Open a **529 Plan** or custodial account early. Even small monthly contributions grow over time. And teach kids about money from day one—financial literacy starts at home.

3. Weddings

You love them. You want to celebrate them. But weddings can wreck your wallet if you're not careful.

Average cost in the U.S.: $25,000–$30,000+

Things people forget to budget for:

- Rings
- Photographer/videographer
- Travel for guests or destination weddings
- Decor, DJ, food, dress, venue
- Bachelor/bachelorette weekends

Tip: Set a budget and stick to it. Consider smaller or backyard weddings, or delay the celebration until you're financially stable. Love don't have to go broke to be real.

4. Buying a Home

Covered in a previous chapter—but don't forget:

- Down payment
- Closing costs
- Furniture and appliances
- Ongoing repairs
- Property taxes and insurance
- Moving costs

Tip: Plan for not just the mortgage—but **everything** that comes with it. That's how people end up house-rich, cash-poor.

5. Moving Out On Your Own

Leaving home is a flex—but rent comes with receipts.
Costs:

- First and last month's rent + deposit
- U-Haul or movers
- Furniture, kitchenware, bedding
- Utilities, Wi-Fi, renters insurance
- Setting up new bills or canceling old ones

Tip: Don't move out just for freedom—move out with a **financial cushion**. Otherwise, you're just trading one struggle for another.

6. Losing a Job

Nobody sees it coming. And for too many of us, it's just one layoff away from real crisis.

Expenses to cover:

- Rent, utilities, food
- Health insurance (if it was through your job)
- Debt payments (credit cards, loans)
- Transportation

Tip: Have an emergency fund with 3–6 months of living expenses. If that's not possible yet, start with 1 month and build from there. Look into unemployment benefits, COBRA, or local support services.

7. Illness or Disability

An unexpected diagnosis can wipe out a lifetime of savings.

Costs to plan for:

- Doctor visits, hospital stays
- Medications
- Time off work
- Transportation and home modifications
- Caregiver support

Tip: Get **health insurance** and **disability insurance**—even if you're young and healthy. One accident or illness can change everything.

8. Death in the Family

In our culture, funerals are often a celebration of life—but too often, they come with **financial trauma**.

Costs:

- Funeral service, casket, burial or cremation
- Flowers, obituaries, food
- Travel for family
- Legal and probate costs
- Unpaid debts or medical bills

Tip: Get **life insurance** and talk about **funeral planning** in advance. Don't leave your people scrambling with GoFundMe links. Planning is protection.

9. Supporting Family

Let's be honest—**we are the emergency fund** in many families.

Whether it's helping a sibling, co-signing for a cousin, or taking in a relative, our culture emphasizes collective support. That's beautiful. But it can also put pressure on your own financial foundation.

Tip: Set boundaries. Create a "family support budget." Say yes when you can—but not at the cost of your own stability. You can't pour from an empty cup.

10. Starting a Business

Launching your dream isn't cheap.

Costs:

- Licenses, permits, insurance
- Equipment, supplies, software

- Branding, website, marketing
- Rent, payroll, taxes
- Legal and accounting fees

Tip: Start small, stay lean, and don't quit your job without a plan. Build while you learn. And treat your side hustle like a business—even before it starts making money.

11. Legal Trouble

Court costs can hit hard—even if you're innocent.

Potential expenses:

- Attorney fees
- Bail or bond
- Court fines
- Missed work
- Expungement costs

Tip: Know your rights. Avoid unnecessary risks. And consider prepaid legal services or local advocacy programs that offer affordable help.

12. Car Accidents and Repairs

Even if you have insurance, it doesn't cover everything.

Costs to expect:

- Deductible (often $500–$1,000)
- Rental car
- Towing fees
- Lost wages if you can't work
- Higher premiums after an accident

Tip: Have a car repair/emergency fund. And always keep your insurance up to date.

Final Word: Don't Let Life Catch You Slippin'

Here's the truth: **most financial emergencies aren't really emergencies—they're just unplanned life.**

And in our community, unplanned often means unprepared.

But it doesn't have to be that way anymore.

You don't need to be rich. You just need to be **aware**, **intentional**, and **ready**. Because the best time to prepare for a storm isn't when it hits—it's when the skies are still clear.

So let this chapter be a reminder:

You might not control every life event.

But you can control how ready you are for it.

And readiness is a form of wealth, too.

Closing Chapter 33: The Game Don't Stop—It Just Changes

So here we are.

You made it through the budgeting.

The investing.

The car buying.

The credit score breakdowns.

The legacy planning.

The tough conversations about family, money, trauma, and trust.

And if you're feeling a little overwhelmed, good. That means this wasn't just surface-level.

It means you're thinking different. Moving different. Planning different.

Because let's be honest—this book was never just about money.

It's about **mindset**.

It's about **healing from financial hurt**.

It's about **taking control of what our communities were never taught**.

For too long, financial literacy was something "other people" had.

Something whispered in boardrooms. Hidden in tax codes. Gatekept behind jargon.

But not anymore.

This book was written so *we*—Black folks, Brown folks, folks from the block, from the barbershop, from the church, from the lunch table, from the dorm rooms and living rooms—could finally have a seat at the table **with a game plan.**

Now That You Know, What Will You Do?

Because here's the thing about financial literacy—it ain't about perfection.

It's about **progress**.

It's about making one better decision today than you made yesterday.

It's about choosing to open the mail instead of ignoring the bills.

It's about checking your bank account instead of pretending everything's fine.

It's about saying, "I don't know—but I'm willing to learn."

This is your moment to flip the script.

Your Future Is Calling—And It Sounds Like Freedom

Real wealth isn't just about stocks or property.

It's peace of mind.

It's waking up knowing the lights will stay on.

It's saying "yes" to opportunities and "no" to desperation.

It's watching your kids grow up with confidence, not chaos.

It's breaking cycles so deep they've got roots in our bloodline.

And listen—**you're already doing it.**

Every page you read.

Every note you took.

Every question you started asking.

That's movement.

Keep the Conversation Going

Don't close this book and go quiet.

Talk about money with your people.

With your kids. With your crew. With your partner.

Start where you are. Share what you've learned. Stay curious. Stay connected.

If something in this book spoke to you, *pass it forward.*

Your story might be the blueprint someone else needs.

And if you ever feel lost or stuck, remember this:

> ***You were never meant to do this alone.***
>
> ***You come from a people who survive. Now it's your turn to thrive.***

Final Word: Wealth Is the Revolution

Owning land is revolutionary.

Budgeting is revolutionary.

Teaching your kids about compound interest is revolutionary.

Getting out of debt and building a legacy is revolutionary.

Protecting your peace and passing something down is revolutionary.

This is how we fight back.

With spreadsheets and bank accounts.

With wills and insurance.

With discipline and information.

With community and courage.

So go build. Go dream. Go budget. Go invest. Go start that business. Go heal.

Go change your last name's financial reputation.

Go be the one who flipped the story in your family.

Because **you are the culture.**

And now, **you are financially literate.**

Important Dates

We weren't always taught how to manage money. Some of us grew up in households where financial talk was kept quiet—or filled with stress. But this is where we change the story. One month at a time.

This calendar is for the hustlers, creators, athletes, and side-grinders in the community—especially those earning income through NIL, freelance work, content creation, or entrepreneurship. Let this guide help you move smarter through the year, stay ready when tax season hits, and stack wisely for your future.

- January – Lay the Foundation

Jan 1: A New Tax Year Begins

- Start tracking every dollar you earn and spend related to NIL or your business hustle.
- Use tools like Google Sheets, QuickBooks Self-Employed, Keeper Tax, or Expensify.
- **Rule of Thumb:** Save **25%–30%** of every payment you receive for taxes.
- **Cultural Tip:** Open a separate business checking account. Keep your hustle money out of your everyday account.

Jan 15: Final Estimated Tax Payment for Last Year

- If you earned more than $1,000 in profits last year with no tax withholding, pay now to avoid penalties.

- **Form to Know:** IRS Form **1040-ES**

Jan 31: Expect Your Tax Forms

- If you did NIL or gig work, expect:
- **Form 1099-NEC** – from brands who paid you
- **Form 1099-K** – from payment apps (Cash App, PayPal, etc.) if over $600
- **W-2** – only if you were on payroll
- Save all these to a digital folder labeled **"2024 Taxes – NIL"**
- February – Get Organized Like a Boss
- Collect receipts from all business-related expenses: gear, travel, training, promo, marketing.
- Track your mileage if you drive for events.
- **Tax Forms You'll Use:**
- **Schedule C (Form 1040)** – reports your self-employed income
- **Schedule SE** – calculates self-employment tax (usually 15.3%)
- March – Business Owner Time

March 15: Deadline for S-Corps or LLCs

- If you set up an LLC or S-Corp for NIL or business income, this is your tax filing deadline.
- **Form to Know:** IRS Form **1120S**
- **Cultural Hustle Tip:** You don't need to be a big-time CEO to benefit from a business entity—sometimes just claiming your creativity the right way puts more money back in your pocket.
- April – Game Time

April 15: The Big Tax Day

- File your federal taxes.
- Make your **1st quarter estimated tax payment** for this year.

- Last day to contribute to an **IRA** or **HSA** for the previous year (if you qualify).
- **If You Need More Time:** File **Form 4868** for an extension.
- **Real Talk:** Even if you're broke, **file your taxes**—not filing is worse than not paying.
- June – Mid-Year Check-In

June 15: 2nd Quarter Estimated Taxes Due

- If your income's climbing, now's the time to adjust what you're saving for taxes.
- Review your budget and schedule time with a tax pro if you need guidance.
- **Mid-Year Move:** Ask yourself—are your financial goals still aligned with how you're living?
- July – Reflection & Repositioning

July 1: NIL Anniversary

- Celebrate your wins and evaluate your money mindset.
- Review contracts, brand partnerships, and rates.
- **Tip:** If you're consistently making money, forming an LLC might help you protect your name and reduce your tax bill.
- September – Tighten Up

September 15: 3rd Quarter Estimated Taxes Due

- Organize your receipts and financial records before the fall rush.
- Start pre-filing strategies now so you're not overwhelmed come January.
- October – Look Ahead to College & Taxes

October 1: FAFSA Opens

- NIL income might impact financial aid—especially for dependent students.
- **Tip:** Talk with a college financial aid advisor or CPA who understands NIL rules and student finances.

October 15: Final Tax Filing Deadline (for those who filed extensions)

- If you asked for more time back in April, it's up.
- November – Power Planning Season
- Schedule a session with a tax professional, accountant, or financial advisor.
- Revisit your budget.
- Make purchases now (camera gear, gym memberships, website renewals, etc.) if they're related to your hustle.
- Consider charitable donations—it's good for the soul **and** the tax return.
- **Reminder:** Track everything. If it supports your business or brand, document it.
- December – Close Strong

December 31: Final Day for Many Tax Moves

- Last chance to:
- Make business purchases
- Secure NIL deals for this tax year
- Contribute to retirement plans like SEP IRAs or Solo 401(k)s
- **Safe Harbor Tip:** If you pay at least **100% of last year's tax** (or 110% if you made over $150k), you can avoid underpayment penalties.
- Year-Round Financial Rules of Thumb – For the Culture

1. **Save at least 25%–30% of every NIL or freelance check for taxes.** Don't let the IRS catch you off guard. Be ready.
2. **Keep business and personal money separate.**

It'll make taxes easier and protect your financial identity.

3. Track everything.

Receipts, mileage, subscriptions, gear, travel—it's all deductible if it supports your work.

4. Build your team.

Find a CPA, tax preparer, or financial advisor who understands Black and Brown entrepreneurs, creators, and athletes.

5. Learn your state's rules.

Your income may be taxed differently depending on where you live, where you perform, and where you were paid.

6. Use tools that work for you.

Free is fine to start. Use what helps you stay organized—Google Sheets, Keeper Tax, MileIQ, QuickBooks.

7. Normalize talking about money.

- With your friends. With your family. With your circle. We're breaking generational silence and building wealth on purpose.

About the Author

Pat Brown, MBA is a former Division I football player turned financial educator, advisor, and champion for communities that have historically been left out of the wealth conversation. A fierce advocate for access, equity, and education, Pat has dedicated over 20 years to helping people—from student-athletes to professionals to everyday families—make smarter money moves, build generational wealth, and change their financial narrative.

After serving as team captain at the University of Kansas and briefly playing in the CFL, Pat saw firsthand how a lack of financial literacy could derail even the most promising careers. He earned his MBA and began a new mission: to be the guide he wished he had when he was coming up.

Since then, Pat has worked as a wealth advisor, insurance specialist, and national financial literacy speaker. He teaches on everything from budgeting and credit to investing, taxes, entrepreneurship, NIL income, and estate planning—with a focus on making the information **relatable, real, and rooted in culture**.

Pat is the founder of multiple financial literacy platforms, each created to meet people where they are:

- **www.FinancialLiteracyForNIL.com** – For student-athletes navigating Name, Image, and Likeness income
- **www.FinancialLiteracyForStudentAthletes.com** – Focused financial education for high school and college athletes
- **www.FinancialLiteracyForCollegeCoaches.com** – Helping coaches manage money and mentor athletes with confidence
- **www.FinancialLiteracyForParentsOfStudentAthletes.com** –

Supporting parents in guiding their student-athletes

- **www.FinancialLiteracyForNILInternational.com** – Tailored education for international student-athletes
- **www.FinancialLiteracyForDoctors.com** – Addressing the unique financial journey of physicians
- **www.FinancialLiteracyForAttorneys.com** – Financial insight and planning for legal professionals
- **www.FinancialLiteracyForProAthletes.com** – Helping professionals in sports protect and grow their wealth
- **www.FinancialLiteracyForTheCulture.com** – A cultural lens on wealth, legacy, and financial empowerment
- **www.FinancialLiteracyForArtists.com** – Teaching creatives how to manage money while staying true to their craft

Whether he's working with universities, community organizations, churches, or national conferences, Pat delivers one message loud and clear: *you don't have to be born into wealth to build it.*

As a husband, father, and lifelong learner, Pat brings his whole self to the work—sharing real stories, hard truths, and practical steps that resonate with people who've never seen themselves in traditional financial conversations. He's not just teaching money—he's changing mindsets.

Because financial literacy isn't just about dollars. It's about dignity, direction, and doing better for the next generation.

The culture deserves wealth too.

And Pat Brown is here to help make that happen.

100 essential questions

100 essential questions to ask financial advisors, CPAs, estate planning attorneys, insurance professionals, and other key players in your financial life. These questions are designed specifically to empower *The Culture*—to help you find professionals who understand your journey, respect your values, and have your best interest at heart.

Questions to Ask a Financial Advisor

1. Are you a fiduciary, and are you legally required to act in my best interest?
2. How do you get paid—flat fee, commission, or percentage of assets?
3. Do you have experience working with clients from culturally diverse backgrounds?
4. How do you support first-generation wealth builders?
5. What's your investment philosophy and how do you explain it to beginners?
6. How will you customize your advice to my specific goals?
7. Do you help clients build credit and manage debt?
8. Can you walk me through how to create a realistic budget?
9. Do you offer one-time consultations or only ongoing relationships?
10. Will you educate me along the way, or just manage my money?
11. Can you help with homebuying or real estate planning?
12. Do you advise on student loan repayment strategies?
13. How do you help clients who are starting from scratch?
14. Will you review my current financial situation in full before recommending anything?

15. How often will we meet or check in?
16. Do you offer financial planning in writing?
17. Can I reach out between meetings if I have questions?
18. What's your approach to emergency savings planning?
19. Will you explain financial concepts in plain, everyday language?
20. What's the first thing you'd help someone like me work on?

Questions to Ask a CPA or Tax Professional

1. Do you work with clients who have multiple income sources?
2. Can you help with both tax preparation and long-term tax planning?
3. What strategies do you use to reduce my tax burden legally?
4. Will you help me track deductions and organize receipts year-round?
5. Do you help with estimated quarterly taxes?
6. What's your fee structure—hourly, flat, per form?
7. Do you offer virtual appointments or just in-person?
8. Will you represent me if I get audited?
9. Can you explain tax laws in plain language?
10. Do you help clients with rental properties or small businesses?
11. How can I avoid surprise tax bills?
12. Can you help with back taxes or past filing mistakes?
13. What tax credits or deductions apply to families or caregivers?
14. How do you stay current with changing tax laws?
15. Will you file in multiple states if needed?
16. Do you offer reminders for deadlines throughout the year?
17. Can you help me decide between forming an LLC or staying a sole proprietor?
18. Do you help with charitable giving and how it impacts taxes?
19. Can you explain how depreciation works in real estate or business?
20. Will you guide me on what records I need to keep and for how long?

Questions to Ask an Estate Planning Attorney

1. Can you explain the difference between a will and a trust?
2. What happens if I pass away without an estate plan?
3. Do you help clients with limited assets plan for the future?
4. Can you assist in setting up power of attorney and healthcare directives?
5. What should I consider when naming guardians for my children?
6. How do you make sure my estate plan reflects my cultural values?
7. Do you offer flat-fee services or charge hourly?
8. What's the process for transferring a home or property to a family member?
9. Can you help avoid or minimize probate?
10. Do you offer digital estate planning for passwords and online accounts?
11. How often should I update my will or trust?
12. What documents do you recommend every adult have?
13. Can I set up a trust even if I'm not wealthy?
14. How do I include charitable giving or community support in my plan?
15. Will my estate be taxed, and can I reduce that burden?
16. Do you coordinate with financial advisors or CPAs on estate matters?
17. How do you help multi-generational families plan together?
18. Can I protect assets from creditors or lawsuits?
19. Do you offer guidance on leaving property or money to non-family members?
20. What's the cost and timeline to create or update an estate plan?

Questions to Ask an Insurance Professional

1. What kind of life insurance is best for someone like me—term or whole life?
2. How much coverage do I really need?
3. Do you offer policies with living benefits or riders?

4. What happens if I miss a payment—do I lose coverage?
5. Can I increase or decrease my coverage over time?
6. Do you help with auto, home, health, and renters insurance too?
7. What discounts or bundles do you offer?
8. Can you help me file a claim if something happens?
9. What's not covered in my current insurance policy?
10. How often should I review or update my policies?
11. Do you explain everything in writing, or just over the phone?
12. Will this policy build any cash value I can borrow from?
13. Do you offer disability or income protection insurance?
14. Can you help my parents or elders with Medicare or long-term care insurance?
15. What's the biggest insurance mistake you see people in my community make?

Questions to Ask a Real Estate Agent or Mortgage Broker

1. Do you specialize in working with first-time homebuyers?
2. Can you walk me through the entire homebuying process?
3. What should I expect for closing costs and fees?
4. How do I know if I'm getting a good interest rate?
5. What's the difference between pre-qualified and pre-approved?
6. Can you help me understand credit requirements for buying a home?
7. How much house can I realistically afford—not just what I qualify for?
8. What first-time buyer programs are available in my area?
9. Can I buy a home with student loans or moderate income?
10. What's your commission and how is it paid?

Questions to Ask Any Professional Before Hiring

1. Do you have experience working with people from my background?
2. Will you explain things in a way I can actually understand?
3. Do you offer payment plans or sliding-scale pricing?
4. What happens if I don't understand something—can I ask follow-ups?
5. Do you work with people just starting their financial journey?
6. Can you provide references or testimonials from past clients?
7. What's your availability for questions or emergencies?
8. What's one mistake you see people in my community make financially?
9. How do you define success for your clients?
10. Will you educate me or just expect me to follow your lead?
11. Do you have any conflict of interest I should know about?
12. How long have you been doing this work?
13. What licenses or certifications do you hold?
14. Are you part of any professional or culturally focused financial organizations?
15. If I work with you, how will I know I'm making progress?

Glossary of Terms

Financial Terms

1. **Asset** – Something valuable you own, like cash, stocks, or property.
2. **Liability** – Money you owe, such as loans or credit card debt.
3. **Net Worth** – Your total assets minus your total liabilities.
4. **Budget** – A plan for how you spend and save money.
5. **Credit Score** – A number showing how responsibly you use credit.
6. **Interest Rate** – The cost of borrowing money or the return earned on savings.
7. **Diversification** – Spreading investments to reduce risk.
8. **Stock** – A share of ownership in a company.
9. **Bond** – A loan you give to a company or government in return for interest.
10. **Capital Gain** – Profit made from selling an investment for more than you paid.
11. **Mutual Fund** – An investment that pools money to buy a mix of stocks and bonds.
12. **ETF (Exchange-Traded Fund)** – A fund that trades like a stock but holds many investments.
13. **Roth IRA** – A retirement account where withdrawals are tax-free.
14. **401(k)** – An employer-sponsored retirement savings account.
15. **Compound Interest** – Interest earned on your original money and on the interest itself.
16. **Inflation** – The rise in prices over time, reducing purchasing power.
17. **Risk Tolerance** – How much investment fluctuation you can handle.
18. **Emergency Fund** – Savings set aside for unexpected financial needs.

19. **Principal** – The original sum of money invested or loaned.
20. **Dividend** – A share of a company's profits paid to shareholders.

Accounting Terms

1. **Income** – Money you earn from work, business, or investments.
2. **Expense** – Money you spend on goods, services, or business costs.
3. **Revenue** – Total income before any expenses are subtracted.
4. **Net Income** – What's left after all expenses and taxes are paid.
5. **Gross Income** – Income before deductions like taxes or retirement contributions.
6. **Cash Flow** – Movement of money in and out of an account.
7. **Profit** – The money left after subtracting expenses from income.
8. **Loss** – When expenses exceed income.
9. **Invoice** – A bill sent to request payment for services or products.
10. **Receipt** – Proof of payment or purchase.
11. **Write-Off** – An expense that reduces your taxable income.
12. **Deduction** – A legal reduction in the income you are taxed on.
13. **Accounts Payable** – Money your business owes to others.
14. **Accounts Receivable** – Money owed to your business by others.
15. **Depreciation** – Loss of value in an asset over time.
16. **Chart of Accounts** – A categorized list of all accounts in a financial system.
17. **Balance Sheet** – A snapshot of a company's financial position.
18. **General Ledger** – The master record of all financial transactions.
19. **Bookkeeping** – The process of recording financial transactions.
20. **Audit** – A formal review of financial records for accuracy and compliance.

Estate Planning Terms

1. **Will** – A legal document stating how your assets should be distributed after death.

2. **Trust** – A legal arrangement where one party holds assets for another.
3. **Executor** – The person responsible for carrying out your will.
4. **Beneficiary** – A person who receives assets from a will, trust, or insurance policy.
5. **Probate** – The court-supervised process of settling an estate.
6. **Power of Attorney** – A legal document giving someone authority to act on your behalf.
7. **Advance Directive** – A document outlining your medical care wishes.
8. **Living Will** – A written statement of your preferences for end-of-life care.
9. **Healthcare Proxy** – Someone you designate to make medical decisions if you're unable.
10. **Guardianship** – Legal responsibility for another person, typically a child or incapacitated adult.
11. **Inheritance** – Assets passed down from someone who has died.
12. **Estate** – Everything a person owns at death, including assets and debts.
13. **Revocable Trust** – A trust that can be changed or canceled by the creator.
14. **Irrevocable Trust** – A trust that cannot be changed once established.
15. **Estate Tax** – A tax on property transferred from deceased persons.
16. **Gift Tax** – A tax applied to large gifts given during someone's lifetime.
17. **Heir** – A person legally entitled to inherit assets.
18. **Trustee** – A person or institution managing assets in a trust.
19. **Grantor** – The person who sets up a trust.
20. **Letter of Intent** – A non-binding document explaining personal wishes.

Insurance Terms

1. **Premium** – The amount paid regularly for insurance coverage.
2. **Deductible** – The amount you pay out-of-pocket before insurance

pays.

3. **Co-Pay** – A fixed amount you pay for medical visits or services.
4. **Coverage** – The extent of protection your insurance provides.
5. **Claim** – A request made to an insurance company for payment.
6. **Beneficiary (Insurance)** – The person who receives insurance money after a loss.
7. **Underwriting** – The process of evaluating insurance risk before issuing a policy.
8. **Policyholder** – The person who owns the insurance policy.
9. **Term Life Insurance** – Life insurance coverage for a specific period.
10. **Whole Life Insurance** – Permanent insurance with a cash value component.
11. **Disability Insurance** – Pays income if you're unable to work due to injury or illness.
12. **Liability Insurance** – Covers damage or injury you may cause to others.
13. **Homeowners Insurance** – Covers damage to your home and personal belongings.
14. **Auto Insurance** – Covers vehicle damage and liability in accidents.
15. **Health Insurance** – Covers medical expenses and services.
16. **Long-Term Care Insurance** – Covers the cost of long-term care services.
17. **Rider** – An add-on feature or change to a basic insurance policy.
18. **Exclusion** – Situations or conditions not covered by a policy.
19. **Grace Period** – Extra time to pay your premium before losing coverage.
20. **Claim Adjuster** – The person who investigates insurance claims and determines payouts.

Additional General and Crossover Terms

1. **Taxable Income** – The portion of income on which taxes must be paid.

2. **Form 1099** – A tax form reporting income from freelance or contract work.
3. **Form W-9** – A tax form you fill out to provide your taxpayer ID to clients.
4. **Schedule C** – The IRS form for reporting business income as a sole proprietor.
5. **Liquidity** – How quickly an asset can be converted into cash.
6. **Asset Allocation** – Dividing investments among different categories to balance risk.
7. **Estate Plan** – The complete strategy for passing down your assets.
8. **Succession Plan** – A plan for passing leadership or ownership of a business.
9. **Term Sheet** – A summary of the key points in a proposed deal or contract.
10. **Joint Account** – A bank account owned by two or more people.
11. **Escrow** – Funds held by a third party until conditions of a contract are met.
12. **Power of Appointment** – Legal power to designate who receives property from a trust.
13. **Umbrella Insurance** – Extra liability insurance that goes beyond standard policies.
14. **Self-Employment Tax** – Taxes paid by freelancers or business owners.
15. **SEP IRA** – A retirement plan for self-employed individuals or small businesses.
16. **Solo 401(k)** – A retirement plan for individuals who work for themselves.
17. **FICO Score** – A type of credit score used widely by lenders.
18. **Amortization** – Paying off debt with regular payments over time.
19. **Escalation Clause** – A clause that increases payment terms under certain conditions.
20. **Financial Statement** – A written record of financial activities and position.

Why This Book Exists

This book exists because too many of us were left out of the conversation when it came to money.

We weren't born into generational wealth. We weren't taught how to navigate taxes, investments, credit scores, or compound interest at the dinner table. For many of us, our introduction to money came through stress, survival, or silence. But now—it's time to break that cycle.

Financial Literacy For The Culture is here to shift the mindset. To put knowledge in your hands. To give you a roadmap for building wealth, protecting what's yours, and walking with confidence in rooms that were never designed for us.

Financial education is a tool of empowerment. It opens doors. It breaks chains. It creates options. And just like in sports, music, or entrepreneurship—your success off the field, off the stage, or out of the system depends on **discipline, strategy, teamwork, and knowing when to bring in professionals.**

How to Use This Book

This book is a guide, not a rulebook.

It's here to help you:

- **Start asking better questions**
- **Build habits that stick**
- **Make informed decisions about your money**
- **Understand the game, so you can stop getting played**

You won't have all the answers overnight—and that's okay. The goal is to become aware, then active, then consistent. Reread chapters. Highlight what speaks to you. Share what you learn. And don't be afraid to admit when you need help.

Need Help? Start Here

When you're ready to take it further, reach out to someone who's walked this walk and knows the struggle **and** the strategy.

Pat Brown, MBA

Former Division I football captain. Financial educator. Trusted advisor.

Pat built this platform because he saw firsthand how people from the culture were being left behind financially—not from lack of hustle, but from lack of access. That stops here.

Contact:

- **Website:** www.financialliteracyfornil.com
- **Email:** info@financialliteracyfornil.com

Want free game in your inbox? **Join the newsletter** to stay up on resources, real-talk money tips, workshops, and support created specifically for *us*.

Final Word: Use This. Don't Shelf It.

This book wasn't made to sit in a binder, on a coffee table, or buried in a downloads folder. **Use it.** Revisit it. Pull it out when you get that new job, that raise, that NIL deal, that tax bill, or that dream.

Share it with your circle. Teach your little cousins. Pass it to your parents. Run it back with your kids. This is your financial playbook—and we only win when we study it, apply it, and teach it forward.

Stay sharp. Stay curious. Stay building.

We've got culture. Now let's build capital.

Disclosure & Disclaimer

Important Notice and Disclaimer

This book, *Financial Literacy For The Culture,* is written with the intent to educate, empower, and encourage individuals—especially those from historically underserved, underrepresented, or underestimated communities—to take ownership of their financial future. The knowledge shared throughout these pages is drawn from the author's personal experiences, professional journey, and over two decades of work in financial services, education, and community empowerment.

However, before going any further, it's important to understand:

Educational Purpose Only

All content in this book is presented solely for general educational and informational purposes. It is not intended as legal, financial, tax, accounting, or investment advice.

This book is here to provide foundational concepts, culturally relevant insights, real-life analogies, and practical strategies that can help you better understand your relationship with money, build wealth, and break generational cycles. But it's not a personalized financial plan. Everyone's financial situation, goals, family dynamics, income levels, and challenges are different.

What works for one person—or one culture, neighborhood, or generation—may not work for another. Always seek personalized advice from licensed professionals before making decisions involving investments, contracts, taxes, or legal matters.

No Legal Advice

Although this book may touch on legal topics such as estate planning, contracts, or business formation, it does not provide legal advice and should not be used as a substitute for working with an attorney.

If you are starting a business, managing family assets, drafting a will, entering into agreements, or have questions about your legal rights, consult a licensed attorney who specializes in that area of law. Laws and regulations vary by state, and only a qualified professional can ensure you're protected.

No Financial or Investment Advice

This book covers budgeting, saving, credit, investing, debt reduction, and long-term planning—but it does so from an educational lens, not as individualized financial advice.

Do not act solely on what you read here without speaking to a Certified Financial Planner™, licensed financial advisor, or fiduciary professional. Every financial move you make should take into account your unique goals, risk tolerance, family needs, and circumstances.

No part of this book guarantees financial success, investment returns, or economic security. The examples and case studies are illustrative only and do not predict or promise outcomes.

No Accounting or Tax Advice

While this book mentions common tax topics—like business deductions, 1099 income, or saving through retirement accounts—it is not written by a CPA, enrolled agent, or tax attorney.

If you are managing side income, running a business, investing, or navigating complex tax situations, please consult with a qualified tax professional. Tax rules vary by state, income level, and filing status. Getting the right advice now can save you money and stress down the road.

No Guarantees or Promises

This book doesn't promise wealth. It doesn't promise financial peace. What it offers is insight, motivation, and a culturally grounded framework for thinking differently about money.

Your path may be filled with student loans, medical bills, job changes, family obligations, or setbacks. But it's also filled with potential, resilience, creativity, and opportunity. The strategies in this book are here to help you navigate that path—but the outcome is ultimately in your hands.

Limitation of Liability

By reading this book, you agree that the author, Pat Brown, MBA, and any affiliated platforms—such as FinancialLiteracyForTheCulture.com and related educational initiatives—are not responsible for any personal financial decisions or consequences resulting from your use of this content.

Neither the author nor any entity mentioned in this book shall be held liable for loss, damages, or other outcomes resulting from the application or misinterpretation of the content shared herein.

Encouragement to Seek Professional Help

This book was written out of love for the culture—and with a deep understanding that systemic gaps in financial education, access, and trust still exist. But knowledge is power, especially when paired with the right team.

If you don't have a trusted advisor, CPA, estate planner, or attorney in your corner, now is the time to start building your circle. Find professionals who understand where you come from and where you're trying to go.

You deserve guidance that reflects your reality—and your vision. Let this book be a spark, not the whole strategy.

Made in the USA
Monee, IL
29 July 2025

22154863R10226